Selected Legal Issues of E-Commerce

Law and Electronic Commerce

Volume 16

The titles published in this series are listed at the end of this volume.

Selected Legal Issues of E-Commerce

Edited by

Toshiyuki Kono

Christoph G. Paulus

Harry Rajak

KLUWER LAW INTERNATIONAL

THE HAGUE / LONDON / NEW YORK

A C.I.P. Catalogue record for this book is available from the Library of Congress.

ISBN 90-411-1898-5

Published by Kluwer Law International,
P.O. Box 85889, 2508 CN The Hague, The Netherlands.

Sold and distributed in North, Central and South America
by Kluwer Law International,
101 Philip Drive, Norwell, MA 02061, U.S.A.
kluwerlaw@wkap.com

In all other countries, sold and distributed
by Kluwer Law International, Distribution Centre,
P.O. Box 322, 3300 AH Dordrecht, The Netherlands.

Printed on acid-free paper

Printed in the Netherlands.

PREFACE

At a time when there are still a number of voices calling for the Internet to remain a law-free zone, a whole bundle of conflicts have already emerged, many of which have found their way to lawyers and the courts in a substantial number of different jurisdictions. It surely now cannot be doubted that the Internet, like any other place in the world where people come together and follow their own interests, needs, indeed cries out for rules to be developed for the handling of such conflicts. Lawyers are the experts for fabricating rules and it is, therefore, not surprising that they have already created a new area of law – commonly called "law of the internet" or "cyberlaw". This area, however, is still far from being strictly defined. It touches on many existing areas of law, but at the same time it deals with a wholly new medium – cyberspace - which itself is subject to constant change and development. Under these circumstances, it is not surprising that in a number of cases the predictions as to how this law will look at some selected moment in the future are vague and uncertain.

This is particularly true for the commercial side of the Internet, for which the term "E-Commerce" has been coined. So rapid has been the development of E-Commerce, that it is now frequently said that this is the future of any commerce and that it carries the potential for enormous growth. Yet, this is but a forecast and one which is not without many question marks – at least for the present. E-Commerce, essentially comprises two major sections – business to consumer ("B2C") and business to business ("B2B") and a cautious assessment at this stage may be that while the B2C side of E-Commerce may never reach its predicted importance, it would appear likely that the B2B area will undergo massive further development. Thus, it is imperative that appropriate people, bodies, organisations, countries and indeed, international organisations prepare, draft and enact rules which are appropriate for a virtual and ubiquitous space which may well defy the traditional borderlines of sovereign states.

This volume contains articles based on presentations given at an international symposium held in late-July 2001 in Miyazaki, Japan. Those who participated work in one way or another in the study and analysis of cyberlaw and some are engaged occupations which are increasingly dependent on internet related activities. All are engaged in the endeavour of developing an appropriate and workable cyberlaw. They should not be read with the expectation of finding definite solutions. We are surely still a long way from resolving the enormous number of complications and tensions which come from the necessary involvement of many different legal systems and anticipated strong presence at an international dimension. The contributors here should rather be read as one collective voice in a huge chorus, which searches for the ideal of a universal consensus to a major new commercial challenge. We anticipate that this will be a search whose future will be a great deal longer than its past.

Toshiyuki Kono
Christoph G. Paulus
Harry Rajak

March 2002

TABLE OF CONTENTS

THE AUTHORS

H. Baum is Senior Research Associate at the Max-Planck-Institut für ausländisches und internationales Privatrecht, Hamburg/Germany; he is specializing in the law of Japan, trade and commercial law, corporation law and capital market law, comparative law and international private and procedure law.

M. Dogouchi is Professor of Law at the Tokyo University in Tokyo/Japan, specializing in private international law and international civil procedure law.

Y. Hayakawa is Associate Professor of Law at the Rikkyo University in Tokyo/Japan. He is specializing in private international law, transnational litigation, international commercial arbitration, cross-border bankruptcy law and the law of e-commerce.

Th. Hoeren is Professor of Law at the University of Muenster/Germany; he is specializing in computer law, banking and insurance law, competition law, and international business transaction law.

H. Kanda is Professor of Law at the Tokyo University in Tokyo/Japan; he is specializing in company law and the law of financial regulation.

T. Kono is Professor of Law at the University of Kyushu, Fukuoka/Japan; he is specializing in private international law, international civil procedure law, cultural property preservation law.

S. Osaki is Head of Capital Market Research Group, Nomura Research Institute, Tokyo/Japan; he is specializing in national and international capital market law.

C. Paulus is Professor of Law at the Humboldt-University at Berlin/Germany; he is specializing in legal history, national and international civil procedure law, national and international insolvency law and the law of e-commerce.

H. Rajak is Professor of Law at the University of Sussex in Brighton/England; he is specializing in company law, insolvency law, business transactions law.

A. Sebok is Professor of Law at the Brooklyn Law School, New York/USA; he is specializing in tort law, legal philosophy and constitutional law.

A. Trunk is Professor of Law at the University of Kiel/Germany; he is specializing in east-european law, international private and procedure law, insolvency law, and information law.

Yabu No Naka

*Thomas Hoeren**

Contents

* Professor of Law, University of Muenster, Germany.

Toshiyui Kono/ Christoph G. Paulus/ Harry Rajak (eds.); The Legal Issues Of E-Commerce
© 2002 Kluwer Law International. Printed in the Netherlands, pp. 1-12.

Kono et al. (eds.), Selected Legal Issues of E-Commerce, 1–12.
© 2002 Kluwer Law International. Printed in the Netherlands.

A.   PREFACE

My concerns are the sudden death of e-commerce companies. During the last year or so, companies which were regarded as the superior winners in the world, the titans of e-commerce seem to have been murdered at a stroke. On one view it may have been the law which caused the economic depression in ebusiness, but in my view, e-Commerce has been killed by the very nature of internet and network economy itself. Here, I am presenting my ideas in the form of a novel with some references to legal sources as hypertext in footnotes.[1] My short text is based on a novel written by Ryunosuke Akutagawa which was the literary source of Kurosawa's famous film "Rashomon".[2] It still has the form of a speech (with only a few footnotes) as it is meant to be published in a conference paper booklet.

B.   THE TESTIMONY OF A WOODCUTTER QUESTIONED BY A HIGH POLICE COMMISSIONER

Yes, Sir. Certainly, it was I who found the body. This morning, as usual, I used the road when I found the body in a grove. The exact location? Several meters off the road. The body was lying flat around, right beside the highway. No. The blood was no longer running. The wound had dried up, I believe.

C.   THE TESTIMONY OF A TRAVELLING BUDDHIST PRIEST QUESTIONED BY A HIGH POLICE COMMISSIONER

The time? Certainly, it was about noon yesterday, sir. The unfortunate man was on the highway to sell a variety of goods and services since several months. He was young, intelligent, dynamic and ambitious for the sake of his business. He struggled very hard to survive. First he was applauded by everybody. He got money, support, public interest. But then the journey got to be exhausting. He lost money. The profits were too low. Only a few people contacted him to make business. So, his journey became more and more hazardous. The name? He called himself "dotcom" so far as I remember.

By the way, Dotcom had a lady accompanying him on a horseback, who I have learned was his wife. A scarf hanging from her head hid her face from view. The lady's height?

---

[1]   However, I strictly avoid any reference to literature as this paper is part of a book which represents conference papers.

[2]   I used, extensively, the English translation of the novel published in London 1997.

Oh, about four feet five inches. Since I am a Buddhist priest, I took little notice about her details.

Little did I expect that he would meet such a fate. Truly human life is as evanescent as the morning dew or a flash of lightning. My words are inadequate to express my sympathy for him.

D. THE TESTIMONY OF A POLICEMAN QUESTIONED BY A HIGH POLICE COMMISSIONER

The man that I arrested? He was wearing a dark blue silk kimono. And he used a bow and strange arrows with hawk feathers – these were all in his possession I believe. The name of the villain? "Kindai ha no arikata". He claims to be innocent.

E. THE TESTIMONY OF „KINDAI HO NO ARIKATA"

Now things have come to such ahead, I won´t keep anything from you. By the way, I am an innocent man. I have never intended to kill the dotcoms. I even tried anything to support them.

How? Well, I used my arrows, the arrows of „kindai ho no arikata", of the modern law, as it should be. I tried everything to regulate e-commerce as extensively and effectively as possible. And I established within two years a new global framework on e-commerce law with clear-cut rules harmonized within Europe taking into consideration regulations on the UN and the US level. I did everything to supply dotcoms with all the necessary legal safeguards they needed.

First, I protected their trademarks against illegal use as part of a domain and gave them a clear-cut guideline how to create a domain without violating the rights of other persons. A company which enters the wide world of the internet needs a domain, more precisely a URL such as "http://www.cocacola.com". These domains are given to everybody who asks for their registration according to the principle "first come, first served". Registrars are private companies acting under the auspices of ICANN; the International Corporation for assigned Names and Numbers. I sharpened the rules of trademark law to protect rightholders against domain grabbing. As the registration and use of domains often violated trademark rights, it was appropriate that harmonized EU principles existed on the protection of trademarks.[3] These rules have been interpreted by courts to apply effectively against the use of trademarks as part of a domain, even in the case of similar wording. This strategy was not only an issue of European regulators, but of the United States which enated their Anticybersquatting Act.[4] In order to get quick decisions in domain controversies, I allowed the establishment of a specific arbitration system based upon the UDRP, the Uniform Dispute Resolution Procedure.[5]

Secondly, I created a globally uniform set of rules in copyright law to protect digital content. I am responsible for at least three important EU directives. The Software Directive[6] maintains a common European standard for the copyright protection of software and grants a range of exploitation rights, including the loading of software in a working memory, the distribution of a computer program and its alteration. The Database Directive[7] provides for a two-fold protection of collections of data by copyight and by a new sui-generis protection system. The sui-generis-right includes the protection of the database producer against linking and meta-searchengines and is granted for at least 15 years. My last and most important work is the so-called InfoSoc Directive, the Directive on Copyright in the Information Society.[8] It contains a new internet exploitation right, based upon the WIPO Copyright Treaty the right of making available content to members of the public not presenting at the place where the act of making available originates. In addition the Directive solved the issue of limitations as it harmonizes the divergent structure of exemptions in the national copyright legislations by implementing an exhaustive mandatory list of possible exemptions. The Directive therefore provides for an exhaustive enumeration of exemptions to the reproduction right and the right of communication to the public. Especially it allows certain acts of temporary reproduction which are transient or incidental reproductions forming an integral and essential part of a technological process carried out for the sole purpose of enabling either efficient transmission in a network or a lawful use of a work.

---

[3]   First Council Directive 89/104/EEC of 21 December 1998 to approximate the laws of the member states relating trade marks, OJ L 040, 11/0271989, p. 1. This directive is the basis for the harmonization of trademark law in the EU.

[4]   Anticybersquatting Consumer Protection Act, S. 1948, incorporated in HR 3194, Public Law Number 106-113, enacted on November 29, 1999.

[5]   Policy adopted on August 26, 1999. See http://www.icann.org/udrp/udrp.htm.

[6]   Council Directive 91/250/EEC of 14 May 1991 on the legal protection of computer programs, OJ L 122 of 17 May 1991, p. 42.

[7]   Directive 96/9/EC of the European Parliament and of the Council of 11 March 1996 on the legal protection of databases, OJ L 077 of 27/03/1996, p. 20.

[8]   Directive of the European Parliament and of the Council on the harmonisation of certain aspects of copyright and related rights in the information society, OJ L 167 of 22. June 2001, p. 10 ; http://europa.eu.int/eur-lex/de/oj/2001/l_16720010622de.html   or   http://europa.eu.int/eur-lex/en/oj/2001/l_16720010622de.html (English Version).

Thirdly, competition law issues have also been dealt with. I installed the EU Directive on certain legal aspects of e-commerce[9] which focuses on the country of origin principle. This principle formerly installed by the European Court of Justice leads to the application of an online marketing law of state where the online provider has his seat. By contrast, and to strengthen this principle, the rules of the countries where a homepage can be accessed cannot be applied any more. This rigid new principle has been promoted in favour of the online industry which only has to look for its home-country marketing laws. According to these principles, information society services should be supervised at the source of the activity in order to ensure an effective protection of public interest objectives.

Fourthly, I regulated e-contracting issues. In the E-Commerce Directive just mentioned I included rules providing that homepages are not a binding offer and that tools for the correction of typing errors have to be provided for. All national laws on written requirements have to be changed in order to increase online contracting. With the EU Signature Directive,[10] I enabled certification-service-providers to develop their cross-border activities with a view to increasing their competitiveness. Therefore, the directive states that certification-service-providers should be free to provide their services without prior authorisation and that the legal effectiveness of electronic signatures and their admissibility as evidence in legal proceedings should be recognised. Advanced electronic signatures which are based on a qualified certificate and which are created by a secure-signature creation device can be regarded as legally equivalent to hand-written signatures. And don´t forget my EU Distance Selling System. The Distance Selling Directive[11] provided for a worldwide unique protection of consumers in eBusiness. The consumer shall be provided with several different kinds of information in good time prior to the conclusion of the distance contract; the information has to be made on durable medium. In addition, the consumer has at least a period of seven working days in which to withdraw from the contract without penalty and without giving any reason and if he or she has not received sufficient information on this withdrawal right, the period is extended to three months.

Fifthly, I have taken care of data protection where new legal tools for data mining and data warehousing became necessary. Personal data, for instance of customers, is of substantial value in e-commerce. This data can be easily recorded, transferred, combined with other data for an extensive personal profile of the customer. Data Mining and Data Warehouse became famous strategies for the dotcoms to survive in the hazardous world

---

[9] Directive 200/31/EC of the European Parliament and of the Council of 8 June 2000 on certain legal aspects of information society services, in particular electronic commerce, in the Internal Market, OJ L 178 of 17/07/2000, p. 1.

[10] Directive 1999/93/EC of the European parliament and of the Council of 13 December 1999 on a Community Framework on electronic signatures, OJ L 13 of 19/01/2000, p.12,

[11] Directive 97/66/EC of the European Parliament and of the Council of 20 May1997 on the protection of consumers in respect of distance contracts, Official Journal L 144, 04/06/1997, p. 19.

of global business. The EU Data Protection Directive[12] and the EU Directive on Privacy and Telecommunications[13] contain rules which guarantee the freedom of the person concerned to decide upon the use of his or her personal data. I used the most restrictive privacy tools of national legislators to build up an effective threshold. The UK idea of notification could be used to create a European system in which all processing of data needs to be notified to the data protection commissioner. I took the French concept that certain sensitive data can only be used with the express consent of the person concerned. I combined it with the German model that any processing of personal data is prohibited unless the person concerned has given his or her consent or a specific statutory provision allows the processing. In addition, I invented a new tool to restrict the exchange of data between Europe and Japan or the United States. According to the EU Data Protection Directive, the transborder data flow to non-EU countries is only lawful if the third state has an adequate level of data protection when compared to the EU standard.

As the sixth and final element, I solved the difficult issue of liability. In the E-Commerce Directive, horizontally structured rules on the liability of host, cache and access providers are included. A service provider can thus benefit from the exemptions for "mere conduit" and for "caching" when it is in no way involved with the information transmitted. The provider of an information society service, consisting of the storage of information, has to act expeditiously to remove or disable access to the information upon obtaining actual knowledge or awareness of illegal activities. And I redrafted the EU rules on the execution of civil court decisions. In addition, I abolished the old Brussels Convention on the recognition and enforcement of judgments in civil and commercial matters and replaced it by a somewhat different EU regulation.[14] This EU Regulation is a legal instrument which is binding and directly applicable.[15]

So – yes. I claim to be innocent. I have done nothing to kill that man. I even supported him to my utmost power.

---

[12]   Directive 95/46/EC of the European Parliament and of the Council of 24 October 1995 on the protection of individuals with regard to the processing of personal data and on the free movement of such data, OJ L 281 of 23/11/1995, p. 31.

[13]   Directive 97/66/EC of the European Parliament and of the Council of 15 December 1997 concerning the processing of personal data and the protection of privacy in the telecommunications sector, OJ L 24 of 30/01/1998, p. 1.

[14]   Council Regulation No. 44/2001 of 22 December 2000 on Jurisdiction and the Recognition and Enforcement of Judgments in Civil and Commercial Matters, OJ L 12 of 16/01/2001, p. 1.

[15]   See the brief explanation of European Union legislative capacity in the contribution to this volume by Professor Rajak.

F.   THE TESTIMONY OF „KINDAI HO NO ARIKATA"

Oh, wait a minute. No torture can make me confess what I don´t know. Your long inquiries, your tortuous questions have, though, made me reconsider my former statements. And I must confess, I might perhaps have caused the death of Dotcom. I did forgot to regulate aspects which may, perhaps, have caused the death of Dotcom.

Firstly, the domain question: My Uniform Dispute Resolution Procedure can only be applied for generic top level domains, such as "com", "net" and "org".[16] Country-based top level domains are mostly not subject of the UDRP (with the exception of states like Coke Island or Antigua). The UDPR is furthermore based on the dubious principle of "bad faith" which is, at least in the light of EU law, to be regarded as irrelevant for granting injunctions. Further problems are caused by the fact that ICANN, the international organisation responsible for organising the assignment of domain names, has just granted new top-level domains, such as "biz" or "info", and this might cause further trademark law conflicts. Finally, trademark is based upon the idea of territoriality, on the concept of nation-based effectiveness of intellectual property rights which leads, inevitably, to insoluble problems where cross-border disputes on domains arise.

I am dissatisfied with my own results in copyright as well. The Software Directive is full of lacunas, such as the difficult regulation on reverse engineering and the somewhat mandatory provision on the use rights for the intended purpose of a computer program. The Sui Generis Right created within the Database Directive has caused a lot of distress with the United States where people fear that this right might include a monopolistic protection of information as such. The InfoSoc Directive has not solved the issue whether the transmission of content in small, internal networks can be classified as a "making available to the public". Furthermore, it hasn´t solved the issue of exemptions insofar as EU member states are free to maintain their divergent traditional exemptions for the sake of non-digital free usage. And apart from these details, the reference of copyright to the concept of territoriality causes major problems in cross-border cases. This principle implies that copyright is violated in every state where the homepage can be accessed. Every e-commerce company has to check any regulation on intellectual property law of every state throughout the world which is of course an impossible task. I knew that this requirement might kill e-commerce but I thought that the application of the territoriality principle wouldn´t lead to much harm.

I am sorry to say that I even failed to solve the competition law needs. Yes, I have installed the country of origin concept, but due to national fears I had to allow so many exceptions and derogations from that principle that the effect of the concept remains

---

[16]   See for further questions related to ICANN the presentation of Yoshihisa Hayakawa.

dubious.[17] Consumer protection has been taken out to a similar extent as criminal law, public health, the delivery of goods, insurance business or copyright. Only minor areas of marketing law remain subject to the country of origin idea. But even there it is unsettled how "country of origin" fits with principles of private international law. For problems of marketing law the concept of the intended marketplace has been established. The law of every country, to which the homepage is purposefully directed, applies. This seemed to be a good limitation to the very general idea of the seat of the user, but even this principle proved to be doubtful. It became unclear how the direction of a homepage, its intended marketplace, could be determined. In addition, the Directive states in the preamble that private international law remains untouched and to the same extent shall not interfere with country of origin ideas. But that's not all. I have forgotten third, non-EU countries like Japan. They cannot profit from the home-state vision; targeting their business globally they have to take care of all the different marketing laws in Europe. This might violate WTO law – an aspect which I didn't consider at all.

And as for my e-contracting regulations, please just forget them. Let me only use the example of my favourite regulations on distance selling to illustrate why.[18] These regulations proved to be ineffective. The Directive contains too many exemptions. Owing to extensive lobbying, an exemption for financial services had to be made, an exemption which could not be justified by any argument. The EU Commission tried to close this gap by drafting a separate directive on distance marketing of consumer financial services; but this draft was and will never be accepted by the Member States. Discussion on this draft stopped in June 2001, so that banking and insurance business will be without specific consumer protection laws when doing e-business.[19] Furthermore, the requirement of the "durable medium" caused severe problems. A homepage is not durable; an e-mail is not durable. "Durable" is electronic information if it is stored on the computer of the consumer. But how could we prove that the consumer really received the message? As that proved to be nearly impossible, most companies simply refrained from adapting the distance selling regulations.

Finally, the withdrawal right led to bizarre situations. For instance, the question arose: how could you give back a car which you ordered via internet? If the car had been used for seven working days, it is no longer a new car any more and cannot be sold as such. Does the trader really have to bear this loss? Or what is happening with books ordered at Amazon? No exceptions from the withdrawal right have been foreseen for books and, as a result, Amazon, an online bookshop in the past, has now become a free public lending library owing to the Distance Selling Directive. My specific concern however is the

---

[17]　This aspect has been considered in detail by Prof. Dr. Alexander Trunk.

[18]　As to further problems in econtracting related to internet auctions cf. the paper presented by Prof. Dr. Toshiyuki Kono.

[19]　For the consequences in regulating securities and exchange see the papers prepared by Dr. Harald Baum and Sadakazu Osaki.

question of private international law. The principle of the seat of the user has been traditionally applied in consumer protection law where the needs of consumers overrule the interests of traders. Take Art. 12 of the Distance Selling Directive. A consumer shall not lose the protection granted by the Directive by virtue of the choice of the law of a non-member country as the law applicable to the contract if the latter has close connection with the territory of one or more Member States. However, which company acting worldwide in the internet can take account of all the consumer protection laws in the world?

With data protection, I have problems, as well. Again, the strength of my new tool was undermined by several trends. First, the EU closed agreements with the United States to solve the issue of transborder data flow. Both states agreed upon the so-called safe-harbour principles, a kind of model contract which has to be used between EU and US companies and which contains the contractual obligation of the US company to implement EU data protection principles. However, these principles were not worth the paper on which they were written. The biggest problem was George Bush, the new US president who rigorously stopped the whole safe harbour discussion in March 2001. Therefore, everyday, EU companies are violating EU regulations by sending personal data to the States but nobody seems to worry – a great victory for Bush and against privacy.

Yes, you are right: Even my liability considerations have proved to cause international problems. The US has integrated a different concept, the notice and take down concept, in their Digital Millenium Copyright Act.[20] The concept is better than mine, I have to admit that. My focus on "knowledge" of a host provider doesn't clarify to what extent and when the necessary knowledge has been obtained by the provider and what is happening if the provider deliberately does everything to avoid knowledge. And, yes, what of my efforts in the area of internal civil procedure law? This is well-suited for solving intra-EU issues. But as to Japan or the US, they just don't work. There has been a long-lasting discussion on a draft for a new Hague Convention on the Execution of Civil Court Decisions.[21] However, the inclusion of provisions on the exclusive competence of certain courts in intellectual property law matters led to major controversies, as did the question of the enforcement of punitive damages decisions. Therefore, the whole Hague discussion stopped in June 2001; it remains uncertain whether it will lead to major results.

Let me finish my confession: I have killed that man. But it was not my intention to do that; it was mere negligence. Therefore, I hope not to be punished too harshly by you.

---

[20]   See the paper presented by Prof Dr. Anthony J. Sebok on „The Invisible Borderlines of Tort on the Internet".

[21]   See the presentation of Prof. Masato Dogauchi on this matter.

G.   The Confession Of A Woman Who Has Come To The Shimizu Temple

This man laughed mockingly as he looked at my bound companion. How horrified my husband must have been. But no matter how hard he struggled in agony, the rope cut into him all the more tightly. In spite of myself I ran stumblingly to his side. Or rather I tried to run toward him, but the villain instantly knocked me down. "Who are you?" he cried in my face, "Who are you, accompanying this man?". My heart burning, I screamed and told them:

> "I am the spirit of the internet.[22] The Net has a nature, and its nature is liberty. The Internet was born at universities in the United States. The first subscribers were researchers, but as a form of life, its birth was its link to the university and university life. The internet is by its nature anarchic, open, free. The real Internet users are weary of governments. They are repulsed by the idea of the placing of something as important as the Internet in the hands of governments. Policy-Making should be taken away from government and placed with a non-profit organization devoted to the collective interest of the Internet."

"You have to suffer as well, but in a different way", the robber cried. And he struck me severely in my face. I called out in spite of myself and fell unconscious. In the course of time I came to, and found that the robber was gone. I saw only my friend still bound to the root of the cedars. I felt that I had changed, that I had lost something precious, my innocence. "Hey", I said to him, "since things have come to this pass, I cannot live with you. I'm determined to die, ... but you must die, too. You saw my shame. I can't leave you alive as you are." This was all I could say. I took my small sword and raised it over my head. One more I said, "Now give me your life. I'll follow you right away." When he heard these words, he moved his lips with difficulty. At a glance I understood his words. Defying me, his looks said only "Kill me". Again at this time I must have fainted. By the time I managed to looked up, he had already breathed his last – still in bonds. Gulping down my sobs, I untied the rope from his dead body. And ... and what has become of me since I have no more strength to tell you. Anyway, I hadn't the strength to die. I stabbed my own throat with the small sword, I threw myself into a pond at the foot of the mountain, and I tried to kill myself in many ways. Unable to end my life, I am still living in dishonour (A lonely smile) Whatever can I do? Whatever can I ... I ... (Gradually, violent sobbing).

---

[22]   The following quotes are taken froim Lawrence Lessig, Code and other laws of cyberspace, New York 2000.

H.   THE STORY OF THE MURDERED MAN, AS TOLD THROUGH A MEDIUM

While the criminal talked, my wife raised her face as if in trance. She had never looked so beautiful as at that moment. What did my beautiful wife say in answer to him while I was sitting bound there? I am lost in space, but I had never thought of her answer without burning with anger and jealousy. Truly she said, ."Then take me away with you wherever you go." This is not the whole of her sin. If that were all, I would not be tormented so much by the dark. When she was going out of the grove as if in a dream, her hand in the robber´s, she suddenly turned pale, and pointed at me tied to the root of the cedar, and said nothing. She just sat in front of the tree where I was almost dying. She could have helped me; but she remained silent as if she had gone crazy. I looked at her, and immediately she understood. She came to me and whispered: I cannot help you. This would violate my ideals. Take for instance your desire, finally to get an instrument for proving electronic orders, the electronic signature. The lawyers did everything to provide you with a clear framework for digital signatures.[23] But I made this device useless, not purposefully, but negligently. You remember, network economy involves the co-operation of all branches of industry. The more people engage, the higher the network effect works. But as to electronic signature nobody wanted to start.

The banking industry was asked to develop and distribute signature units on the banking cards; but they refused. That has to do with the different technical standards within the banking community ranging from E-Cash to SET. Furthermore, the banks were unwilling to finance signature tools in favour of other industrial branches. The state, itself, also refused the nationwide implementation of signature tools as there is no money in the state budget. The user, himself, refused to buy signature-reading devices as there are no reasonable advantages for him to justify such an investment. As a matter of fact, there is no reason why somebody should buy chip cards with a digital signature if he is now bound by a contract whose formation he could deny without such a signature. So, nobody is using digital signatures, at least in Europe; this technique is dead before it has even been borne.

Similar network effects can be traced back to the discussion on Ecash, one of the fashionable topic in 2000, but now dead. That has nothing to do with law, as the legal framework on Ecash was lucidly structured by EU and US regulations.[24] But nobody wanted to bear the risk of losing ecash and getting no equitable refund. The banking institutions wanted to shift all risks to the traders and the customers; but both groups – simply by ignoring the new technology – did not co-operate in absorbing all the risk.

---

23   An overview of Japanese regulations on electronis signature and form requirements can be found in the paper of Prof. Hideki Kanda.

24   This topic has been dealt with by Prof. Dr. Mads Andenas in his speech.

Furthermore, I have to admit that my conception itself can be questioned. The internet has never been an academic institution, but a militaristic idea. The stress on cyberanarchy disguises the non-democratic features of my dream. Organisations such as the privately organized and US-controlled ICANN demonstrate that behind these informally working organisations there is a bizarre jungle of business interests and uncontrolled state interference. Perhaps my ideas are even preventing technological progress. The internet is – technically regarded - old-fashioned, not adapted to the needs of ebusiness. Video transmissions or internet telephony are practically impossible owing to the inherent technical restrictions of the Internet. I am so sorry; I cannot act against my own nature and help you. I have to let you die."

This is what my wife said to me before I died.[25] She seemed to feel helpless, ashamed, guilty. But I had no time to take care. Once and for all, I sank down into the darkness of space.

---

[25]   This end of the story leads to questions of insolveny law dealt with by Prof. Dr. Christoph Paulus und Prof. Dr. Harry Rajak.

MAKING UNIFORM RULES IN THE ERA OF E-TRANSACTIONS

*Yoshihisa Hayakawa**

Contents

---

*   Associate Professor of Law, Rikkyo University Faculty of Law, Tokyo, Japan; Japanese delegate for the e-commerce WG of UNCITRAL for the thirty-sixth and thirty-eights sessions; Japanese delegate for the Special Commission for the Indirect Held Securities of the Hague Conference on Private International Law.

TOSHIYUI KONO/ CHRISTOPH G. PAULUS/ HARRY RAJAK (eds.); THE LEGAL ISSUES OF E-COMMERCE
© 2002 Kluwer Law International. Printed in the Netherlands, pp. 13-23.

T. Kono et al. (eds.), Selected Legal Issues of E-Commerce, 13–23.
© 2002 *Kluwer Law International. Printed in the Netherlands.*

A.   INTRODUCTION

Information technology has become a necessary tool for the contemporary scene. With it we can easily contact any natural person or legal entity all over the world. It has greatly facilitated worldwide "e-transactions".

As desirable rules for e-transactions are sometimes different from rules for ordinary transactions, new legislation for e-commerce is being contemplated, drafted and enacted by many countries. Japan, for instance, established its own law for electronic signature in 2000.[1] An act for electronic contracting was passed in 2001.[2] An act for limiting the liability of Internet Service Provider was established in 2001.[3] And we can find similar initiatives in many countries.

The fact that each state has begun to make its own new legislation would seem to be favorable for e-transactions. Yet, from another viewpoint, this is disturbing for the future development of e-transactions. It will result in the situation of many different rules for e-transactions existing in many jurisdictions. Even if we can easily cross borders with IT gears, such a legal diversity will make us hesitate to do so for the possible risks in unfamiliar legal systems of foreign countries.

In order to avoid the risks of legal diversity, many international organizations have begun to work in seeking worldwide uniform rules of e-transactions. Such activity, which is, of course, desirable for the future development of e-transactions is described in the following chapter. Thereafter, given that some concerns are raised as to the consequence of these activities, we will examine the real motives of the international organizations and analyse the negative features of current activities for the making of uniform rules of e-transactions. Finally, several factors will be considered relevant to the making of uniform rules for e-transactions.

B.   OVERVIEW OF THE ACTIVITIES FOR MAKING UNIFORM RULES

I.   UNCITRAL

One of the most famous international organizations in the area of making uniform rules is the United Nations Commission on International Trade Law (UNCITRAL). This

---

[1]   Law Concerning Electronic Signatures and Certification Services, Law No.102 of 2000.

[2]   Law concerning Exceptions of the Civil Code Related to Electronic Consumer Contracts and Electronic Notice of Acceptance, Law No.95 of 2001.

[3]   Law on Restrictions on the Liability for Damages of Specified Telecommunications Service Providers and the Right to Demand Disclosure of Identity Information of the Sender, Law No. 137 of 2001.

organization has several working groups, one of which is devoted to electronic commerce (the Electronic Commerce WG). This WG arose out of a group set up between 1973 and 1987 to establish uniform rules for international negotiable instruments. Between 1988 and 1992, it worked on uniform rules for international payment and in 1992, it changed its name to the Electronic Data Interchange (EDI) WG and began to examine appropriate uniform rules for one kind of e-transactions. In 1997, it began to call itself the Electronic Commerce WG. Hitherto it has contributed to establishing two model laws in this field: *UNCITRAL Model Law on Electronic Commerce with Guide to Enactment with additional article 5 bis as adopted in 1998*; and *UNCITRAL Model Law on Electronic Signatures*. And it has now started its new project for a draft convention on electronic contracting.[4]

Other working groups of UNCITRAL also touch on issues related to e-transactions. The International Contract Practices WG, for instance, has contributed to the development of the *Draft Convention on Assignment of Receivables in International Trade*. The International Arbitration and Conciliation WG has examined the "in writing" problem on arbitration agreement in electronic commerce.[5]

II.   The Hague Conference On Private International Law

The Hague Conference on Private International Law has a long established reputation for having contributed to uniform rules. Its main target is not making uniform substantive rules but the establishment of uniform conflict-of-law rules.[6]

Historically, this organization has worked mainly in the field of transnational judicial proceedings or the field of international family law. Since 2001, however, it has started a new project - the *Draft Convention on the Law Applicable to Certain Rights in respect of Securities Held with an Intermediary.*[7] In contemporary securities transactions, most of the securities are immobilized or dematerialized and are only to be found electronically booked on the computer network of financial institutions. In other word, nowadays, many securities transactions have become a kind of e-transactions and this has drawn the Hague Conference on PIL into the field of e-transactions.

Even in the traditional field where this organization has worked for a long time, issues on e-transactions have emerged at various phases. In the series of discussions leading to the *Draft Convention on International Jurisdiction and Foreign Judgments in Civil and*

---

4   For more details of UNCITRAL, *see* http://www.uncitral.org/en-index.htm
5   In the thirty-eighth session of the Electronic Commerce WG, the problems of online dispute settlement were discussed as an alternative to the possible future work in UNCITRAL.
6   For more details of Hague Conference on PIL, *see* http://www.hcch.net/
7   *See* http://www.hcch.net/e/workprog/securities.html

Commercial Matters, for instance, one of the most serious topics was the treatment of e-transactions, raising issues such as whether or not international jurisdiction rules for ordinary transactions would also work for e-transactions? This serious problem is, in fact, still being debated in the Hague Conference.[8]

III. The OECD

The OECD has, over a long period, contributed to the making of worldwide uniform rules, and from a very early stage, it paid attention to e-transactions.[9] In 1997, it established *Implementing the OECD Privacy Guidelines in the Electronic Environment.*[10] In 1998, it established *Electronic Commerce: Taxation Framework Conditions.*[11] and in 1999, it drafted the *Guidelines for Consumer Protection in the context of Electronic Commerce*[12] And it has promoted online dispute resolution by organizing several workshops or symposiums.[13]

IV. WIPO

The World Intellectual Property Organization has worked for the establishing of uniform rules, mainly in the field of intellectual property. Having considered that recent developments in e-transactions enlarge the possibilities for the infringement of another's intellectual property anywhere, WIPO started projects for establishing uniform rules of e-transactions in this field. In 2001, for instance, WIPO established the Joint Recommendation concerning Provisions on the *Protection of Marks, and Other Industrial Property Rights in Signs, on the Internet.*[14]

WIPO, has also been active in the fields of Arbitration and Mediation. It drafted *Dispute Avoidance and Resolution Best Practices for the Application Service Provider Industry* for IT business entities.[15] For online dispute resolution, it presented a report to the Internet Corporation for Assigned Names and Numbers (ICANN), an international

---

[8]   *See* http://www.hcch.net/e/workprog/jdgm.html
[9]   *See* http://www1.oecd.org/subject/e_commerce/
[10] *See* http://www1.oecd.org/dsti/sti/it/secur/
[11] *See* http://www1.oecd.org/daf/fa/e_com/framewke.pdf
[12] *See* http://www1.oecd.org/dsti/sti/it/consumer/
[13] Section B of the Part VI of the *OECD Guidelines for Consumer Protection in the context of Electronic Commerce*, above mentioned, strongly encouraged consumers to use ADR for resolving B to C disputes. The conference *Building Trust in the Online Environment* held at The Hague in December 2000 was jointly organized by the OECD, the Hague Conference on PIL and the International Chamber of Commerce (ICC). For more details, *See* http://www1.oecd.org/dsti/sti/it/secur/
[14] http://www.wipo.int/about-ip/en/
[15] http://arbiter.wipo.int/asp/index.html

administrative body of Internet Protocol and domain names, and largely contributed to the establishing of the online dispute resolution scheme of ICANN for the cybersquatting disputes of domain names,[16] as well as encouraging this movement by organizing several workshops and symposia.[17]

V.   Other International Organizations

The International Telecommunication Union (ITU) has served as a leading international organization in the field of telecommunication. At the early stages of the expansion of Internet, the ITU did not pay any attention to the problems of the Internet because the Internet is a computer network based upon a uniform protocol standardized produced by *private entities*. Nowadays, however, the ITU has begun to work for making uniform rules for e-transactions developed on the Internet,[18] as is evidenced by the noteworthy symposium for the *Multilingual Domain Names* which was jointly organized by the ITU and the WTO in December 2001 is noteworthy.[19] The ITU has recognized the Internet as an established global standard for computer network and now, clearly intends to be involved with the making of uniform rules for the core part of the network system.

The International Organization for Standardization (ISO) is an international body for making uniform standards mainly in the fields of technology. Recently, complaints from consumers involved in e-commerce transactions have drastically increased and the ISO has begun a project for making uniform rules for complaints handling,[20] a project which aims to establish a uniform standard for the correct handling by business entities of such complaints.

The World Trade Organization (WTO) is an international organization mainly devoted to the making of uniform rules of international trade between nations. It, too, has begun to get involved with problems on e-transactions.[21] One of the related topics discussed in the WTO is the treatment of the transactions of digital contents. Roughly speaking, the WTO has two different rules of international trade, one for the trade of goods and the other for services. Should transactions of digital contents, for example music files or motion picture files, delivered on the computer network be classified as the former or the latter?

---

[16]   http://wipo2.wipo.int/process1/report/ After the establishment of this dispute resolution scheme by ICANN, the Arbitration and Mediation Center itself joined this scheme as one of dispute-resolution service providers.

[17]   Especially, the *International Conference on Dispute Resolution in Electronic Commerce* held at Geneva in November 2000 is important. For more details, *see* http://arbiter.wipo.int/events/conferences/2000/index.html

[18]   http://www.itu.int/ECDC/

[19]   http://www.itu.int/mdns/

[20]   http://www.iso.ch/iso/en/comms-markets/consumers/iso+theconsumer-06.html

[21]   http://www.wto.org/english/tratop_e/ecom_e/ecom_briefnote_e.htm

This is one of the critical issues discussed in the WTO, as well as other problems on e-transactions in the field of tariffs, conflict-of-laws, intellectual property and capacity building.[22]

Other international organizations that have worked for making uniform rules in various fields, for example, the International Institute for the Unification of Private Law (UNIDROIT), seem to be biding their time before joining in the process of contributing to the making of uniform rules of e-transactions.[23]

VI. Private Organizations

One of the remarkable features of e-transactions is the influence of private organizations in the process of making uniform. This is partly due to the fact that the Internet is a global computer network developed not by governmental bodies but by private entities. Among such private organizations, the most influential is ICANN which operates as an ultimate administrative body of Internet Protocol and domain names for which it has made a number of remarkable sets of rules,[24] especially, the *Uniform Dispute Resolution Policy* and the *Rules for Uniform Dispute Resolution Policy*.[25] These are sets of rules for establishing an online dispute resolution scheme for the cybersquatting disputes on domain names. It is quite remarkable that this private organization used WIPO, an authoritative inter-governmental organization, as an advisory body,[26] and that it has, since the establishment of these rules, engaged this inter-governmental organization, as one of the dispute-resolution service providers for its dispute resolution scheme.[27]

Another of the active private organizations is the International Chamber of Commerce (ICC).[28] The ICC has contributed to the making of uniform rules for business, for example, the *INCOTERMS*, or *Uniform Customs and Practice on Documentary Credits (UCP),* and it has provided services of dispute resolution using its *Rules of Arbitration* and its *International Court of Arbitration*.[29] Since the very beginning, this business

---

[22]   Ministry of Trade and Industry of Japan made a proposal titled as *Towards eQuality: Global E-Commerce presents Digital opportunity to close the Divide Between Developed and Developing Countries* in the WTO in 2001. For more details, see http://www.meti.go.jp/policy/trade_policy/wto/data/proposal_e-commerce_j.htm#tyu_12

[23]   For more details of UNIDROIT, *see* http://www.unidroit.org/

[24]   http://www.icann.org/

[25]   http://www.icann.org/dndr/udrp/policy.htm http://www.icann.org/dndr/udrp/uniform-rules.htm

[26]   *See supra* note 16.

[27]   http://www.icann.org/dndr/udrp/approved-providers.htm

[28]   http://www.iccwbo.org/

[29]   http://www.iccwbo.org/home/menu_international_arbitration.asp
         http://www.iccwbo.org/index_court.asp

organization has paid attention to e-commerce and has tried to make several sets of rules or guidelines for e-business and to make dispute resolution schemes for e-business.[30]

In terms of a specific project for specific transactions, the project for establishing the BOLERO system is noteworthy. This seeks to establish rules for dematerialized bills of landing (B/L).[31] Many private companies and financial institutions all over the world have joined the framework of this type of e-transaction.

In addition to those more fully described above, other private organizations working for the promotion of e-transactions include the Internet Law and Policy Forum (ILPF),[32] Global Business Dialogue on Electronic Commerce (GBDe),[33] and Global Information Infrastructure Commission (GIIC).[34]

C.   THE BACKGROUND TO THE MAKING OF UNIFORM RULE

Why are so many organizations so active in the search for uniform rules governing internet transactions? Partly, it must be said, because there is a worldwide consensus that legal diversity in the governance of internet transactions will be a serious obstacle to its future development. In order to enable this new type of transactions to exert its own power to the full, global uniform rules have to be provided as a basic infrastructure.

This in turn means that an organization may acquire a great reputation and influence if it succeeds in establishing uniform rules in a specific area of e-transactions and this, too, may be seen as a reason for the search by so many organizations for the holy grail of uniform rules in the fields of e-transactions.

While in general, it is desirable for the sound development of one industry that many entities try to enter and work within that industry, here we are concerned with the industry of making uniform rules. And if each entity makes its own "uniform rules" independently in many places, we must question whether this is an appropriate process for the devising of generally applicable uniform rules.

---

[30]   http://www.iccwbo.org/home/menu_electronic_commerce.asp;   *supra*   note   13;   *See   also* http://www.iccwbo.org/home/bdrs/adr/b2cadr_survey.doc
[31]   http://www.bolero.net
[32]   http://www.ilpf.org/
[33]   http://www.gbde.org/
[34]   http://www.giic.org/

D.   PROBLEMS ARISING OUT OF THE MAKING OF UNIFORM RULES

I.   Conflict Of Uniform Rules

Many international organizations are making different "uniform rules" to cover the same problem. While each target is slightly different from others and the purpose or function of each set of rules is strictly different from the others, there would now seem to be several conflicts of uniform rules in various areas. The BOLERO project, for example, works for establishing of uniform rules for dematerialized Bills of Lading, the king of transport documents. Another project, however, - the Trade and Settlement EDI System (TEDI) project[35]- is seeking uniform rules to cover dematerialized transport documents. Separately, each is making its own schemes for the same problem.[36]

Of course, each organization tries to avoid such overlap and potential conflict. At the Hague Conference on PIL meeting in January 2001 of the Working Group of Experts for the *Draft Convention on the Law Applicable to Certain Rights in respect of Securities Held with an Intermediary*, for instance, the Secretariat of UNCITRAL made a statement that the Indirectly Held Securities project of the Hague Conference should be progressed out of regard for the *Draft Convention on Assignment of Receivables in International Trade* of UNCITRAL. Yet, contrary to this, at the thirty-fifth session of the Commission of UNCITRAL in June 2001, the Secretariat of the Hague Conference made a statement seeking to remove part of the draft UNCITRAL convention in order to avoid the overlap between the draft UNCITRAL convention and the draft Hague Conference convention.[37]

Mutual concessions may be a step forward but they do not always work in this industry. At the January 2001 meeting of the Hague Conference, the Secretariats of both UNIDROIT and UNCITRAL made long statements stressing the importance of establishing uniform substantive rules on the matter of indirectly held securities. The future looks like a tug of war on this issue between these organizations.[38]

---

[35]   http://www.tediclub.com/english/fruits.html

[36]   In the thirty-eighth session of the Electronic Commerce WG of UNCITRAL, the original document fo the WG discussion only mentioned the name of the BOLERO. On this occasion, some delegate: strongly emphasized the existence and importance of the TEDI project.

[37]   There were similar discussions to avoid overlap situations in the thirty-eighth session of the Electronic Commerce WG of UNCITRAL.

[38]   For the thirty-ninth session of the Electronic Commerce WG of UNCITRAL, the ICC immediately submitted its opinion about the project of UNCITRAL for making a draft convention for electronic contracting. *See supra* note 4.

II.   Speed In The Making Of Uniform Rules

Another problem to be found in the activities of these organizations is the speed (or lack of it) with which they work. There can be no doubt that this is a field where change is rapid owing to the continual development of information technology. Rules for e-transactions need to be established quickly and continually modified. Yet, the modus operandi of traditional international organizations is very different. The project for the *UNCITRAL Model Law on Electronic Signatures*, for instance, started in 1996 and the model law was finally agreed in 2001. During these five years, states all over the world were deeply involved in e-transactions and rules for electronic signature were sorely needed. Many states, including Japan, established their own national laws on electronic signature as quickly as possible long before the completion of the model law, resulting in legal diversity on this matter and the depreciation of the model law as a set of uniform rules.

Considering these circumstances, the Hague Conference on PIL organized its project for making the *Draft Convention on the Law Applicable to Certain Rights in respect of Securities Held with an Intermediary* commendably quickly. To speed up the process of making the draft convention, telephone conferences were frequently held and comments were almost always invited by e-mail before the physical meetings.[39] The most remarkable progress from this viewpoint, however, was that made in the ICANN project for the *Uniform Dispute Resolution Policy* and the *Rules for Uniform Dispute Resolution Policy* . This newly established private organization made these rules within one year. The speeded up process, supported by information technology might have been open to criticism according to the traditional practice for the making of worldwide uniform rules, but it is true that the rules in question were effective in sorting out cybersquatters and in maintaining order in some parts of the e-transaction world.[40]

III.   Involvement Of Private Organizations

Can it be said that the involvement of private organizations has only a positive effect on making uniform rules? Many have concerns about the neutrality of such private organizations. Most of the organizations are associations of business entities or funded by business entities. Are these always neutral enough, for example, in the interests of consumer protection in e-transactions? Are they sufficiently unbiased when it comes to issues such as privacy in e-transactions?

---

[39]   *See supra* note 7.

[40]   *See supra* note 25.

To avoid such concerns, ICANN, for instance, has tried to let ordinary people join as members or directors and it has tried to ensure that it is democratically organized.[41] However, many of the private organizations involved have close relationships with appropriate business industries.

E.   CONCLUSION

The recent development of e-transactions has had a great impact on the process of making worldwide uniform rules. It has stimulated the activities of many international organizations and it has caused the traditional process of making uniform rules to be re-examined. Yet it must be said that while the existence of several uniform rules is desirable in the light of competition, too many uniform rules on the same topic, will be self-defeating and lead to the necessary creation of conflict of uniform rules. One idea for avoiding such overlapped situations is a joint venture of some international organizations for making uniform rules, something which, at the level of organizing a conference or workshop, is not so exceptional.[42] Indeed, as the next phase of the search for uniform rules gets underway, projects jointly organized by some organizations are beginning to emerge.[43]

While we must take care in what we are doing, speed in the making of uniform rules is essential, especially for e-transactions. The traditional process of making uniform rules must be radically revised for e-transactions and an important element in this regard is the use of information technology for inviting comments and holding discussion.

Finally, we should emphasize that for e-transactions, private organizations have been very active in making uniform rules. This has stimulated the traditional activities of inter-governmental organizations and we should encourage the activities of the private organizations. At the same time, however, we must seek to ensure the neutrality of their

---

[41]   http://www.icann.org/participate/
[42]   *See, e.g., supra* note 13.
[43]   For instance, the project of the international interests of mobile equipment is jointly organized by the UNIDROIT and the International Civil Aviation Organization (ICAO). *See* http://www.unidroit.org/english/workprogramme/main.htm

activities. Whatever else is the case, there can be no doubt that no time must be lost in searching for effective uniform rules in the era of e-transactions.

European Directives In The Field Of Electronic Commerce: Interplay With German Law

*Alexander Trunk**

Contents

---

*   Professor of Law, Director of the Institute of East European Law, University of Kiel, Germany.

TOSHIYUI KONO/ CHRISTOPH G. PAULUS/ HARRY RAJAK (eds.); THE LEGAL ISSUES OF E-COMMERCE
© 2002 Kluwer Law International. Printed in the Netherlands, pp. 25-39.

T. Kono et al. (eds.), Selected Legal Issues of E-Commerce, 25–39.
© 2002 *Kluwer Law International. Printed in the Netherlands.*

A.   INTRODUCTION

Today the European Union is one of the major players in the field of legislation on electronic commerce. There are numerous pieces of European Community legislation on electronic commerce,[1] and several initiatives are still pending. Although it is not unjustified to accuse the EC of over-regulation in some fields,[2] EC legislation on e-commerce is too recent and too sketchy to carry much responsibility for the current dot.com-crisis. The aim of the European Union is certainly not to "kill" e-business, but to create a favourable climate for this sector of the economy, and this includes adequate, internationally compatible legislation. Whether the EU's approach is satisfactory in this respect, is of course a matter of discussion, and EU legislation on e-commerce is far from perfect. This has many reasons: online technology develops rapidly and poses new legal questions. Lawyers need some time to understand the problems raised by technology, and sometimes there is a communication gap between the developers of the technology and lawyers, who have to deal with the legal implications of technology. If one does not really understand what a cookie is, how shall one then correctly answer, for example, data protection questions about cookies?[3]

EU legislation reflects legal developments in the United States, the motherland of the Internet, as well as in the EU member countries and also developments in other countries. On the other hand, the EU wishes to place its own stamp on the discussion, thereby stimulating national legislation and contributing to international cooperation. European Community legislation on e-commerce is therefore not a one-way strategy imposing regulations and directives upon the EU member states, but it is rather a constant dialogue between the member states and the EU.

I will try to show this by the example of the interplay between EU law and German law, as German law has had a certain impact upon EU legislation in this field. My purpose is not so much to discuss the EU provisions themselves, but their interaction with one member state's legal system. I will start with an overview of EU and German legislation on e-commerce (or, more broadly, the law of information technology), and I will then review in greater depth one or two issues of current significance in this discussion, in particular with regard to the European E-Commerce Directive.

---

[1]   For an overview see, e.g." Legislation" (e-commerce) on the website of the Information Society Directorate-General   of   the   European   Commission, http://europa.eu.int/ISPO/ecommerce/legal/legal.html.

[2]   The Community itself is trying to streamline its legislation, see the White Paper, *European Governance* of 25 July 2001, accessible at http://europa.eu.int/comm/governance/index_en.htm.

[3]   For a discussion about data protection law with regard to cookies cf. Moos, in: Kröger/Gimmy (ed.), Handbuch zum Internet-Recht (2000), p. 430 et seq.

B. OVERVIEW OF EUROPEAN AND GERMAN LEGISLATION IN THE FIELD OF ELECTRONIC COMMERCE

Impressed by the economic development of the IT sector in the United States, the European Union and its Member States started at about the same time to develop new legislation to support development of this "emerging market". Germany took a proactive position, with the Bundestag passing the so-called Multimediagesetz (Multimedia Act), ("Law on Information and Communication Services", IuKDG)[4] in 1997. Differently from what one might perhaps expect, this law is not a systematic Code of legislation, but a common denominator for several loosely connected laws, dealing with some major aspects of information technology law, in particular with digital signatures and with the liability of Internet service providers.

At about the same time, in April 1997, the European Commission published a Communication ("A European Initiative in Electronic Commerce"[5]), in which it declared its objective as being to pass appropriate legislation for e-commerce by the year 2000. The main focus of this initiative is of an economic nature: The Commission hopes to strengthen the New Economy sector in European business, thereby creating new jobs and economic growth. Out of the declaration of 1997 sprang a number of directives particularly devoted to what the Commission calls "Services of the Information Society".[6]

I will first deal with these specific e-commerce related directives. After that I will turn to the second category of such EU legislation which applies to e-commerce transactions, although it is not formally limited to them.

---

[4] Law of 22 July 1997, Bundesgesetzblatt (BGBl.) 1997 I pp. 1870 et seq., recently revised by law of 14 December 2001 (Gesetz über rechtliche Rahmenbedingungen für den elektronischen Geschäftsverkehr), BGBl. 2001 I, pp. 3721. English translation of the original version of the law available at http://www.iid.de/iukdg/gesetz/iukdge.html.

[5] COM(97) 157, accessible at http://europa.eu.int/ISPO/ecommerce/legal/documents/com97-157/ecomcom.pdf. Instead, often the Bangemann report of 1974 („Europe and the Global Information Society") is cited as the key initial document, Lloyd, Information Technology Law, 3rd ed. (2000), p. 19 at 1.51.

[6] By way of a rather intransparent legislative technique, Information Society Services are not defined in the substantive directives relating to these services (in particular the E-Commerce Directive 2000), but in the purely technical Transparency Directive 98/34/EC (Official Journal EC L 204/37, amended by Directive 98/48/EC, Official Journal EC 1998 L 217/18) which deals with EC member states' information to the EC about newly introduced or amended technical standards, see Lloyd, Information Technology Law, 3rd ed. (2000), p. 562.

I.   European Legislation On E-Commerce

Within the European Commission, primary responsibility for the regulation of e-commerce lies with the newly established Information Society Directorate General,[7] though other Directorates General may also be competent to deal with information technology issues relating to their special missions (e.g. consumer protection, financial services, justice and home affairs).

1.   Special E-Commerce Directed Legislation

a)   E-Commerce Directive 2000

The most basic of the IT-related directives is the already mentioned Directive of 8 June 2000 on "Certain Legal Aspects of Information Society Services ... in the Internal Market", the so-called E-Commerce Directive.[8] Like many other European directives, it cuts across the traditional distinctions between public, civil and criminal law. Similar to the German Multimediagesetz of 1997, the directive provides for the freedom to offer "Information Society Services" without an advance licence[9] and establishes unified rules on the liability of service providers (art.12 - 15). It goes beyond the German Multimediagesetz of 1997 in so far as it imposes certain information duties upon service providers (art.5 - 7, 10) and regulates some aspects of online contracting (art.9, 11). Most important, however, there is an express guarantee of "home country (and no other) control" to service providers established within the European Community (art.3). [10] This is meant to strengthen the European internal market, as service providers have to obey the laws of their place of establishment and are - at least in principle - relieved from the burden of checking the rules in other EU member states where they might wish to market their services.

b)   Electronic Signatures Directive 1999

An important aspect of information technology is that of electronic (or digital) signatures. This serves as a tool to prove the integrity and authenticity of an electronic document and

---

7   See the website of this DG at http://europa.eu.int/comm/dgs/information_society/index_en.htm.

8   Official Journal of the EC 2000 L 178/1.

9   Art.4 of the Directive, in contrast with telecommunications law and radio and TV law, where there limited frequency space. As new technologies allow the use of one frequency for a large number purposes and Internet services start to fulfil similar "public information" functions as radio/TV, the requirements of authorisation and control of "..internal balancing of views" so far imposed on radio/TV providers might in the future be substituted by general rules of competition and the civil law.

10   Cf. the formulation in the European Initiative in Electronic Commerce, as quoted by Kelleher/Murray IT Law in the European Union (1999), p. 86 at.8.04.

can therefore be used to fulfil certain legal requirements as well.[11] It has a very broad potentiality of application, far beyond the area of contract law, where it is most often discussed, extending, for example, to company law, banking law, procedural law or administrative law. I do not have to explain technicalities of electronic signatures at this place.[12]

Electronic signatures are the object of a particular European directive, the Electronic Signatures Directive of 13 December 1999,[13] which was passed even before the more general E-Commerce Directive 2000. The structure of the Signatures Directive is similar to the E-Commerce Directive. Like the E-Commerce Directive, it includes a provision on the freedom of certification service providers from advance licence requirements (art.3) and a provision on home country control (art.4).[14] The remaining provisions dealing mainly with the legal effects of electronic signatures and with liability issues (art.5 - 8).

In Germany the corresponding legislation is split into two parts. In the first place, there is the more technical or structural requirements as to electronic signatures which are fixed in the Signaturgesetz (Signature Act), which was originally passed, very early, in 1997 as part of the Multimediagesetz. This Act was radically amended on 21 May 2001[15] to adopt the requirements of the EU Signatures Directive. The Signature Act is complemented by a Government Ordinance, the first version of which dated from 1997, but which has recently been adapted to the new Signature Act 2001.[16]

Secondly, the legal consequences of electronic signatures are laid down in other legislation, depending on the legal sphere in which electronic signatures might be useful. Significantly, the Bundestag has recently passed special legislation modifying the Civil Code (and other private law legislation) to take account of electronic signatures.[17] This

---

[1] Cf. Smedinghoff, Online Law (1996), pp. 53 et seq.

[2] See e.g. Tanenbaum, Computernetzwerke (1997), pp. 632 et seq.

[3] Official Journal of the EC 2000 L 13/12.

[4] Both directives start with provisions on their range of application and on interpretation.

[5] That is the date of the Bundesgesetzblatt where the law was published: BGB1 2001 I no.23, p. 904 et seq. (the law entered into force on 22 May 2001). The Bundestag passed the law on 25 February 2001, the Bundesrat gave its consent on 9 March 2001. An English translation of the Signaturgesetz 2001 is available at http://sicherheit-im-internet.de/download/026-Signaturgesetz_englisch.doc.

[6] Signature Ordinance of 16 November 2001, BGBl. 2001 I p. 3074, An English translation is available at http://www.bmwi.de/Homepage/download/infogesellschaft/SigV_E.pdf. The foregoing Ordinance of 22 October 1997 was published in BGB1 1997 I p. 1870 et seq.

[7] Act of 13 July 2001 on the Adaptation of the Provisions on Form in Private Law and Other Provisions to Modem Legal Transacting, BGB1 2001 I no.35, p. 1542 et seq.; cf. also the draft of this law on the Website of the German Federal Ministry of Justice, at http://www.bmj.bund.de/ggv/ggv_i.htm/bgbrege1.pdf.

law entered into force on 1 August 2001. Similar legislation is planned in the fields of administrative law and criminal law.[18]

2. More General EU Legislation Applying To E-Commerce

So far, the E-Commerce Directive 2000 and the Electronic Signatures Directive 1999 are the main examples of EU legislation specially designated for the IT sector. Although further IT-specific directives may be expected in the future, e.g. with regard to electronic payments,[19] data protection[20] and consumer protection,[21] the bulk of EU legislation regulating e-commerce is not IT-specific.

Of particular importance to e-commerce are the European Community's Data Protection Directive of 1995[22] and EU consumer protection legislation, namely the Unfair Contract Terms Directive of 1993[23] and, more recently, the Distance Selling Directive of 1997.[24] While the Unfair Contract Terms Directive applies to all consumer contracts, the Distance Selling Directive comes somewhat closer to the specifics of e-commerce. However, it covers most forms of distance selling, reaching from mail or telephone orders to online contracts. There is a traceable line of increasing specialization from "general" legislation (in particular fields like consumer protection or data protection) through "distance contracts", towards "e-commerce" in general or even more the specific types and activities of e-commerce.

The political question is, of course: When do we need specific e-commerce legislation and when is it sufficient or even preferable to put e-commerce in the framework of general legislation? The question can certainly not be answered in a generalized manner. The answer depends, among other factors, on the perceived specific nature of e-commerce, on the necessity of detailed legislation and also on the context of a legal system. Even if it may be right to create an IT-specific directive at the EU level, it may be

---

[18] Cf. the draft of a 3ʳᵈ law amending legal provisions in the field of the law of administrative procedure (version of 16 July 2001), accessible at http://www.bmj.bund.de (at Gesetzgebungsvorhaben).

[19] Cf. e.g. the Commission Recommendation 97/489/EC of 30 July 1997 concerning transactions by electronic payments and in particular the relationship between issuer and holder, Official Journal EC 1997 L 208.

[20] Cf. the proposal for a Directive concerning the processing of personal data and the protection of privacy in the electronic communications sector, COM/2000/385 final (accessible at http://europa.eu.int in the Eur-Lex database).

[21] IT-relevant, but not IT-specific: the proposal for a Directive on the distance marketing of consumer financial services (COM/1999/385), accessible at http://europa.eu.int/ISPO/ecommerce/legal/consumer.html), discussed by Kelleher/Murray p. 150 et seq.

[22] Directive 95/46/EC of 24 October 1995, Official Journal EC 281/31, discussed by Kelleher/Murray p. 222 et seq.

[23] Directive 93/13/EC, Official Journal EC 1993 L 95/29.

[24] Directive 97/7/EV, Official Journal EC 1997 L 144719.

preferable to integrate such a directive into a more general framework on the national level. One can see this in the approach which has been taken by Germany in transposing - maybe even transgressing - European e-commerce legislation.

II. German Legislation On E-Commerce

As mentioned before, the relationship between the European Union's legislative procedure and its member states can be seen as a constant dialogue. This is particularly true in an emerging field like information technology law. Usually national legislators are quicker and more flexible than the EU, but sometimes the more bureaucratic character of the EU legislative process may speed-up developments.

In contrast with EU legislation, member states' legislation on e-commerce is - to a far larger degree,- integrated within general legislation. This is self-evident as national legal systems, in particular on the Continent, have broad, well formed laws or even Codes on all legal subjects. Coherence within such a system - which includes the traditional distinction, at least on the Continent, between public, private and criminal legislation - is furthered when rules on e-commerce are integrated within existing legislation. Nevertheless, sometimes specific e-commerce legislation may help to develop certain areas of the law.

1.   Specific IT-Legislation

The German Multimedia Act of 1997 (Informations- und Kommunikationsdienste-Gesetz, IuKDG)[25] served as an eye-opener to the German legal community with regard to e-commerce, although it was a somewhat belated follow-up to American[26] and even international quasi-legislation which emerged from discussions at UNCITRAL.[27]

The Multimedia Act consists of several subdivisions, the most important of which being the so-called Teledienstegesetz (Teleservices Act 1997) as the basic regulation,[28] a special Act on Data Protection in Teleservices (Teledienstedatenschutzgesetz 1997)[29] and

---

[25]   Supra footnote 4.

[26]   E.g. the Signature Acts of some U.S. states (Utah Digital Signature Act 1995 and others), cf. Smedinghoff, Online Law (1996), pp. 53 et seq.

[27]   UNCITRAL Model Law on Electronic Commerce 1996 (with amendment 1998), accessible at http://www.uncitral.org/en-index.htm.

[28]   The Teleservices Act is contained in art.1 of the Multimedia Act (IuKDG) of 1997; the Act is commented in: Rossnagel (ed.), Recht der Multimedia-Dienste (Looseleaf), Section 2.

[29]   This Act is contained in Art.2 IuKDG 1997; the Act is commented on in Rossnagel (ed.), Recht der Multimedia-Dienste (Looseleaf), Section 3. As to the recent amendment of 2001 (Signature Act 2001), see supra footnote 15 and infra footnote 31.

the Signature Act (Signaturgesetz 1997),[30] which established rules on digital signatures in Germany. The last of these dealt in considerable detail with the structural requirements of digital signatures (such as authorization and control of certification authorities), but almost left out, entirely, the legal consequences of digital signatures. The consequence has been that digital signatures have been little used in German practice so far, as business and consumers did not see any particular advantages they could get by using them. This will probably change in the near future as the Signature Act was modified in May 2001 to implement the European Electronic Signatures Directive[31] and the German Civil Code (Bürgerliches Gesetzbuch, BGB) has most recently been amended to ensure that so-called "qualified" electronic signatures fulfil the requirements of "writing" under art. 126 of the Code.[32] It is important to note that not all electronic signatures fulfil the writing requirements of the Civil Code, only those that are based on private-public key encryption and involve certification of the public key by a publicly controlled certification authority.[33]

The constitutional division of power in Germany also serves to complicate matters. At about the same time as the Bundestag passed the Federal Multimedia Act, the German Lände concluded a Treaty on so-called Media Services (Mediendienste-Staatsvertrag, MDStV).[34] Legislation on the press, on radio and TV falls under the domain of the Lände, which did not wish to see their legislative power in this regard diminished by leaving regulation of the Internet completely to the Federal legislator. However, the borderline between teleservices (covered by federal law) and media services (covered by the Lände treaty) is very unclear. Teleservices are defined as having a mainly individual purpose, while media services are said to have an orientation towards the public.[35] Whether, for example, webpages are covered by the Teleservices Act or by the Lände Treaty is still in dispute.[36] The practical relevance of this dispute is, fortunately enough, limited, as the Federal Government and the Lände agreed on a nearly identical wording of the Multimedia Law and the Lände Treaty. This distinction between teleservices and media services is in no way reflected by EU legislation. Therefore, when the EU E-

---

[30]   Art.3 IuKDG; comment in Rossnagel (ed.), Recht der Multimedia-Dienste (Looseleaf), Section 5.

[31]   Signature Act 2001: Act of 16 May 2001 on framework conditions for electronic signatures (Gesetz über Rahmenbedingungen für elektronische Signaturen), BGBl. 2001 I pp. 876 et seq. This law implements the EC Signatures Directive 1999 and repeals the Signature Act 1997.

[32]   For more details, see infra at footnote 42. The Act entered into force on 1 August 2001.

[33]   For an analysis of the Act see Hähnchen, Das Gesetz zur Anpassung der Formvorschriften des Privatrechts an den modernen Rechtsgeschäftsverkehr, NJW 2001, pp. 2831 et seq. and Rossnagel, Das neue Recht elektronischer Signaturen, NJW 2001, pp. 1817 et seq.

[34]   The text is published e.g. at Geppert/Rossnagel, Telekommunikations- und Multimediarecht, 3rd ed. (2001), pp. 161 et seq., and is also accessible e.g. at http://www.datenschutz-berlin.de/recht/de/stv/mdstv.htm.

[35]   Cf. sec.2 Teleservices Act and sec.2 Media Services Treaty.

[36]   Cf. e.g. Holznagel, Vorfragen zu Rundfunk-, Medien- und Telediensten, in: Hoeren/Sieber (ed.) Handbuch Multimedia Recht (Looseleaf), Section 3.2., pp. 19 et seq., Spindler, Haftungsrecht, idem Section 29, pp. 28 et seq.

Commerce Directive is transposed into German law,[37] both the federal Multimedia Law and the Lände Treaty on Media Services will both have to be modified accordingly.

2.   General Legislation

As already mentioned, most of the law of e-commerce in Germany is part of general, non IT-specific legislation. This is true for all branches of the law, whether civil, administrative or criminal law. In particular, conclusion and performance of an online contract falls under the rules of the Civil Code, with special laws on the control of unfair general conditions of contracts (contracts of adhesion) and on some aspects of consumer protection, for example the EU Distance Selling Directive which was implemented in 2000 by the Distance Selling Act.[38] Delictual liability for online behaviour is covered by the Civil Code, with special regulation for unfair competition outside the Code (Law on Unfair Competition). Similarly, the use of electronic means of communication in procedure is governed by the Procedural Codes, e.g. the Code of Civil Procedure or the Insolvency Code.

This approach has worked reasonably well in most situations. For example, online contracting has always been possible, even though numerous details (such as the time when an offer or acceptance via email become binding) are still open to discussion. In civil procedure, the Federal Supreme Court has accepted the filing of actions by computer fax[39] and it is expected that this jurisprudence will be extended to filing by email.[40] Nevertheless, some general provisions have been regarded as unsatisfactory, or

---

[37]   This is to be expected in the near future. On the federal level, the relevant laws have already been passed: Gesetz über Rahmenbedingungen für den elektronischen Geschäftsverkehr of 9 November 2001, publication in the Bundesgesetzblatt is imminent. Some provisions of the Directive have been included in the Act of 26 November 2001 on Modernization of the Law of Obligations (Schuldrechtsmodernisierungsgesetz), BGBl. 2001 I pp. 3137 et seq., accessible at http://www.bundesanzeiger.de.

[38]   Act of 27 June 2000, BGBl. 2000 I pp. 897 et seq. The Act will be integrated in the Civil Code as from 1 January 2002 by the Schuldrechtsmodernisierungsgesetz of 26 November 2001, BGBl. 2001 I pp. 3137 et seq.

[39]   Decision of the Common Senate of the Federal Supreme Courts of 5 April 2000, NJW 2000, p. 2340.

[40]   Filing by BTX, the predecessor of email based on proprietary technique of Deutsche Telecom, was accepted by the Federal Supreme Administrative Court, NJW 1995, p. 2121. However, the Act of 13 July 2001 on the Adaptation of the Provisions on Form in Private Law and Other Provisions to Modern Legal Transacting, BGBl 2001 I pp. 1542 et seq., which expressly permits electronic filing, requires that the Federal Government and the Länder open this possibility by particular ordinances (sec.130 subsection 6 Code of Civil Procedure as amended by the Act of 13 July 2001). Moreover sec.130 subs.6 seems to require a qualified (!) electronic signature in the sense of the Signature Act 2001, which would put a rather strict burden on the parties. It seems that the new law closes the door to electronic filing "below" the formal requirements of the new law, but the Act might be interpreted in the sense that the Federal Government and the Länder may relax the formal requirements, including e.g. PGP signed documents or perhaps even unsigned emails.

insufficiently clear, and have therefore either been superseded by special legislation or modified or clarified in order to serve better, the needs of the information society.

The most prominent example of special e-commerce legislation superseding general legislation is sec.5 of the Teleservices Law 1997 (part of the Multimedia Act 1997), which intends to protect internet service providers from civil (as well as administrative and criminal) liability for illegal content, which is accessible through their services.[41]

An example of a modification of the general law by introducing into existing legislation an additional, IT-specific rule are the new sections 126 (3) and 126a of the Civil Code (BGB),[42] which provide that "qualified" electronic signatures fulfil the writing requirements in civil law. In principle, one could have interpreted the Civil Code writing requirements in this sense even before the introduction of this specific provision, but there was near unanimous opinion among scholars that the particular risks of electronic signatures, for example, the misuse of signature chipcards by third persons, would inhibit such an interpretation.[43] The new section126 (3) and sec.126a, BGB, had to be introduced in order to implement art.5 (1) of the EU Signatures Directive, 1999.

With the similar purpose of strengthening the legal position of electronic signatures, a new provision, art.292a, has been introduced into the Code of Civil Procedure.[44] This creates a presumption that an electronic document, which is signed with a qualified digital signature, originates from the person indicated in the signature.[45] Of course, the risks linked with electronic signatures cannot simply be defined away by legislation.

C. INTERPLAY BETWEEN THE E-COMMERCE DIRECTIVE AND GERMAN LAW

I now turn to some particular topics with regard to the implementation of EU directives, which are at present under much discussion in Germany. I will limit myself to the E-Commerce Directive,[46] which was to be implemented by17 January 2002. In order to stress the importance of this directive, the German Government decided to prepare a particular Act on a Legal Framework for Electronic Commerce (EGG = Gesetz über rechtliche Rahmenbedingungen für den Elektronischen Geschäftsverkehr), which amends

---

[41]   For a discussion of some aspects of this section, see infra at footnote 56.
[42]   Introduced by the Act of 13 July 2001, supra footnote 17.
[43]   See e.g. Palandt (-Heinrichs), Bürgerliches Gesetzbuch, 60th ed. (2001), sec.126 at no.7.
[44]   Introduced by the Act of 13 July 2001, supra footnote 17.
[45]   There are several other new provisions on the use of information technologies in court proceedings, e.g. sec.128 a Code of Civil Procedure as amended in 2001 (permitting online video conferences) and sec.174 Code of Civil Procedure as amended in 2001 (permitting service of documents by email etc.).
[46]   Supra footnote 8.

the Multimedia Act 1997, in particular its main component, the Teleservices Act 1997. The Electronic Commerce Act 2001 was passed by the Bundestag on 9 November 2001 and entered into force on 21 December 2001.[47]

I.   Rule Of Provider Origin

The main purpose of the Directive is to make life (that is to say, business life) easier for any provider of information society services ("ISP"), who has an establishment in the European Union. By this Directive the European Union hopes to stimulate the development of the IT sector in the EU. The term, "ISP" is, it should be remembered not limited to the Internet in its technical sense.[48] The main legal principle by which the Directive intends to further the business of ISPs is by the rule of the provider's origin, a matter which is established in art.3 (1) and (2). The relevant articles read as follows:

Art. 1 Objective and scope.
(4)   This directive does not establish additional rules on private international law ... .

Art. 3 Internal Market
(1)   Each Member State shall ensure that the information services provided by a provider established on its territory comply with the national provisions applicable in the Member State in question which fall within the coordinated field.
(2)   Member States may not, for reasons falling within the coordinated field, restrict the freedom to provide information society services from another Member State.
(3)   Paragraphs 1 and 2 shall not apply to the fields referred to in the annex.

The annex referred to in art.3 (3) of the Directives mentions eight matters, which do not fall under art.3, among them copyright, the freedom of choice of law by the parties of a contract, and consumer contracts.

---

[47]   Act of 14 December 2001, BGBl. 2001 I pp. 3721 et seq.

[48]   Art.2 lit.a) E-Commerce Directive 2000 refers to the definition of Information Society Services under art.1 lit.2 Transparency Directive 1998 (supra footnote 6, which describes them as „any service normally provided for remuneration, at a distance, by electronic means and at the individual request of a recipient of services". See Lloyd, Information Technology Law, 3rd ed. (2000), p. 562.

Article 3 of the Directive has been implemented by section 4 of the Teledienstegesetz (TDG, Teleservices Act), as amended by art.1 of the Electronic Commerce Act 2001, and which reads as follows:[49]

> Sec.4 TDG 2001: Principle of origin
> (1) Service providers established in the Federal Republic of Germany and their teleservices are governed by the requirements of German law, even if the teleservices are professionally (geschäftsmäßig) offered or provided in another (sc. Member State of the EU).
> (2) The freedom of services with regard to teleservices offered or provided in the Federal Republic of Germany by providers established in another State (of the European Union) is not restrained.
> (3) Subsections 1 and 2 do not apply ... [then follows the list of exceptions mentioned in the Annex to the Directive]

In order to understand these provisions one must recall the perceived evil, which is intended to be cured by the Directive. E-commerce is regulated differently in each EU Member State, not only with regard to substantive law (for example, as to provider liability), but also because of the rules of private international law. Each Member State has a set of rules on private international law (conflict of laws), which determine the national legal system that is to be applied to a case with an international element. Some of these conflicts rules are unified in the European Union, namely the law applicable to contracts.[50] Other conflicts rules are not unified, for example, the law of cross-border torts. The result is that an ISP who wishes to market its services throughout the EU, has to take into account the appropriate laws of all fifteen EU Member States. As the Internet has an essentially worldwide orientation, in particular as websites can be read worldwide, ISPs are at much higher risk of their activities being governed by foreign law (or a multitude of foreign laws) than are other business entities. The Directive is designed to cure this structural disadvantage of ISPs by prescribing that only the legal system of the country where the provider is established, should apply.

There is, of course, a problem in this "cure" By cutting through the established conflicts rules of the Member States, even those unified in the Rome Convention of 1980 on the Law Applicable to Contractual Obligations[51] (or a future Regulation on this subject), the Directive chooses a connecting factor ("establishment") that is only linked with the ISP. The exclusive application of the law of origin of the ISP neglects the interests of other interested parties, who may, with justification, expect that their own law applies. This

---

[49]   German version accessible at the website of the Federal Ministry of the Economy, http://www.bmwi.de/Homepage/download/infogesellschaft/EGG-Entwurf.pdf. Translation by the author.

[50]   Cf. North/Fawcett, Cheshire and North's Private International Law, 13th ed. (1999), pp. 535 et seq. (on the Rome Contracts Convention 1980).

[51]   Official Journal of the EC 1980 L 266/1.

becomes particularly evident when one takes the example of a non-EU ISP, who has a secondary establishment in one EU Member State (e.g. Luxembourg), whose activities are therefore covered by the Directive,[52] and who publishes on its website, defamatory information about a person living in another EU Member State (for example, the United Kingdom). To apply Luxembourg law only, would run counter to the basic idea in international torts law that the victim of a tort should be able to rely on the protection of a country with which the victim is closely linked.

One might be prepared to accept this rule, even it were regarded as inadequate and unjust, were there not a confusion within the E-Commerce Directive itself. This confusion is caused by article 1 (4), in terms of which "[the Directive] does not establish additional rules on private international law". A similar formula is used in recital 23 in the introduction to the Directive.[53]

To take this formula at face value would mean that article 3 has little, if any, meaning with regard to private law, because it clearly states that the existing national or EC conflicts rules are maintained. Yet, this can hardly have been the intention of the European legislator, given that the Annex to the Directive expressly excepts the choice of law by the parties (see article 3, Rome Convention on the Law Applicable to Contractual Obligations). It would have been quite unnecessary to refer to choice of law by the contracting parties as an exception, if the principle of the law of origin did *not* normally supersede national conflicts rules. Articles 3 and 1 (4) of the Directive, read together, suggest grave insecurity on the part of the drafters of the Directive as to the range of the principle of origin.

The German legislator has tried its best to mould these conflicting provisions of the Directive into a usable legislative form. Section 4 (1) and (2) of the Teleservices Act 2001 establishes two conflicts rules, one for domestic service providers, the other for providers established in other EU Member States.

As to domestic[54] providers the Act says in article 4 (1) that the "requirements" of German law apply, even if the ISPs do business in other EU countries. This raises a number of questions:

Does the reference to German law include German conflict of laws rules? This was suggested during the legislative process by some authors,[55] but this would have the

---

[52] "Establishment" is defined in art.3 (c) of the Directive and can be understood quite broadly (the mere presence of technical means and technologies to offer Internet services is expressly excluded, but a leased server with some personnel might suffice).

[53] Similarly: sec.2 subs.6 German Teleservices Act 2001.

[54] "Domestic" refers to the place of (primary or secondary) establishment; this can include third-country or even EU providers having a secondary establishment in Germany.

effect to reduce the meaning of the Act for conflict of laws issues so considerably that this interpretation seems hardly compatible with the Directive.

If one accepts that article 4 (1) has some relevance to conflict of laws issues, what is then the range of issues covered by art.4 (1)? One might try to use the notion of "German law requirements", to which art.4 (1) refers, as a tool of interpretation. However, if one understands this notion in the sense of rules "placing burdens" on the provider, provider privileges (articles12 et seq. of the Directive) might be excluded from the provider origin rule, and this would again seem to be in conflict with the Directive. It is submitted that, at the very least, provider liability rules as expressed in articles12 - 15 of the Directive (implemented by sections 8 - 11 of the Teleservices Act 2001) are covered by the provider origin rule. Beyond that it seems doubtful whether the provider origin rule applies to all tort liability.[56] Arguably, one might distinguish between intentional and negligent behaviour (intentional behaviour: ordinary conflicts rules, negligent behaviour: provider origin rule), but there is no indication of such a distinction in the text of the Act or of the Directive.

A further question is raised with regard to third-country-related provider activities. Non-EU-activities are not covered by section 4 (1) of the Teleservices Act, which, in this respect, closely follows article 3 (1) of the Directive. Does this mean that EU providers approaching clients in third countries, for example, the United States or Japan, cannot rely on the liability rules of article 12 et seq. of the Directive? The provider-favourable purpose of the German Electronic Commerce Law would seem to favour an analogous application of section 4 (1) of the Teleservices Act to such situations. *De lege ferenda* at least, such third-country constellations could also be brought under article 3 of the EU Directive.

Similar questions might be raised with regard to section 4 (2) of the Teleservices Act 2001, which prohibits "restraints" on the activities of ISPs, which are established in other EU countries. The wording of this subsection is even less clear about its relevance to private international law than section 4 (1), but it would hardly be convincing to have different conflict rules for German and non-German (EU-internal) ISPs. The need of ISPs to be protected against the application of a multitude of tort laws does not depend on the provider's place of origin. Applying different conflicts rules to domestic and other EU

---

[55]   See e.g. Ahrens, Das Herkunftsland in der E-Commerce-Richtlinie, Computer und Recht 2000, pp. 835 (837 et seq.). Another indication in this sense is that the Act changed the wording of sec.4 subs.1 from „domestic" law (a term which in private international law normally excludes conflicts rules), which had been used in the draft law of 14 February 2001 prepared by the Federal Ministry of Justice, to the more general "German" law. This might also explain why the final version of the law has dropped sentence 2 of sec.4 (1) of the draft law, which had expressly (with some unclear exceptions) reserved private international law rules.

[56]   Choice of law by the parties is expressly excluded from the provider origin rule under art.3 (3) and the Annex to the Directive. It is less clear, however, whether the exception also covers the conflict rules applicable to contracts outside an express or tacit choice of law (law of the place of characteristic performance etc.).

Internet Services Providers would not only run counter the purpose of the Directive, but might also be seen as a discrimination forbidden under EC primary law (art.12 EC Treaty or particular anti-discrimination provisions).

II. Provider Liability

Another very interesting topic of discussion is the unified provisions on provider liability laid down in articles 12 - 15 of the Directive. The main elements of these provisions are the liability privileges in articles 13 and 14 of the Directive. Providers which only "transmit information given by their users" or "provide access to a communication network" are normally not liable for their users' illegal behaviour (such as transmitting offensive materials). Also, providers who grant users the possibility of storing information on their systems (for example, Webspace providers) are liable only if they positively knew that illegal information was stored. These provisions have taken a number of elements from the structure of the existing German liability privilege in section 5 of the German Teleservices Act 1997, which, in turn is one of the most disputed and enigmatic provisions of the Multimedia Act 1997.[57] The liability provisions in sections 8 - 11 of the Teleservices Act 2001 go beyond the Directive in the sense that they do not limit the provider privilege to entities established in the EU. They also protect providers from other countries.

D. CONCLUSION

The European Community has produced two significant directives on e-commerce in the last few years: the E-Commerce Directive 2000 and the Electronic Signatures Directive 1999. Germany has already implemented the Signatures Directive and is implementing the E-Commerce Directive in the near future. In several respects German e-commerce law has inspired the EU E-Commerce and E-Signature directives. When implementing the Directives, Germany has sometimes gone beyond the Directives in creating unified rules for ISPs from the EU and other countries. However, for the time being the bulk of German law applicable to e-commerce is not of an EU background, but autonomous legislation based on comparative experiences.

---

[57] For a detailed analysis see, e.g. Bleisteiner, Rechtliche Verantwortlichkeit im Internet (1998) passim and Spindler, Haftungsrecht, in: Hoeren/Sieber (supra footnote 35), Section 29.

Internet Auction And Its Critical Analysis From The Viewpoint Of Contract And Commercial Law

*Toshiyuki Kono**

Contents

---

* Professor of Law, Kyushu University, Japan; member of UNESCO experts committees.

Toshiyui Kono/ Christoph G. Paulus/ Harry Rajak (eds.); The Legal Issues Of E-Commerce
© 2002 Kluwer Law International. Printed in the Netherlands, pp. 41-55.

T. Kono et al. (eds.), Selected Legal Issues of E-Commerce, 41–55.
© 2002 *Kluwer Law International. Printed in the Netherlands.*

A.   Introduction

While "auction" has been an object of analysis by economists,[1] lawyers have not discussed it much. This paper focuses on the Internet auction and analyzes it from a legal point of view.

If one defines "Internet Auction" very broadly, it includes not only auctions between regular citizens or those as the platform for B2C (business to consumer), but also the platform for B2B (business to business) transactions. There are some few instances of a legal analysis of B2C auctions, but it is a little too early for a discussion of B2B auctions. Platforms for B2B will further develop in various ways, and although one could discuss at least some basic issues of B2B auctions, it will be the Internet auction as platform of B2C that will be the main thrust of this paper.

The legal control of auction business, irrespective of the use of the Internet, varies from country to country. In Germany, for example, article 34b of the Gewerbeordnung requires the permission of the appropriate administrative organs in order to carry on auction business of movables, real property or foreign rights (Versteigerergewerbe). Moreover, the Versteigerungsverordnung, (the administrative ordinance), was introduced with the intent of implementing this regulation. On the other hand, in Japan there is no equivalent legislation. Only the Law on Antiques Business (Kobutsu Eigyo Ho) requires the permission of the prefectural Committee for Public Security (Koan Iinkai) to run an antiques market as a place for transactions by professionals only. This requirement is based on the police controlling and monitoring the flow of antiques and second hand goods, and there is no other law that regulates auctions where at least one party is a non-professional. Therefore any control, if necessary, must be made based on the Civil- and Commercial Codes. For countries such as Japan, which do not have special legislation for auction business, the analysis of the Internet auction from a contractual point of view is crucial, since the contractual structure is the most fundamental legal component of the auction. Also the results of the analysis could be shared with lawyers in other jurisdictions because of the universal character and structure of contract.

Although there are various types of Internet auctions, this paper will focus on particular auction sites, which describe themselves as "venue", such as eBay or Yahoo!Auctions, since this seems, at present, to be the most popular business model of the Internet auction and their business is carried on worldwide. It is, in other words, a typical example of electronic commerce in the context of globalization.

---

[1]   For example, William Vicekrey, "Counterspeculation, Auctions, and Competitive Sealed Tenders", in Public Economics, selected papers by William Vickrey, (ed. Richard Arnott, Kenneth Arrow, Anthony Atkinson and Jaques Drze, (1994), pp. 55-84.

B.   AUCTIONS BETWEEN REGULAR CITIZENS OR B2C

The most popular type of Internet auction is the platform type like eBay or Yahoo! Auctions. To participate in transactions on this platform, that is, to offer goods at the auction or to bid, registration and obtaining an ID and password is required. Usually only one person accepts the highest bid, while under the so-called Dutch auction system[2] several persons can accept the bids. The price is determined by competition: the highest bidder wins. For the bidder there are two methods of bidding, first manually inputting his or her bidding price, secondly to offer his or her maximum bid, and leave it to the software automatically and gradually to raise the price towards the limit, depending on the bids of others. If nobody bids more than this maximum bid, this bidder wins. Since it is a "competition", one might expect to see what the current highest bid is, but in this case, the other bidders cannot see the maximum bid. At some auctions, for example, eBay, even the currently highest bid is not shown to other potential bidders. There may be new forms of auctions in the future, but these features of the auctions are the basis of our discussion.

I.   The Legal Status Of The Internet Auctioneer

(1)   The auctioneer in the traditional auction:

According to the terms and conditions of the traditional auction house, auctioneers are deemed to be the agents of the seller.[3] They offer as their service an expert opinion about the items sent for sale and store them until the date of the auction. As for bidding methods, besides the conventional way of bidding in an auction room, bidding may be by fax or by phone. When bidding by fax, the bidder gives a maximum bid price, which is very similar to the system of bidding with a maximum hammer price on an Internet auction. To bid by phone, the bidder tells his or her agent, who is an employee of the auction house, "yes" or "no". The agent will raise the bid within whatever discretion has been conferred. If another bidder offers a higher bid, the agent will say to the principal something like "there are so-many pounds against you". The bidder must then decide whether to raise the bid to compete further or to withdraw from the transaction. This is similar to bidding at an Internet auction site by inputting the bidding price manually, although saying "yes" or "no" is much easier. These services at a traditional auction house are free of charge, unless the bid is successful, in which case the auctioneer charges both the seller and the successful bidder in accordance with the sales price.

---

2   Historically it meant the type of auction, where the first bidder wins, while price is going down. See, op.cit. at 61.

3   For example, according to the terms and conditions of Phillips Son & Neal Limited, the auction house acts "as auctioneers and agents for the vendor...".

(2) At an Internet auction, there are several pricing strategies, for example:

(a) participation may be free to all participants (seller and buyer), unless either uses a special service (as, for example, with eBay Japan);

(b) it may be free only to the buyer, while the seller must pay a certain amount as a fee. In addition, at the fall of the hammer, the buyer has to pay a certain percentage of the hammer price (this is also available on eBay);

(c) all participants have to pay a fixed amount in fees (e.g. Yahoo! Japan).

These can be classified into two types, charging a fixed fee or charging fees by reference to the hammer price.

The fact that the participants have to pay the auctioneer means that there must be some contractual relationship between the auctioneer and the participants, the terms of which being that the auctioneer provides a service, and the participants pay for it.

Yet, what is the service, given that an Internet auctioneer does not provide an expert opinion nor does he or she store the items? Given, also, that in a traditional auction house, bidding by fax or by phone is free of charge, unless the bid is successful? As long as these bidding methods are offered free in the auction business, consumers will not consider it worth paying, even if the service is offered on the Internet where the only palpable difference is the automated system of the Internet auction.

It might be argued that since, according to the terms and conditions of the major auctioneers, the auction site is described as "venue",[4] the fees could be considered as entrance fees, thereby establishing the contractual relationship between internet auction site and the buyer or seller. But this understanding is based on a simple paraphrasing "auction site as a virtual venue" and it legally does not mean anything, since legal obligation and its fulfillment are not the matter of the virtual world, but that of the real world. The attempt to use entrance fees to establish this binding legal obligation is neither persuasive nor logical as an explanation of the relationship between participants and auctioneers.

In my view, the legal relationship between the auctioneer and participants should be understood as follows: in order to participate in transactions on an Internet auction site, all participants must access the auction site first. In any case, they have to be able to use the software designed for the auction. Thus, in the first place, a contract to use this software must be concluded by the participants and the auctioneer. The application for an ID and password can be considered as the offer and the mail from the auctioneer, providing the ID and password, arriving in the mail server of the participants or of the

---

[4] Vgl. http://www.yahoo.com/info/terms/, http://pages.ebay.com/help/community/png-user.html

participant's Internet provider, is the acceptance which brings the contract comes into existence. The original value of the Internet auction is, as stated above, the automated bidding system. The automation and the software developed for the auction is not separable. Hence what participants are paying to the auctioneer is to be interpreted as fees to use the software.

The legal relationship between the auctioneer who charges a fixed amount and the participants should be considered as the contract to use the auction software. A problem may be said to arise by reason of the fact that eBay Japan does not charge anything to all participants, but it does charge, when a special service is used. But this free use should be considered simply as the provision of an incentive to use the fee-paying services.

(3)   If we understand that the contract to use the software is being effected between the Internet auctioneer and the participants, a further problem arises with a provision to be found, for example with Yahoo!Japan, which states that no warranty is given by Yahoo, even if the contents, system or program of Yahoo!Auctions are not safe or free from error or malfunction or even if all errors or malfunctions are not completely corrected.[5]

However, as long as participants have paid the fees to use the software, it is a contractual obligation of the auctioneer, properly to maintain the system of auction at least to the extent of the functioning of the software and its server. Any such disclaimer as described in the preceding paragraph would, therefore, contravene the principles of good faith.[6] The terms and conditions of other auctioneers might be less specific that that of Yahoo!Japan, but still might raise the same issue. The following general disclaimer of warranty might be seen as an example:

> "You expressly understand and agree that: a. your use of the service is at your sole risk. The service is provided on an 'as is' and 'as available' basis. Yahoo expressly disclaims all warranties of any kind, whether express or implied, including, but not limited to the implied warranties of merchantability, fitness for a particular purpose and non-infringement" (yahoo!auctions[7]);

alternatively,

> "We offer our web-site and services on an 'as is' basis without any express, implied or statutory warranty or conditions" (eBay Japan[8]); "We... provide

---

5   http://www.yahoo.co.jp/docs/info/terms/, at 16.
6   In Japan, it would violate the Consumer Contract Law also.
7   http://www.yahoo.com/info/terms/, at 17.
8   http://www.ebayjapan.co.jp/help/community/png-user.html, at 11.

our web site and services 'as is' and without any warranty or condition, express, implied or statutory." (eBay[9]).

(4)   When a bid is successful at eBay, the seller must pay, besides the fixed "insertion" fees, a certain amount of money, depending upon the final bid. It can be interpreted as an honorarium to eBay and therefore the contractual relationship between the participants and the auctioneer is not simply the contract to use the software. Since the way of calculating the honorarium is very similar to that of the traditional auction house charge, (although the traditional auction houses charge is to both seller and buyer), we might understand the contractual relationship on the internet auction as the same as that of the traditional auction house, namely a brokerage contract. It could be interpreted also as "contract for work and services", in which the party undertakes to bring about a particular result. However, the Internet auctioneer does practically nothing. Its software does everything. Owing to the lack of the auctioneer's efforts to bring about a particular result, it cannot be understood as a contract for work and services and it should be interpreted as the brokerage contract.

Given that there is not much difference between the traditional auction contract and the internet auction contract under which participants can use the software, what might be the contractual effect of the honorarium which has to be paid by a seller to eBay? It may, for example, render contractually enforceable certain implied terms. It might be argued, that in the case of a successful bid, the seller expects a more convenient auction system, safer payment system and more secured delivery service than other auctioneers offer and that the failure to deliver any of these might amount to a breach of contract. From the economic point of view, it is not worth paying the honorarium, unless more service is offered. In future, users will examine whether auctioneers offer satisfying services for the payment and if the payment and services are well balanced. If some auctioneer offers services to provide an expert's opinion or storage space, it has enough reason to charge the honorarium. The disclaimer of warranty, however, is more problematical.

(5)   The Internet auctioneer may view itself as a mere "venue" with the inference that it is completely free from any warranty or liability. Yet, as already argued above, "venue" is nothing but a synonym of a "virtual world" or "virtual market" something which, legally, means nothing Thus any reduction in liability or the freedom from liability is meaningless. One must still seek an appropriate basis in contract for the internet auction's or auctioneer's liability.

If the software or server of the auctioneer has a defect or if the management of the server is bad, it may cause additional loss to the bidder. The auctioneer may, for example have failed to install anti-virus "vaccines" for an unreasonably long period with the effect that the bidding of a particular bidder was disturbed and, consequently, unsuccessful. As a

---

[9]   http://pages.ebay.com/help/community/png-user.html, at 11.

result, the bidder may be forced to purchase the same goods elsewhere at a higher price. Theoretically this bidder could seek compensation.

What then would be the status of a limitation of liability clause in the terms and conditions on which the bidder sought to participate in the internet auction?. Yahoo, for example, requires its participants to accept the following clause,

> "Limitation of liability: you expressly understand and agree that yahoo shall not be liable for any direct, indirect, incidental, special, consequential or exemplary damages, including but not limited to, damages for loss of profits, goodwill, use, data or other intangible losses (even if yahoo has been advised of the possibility of such damages), resulting from the use or the inability to use the service...".[10]

This clause may seem too favourable to the auctioneer. Yet, should the same criteria be applied to internet auction contractual liability as to other, regular compensation cases? The fee paid for the use of the software is usually very low and one might, therefore, have thought that there should have to be very unusual circumstances to justify compensation for the bidder's additional loss. Further, it must be remembered that the Internet auction is still at the very early stage of its development and that the imposition of a wide-ranging liability on the auction or auctioneer might kill this development.

(6)   Two small points should also be mentioned. First, there are guidelines on the website of many Internet auctioneers, in addition to the terms and conditions. These guidelines sometimes contain provisions, which could be said to form a part of the terms and conditions (this is, for example, the case with Yahoo!Japan). The word "guideline", of course, is usually used to describe principles without binding power and this use of it may, therefore, be misleading. Secondly, the terms and conditions of some auctioneers in non-English speaking countries appear to be a direct translation from the English version (for example in the case of eBay Japan). Sometimes, the translation is so bad that the meaning of some of the provisions is not at all clear. This must be revised by legal professionals as soon as possible.

(7)   Finally, there is the issue of the choice of law and jurisdiction clauses, which are usually included in the terms and conditions. In the case of Yahoo!Japan, the applicable law is Japanese law and the Tokyo District Court has jurisdiction over disputes between Yahoo Japan and the participants. On the other hand, eBay Japan adopts Californian law and disputes are to be submitted to commercial arbitration in the USA. Clearly, auctioneers expect to attract sellers and bidders from abroad.

---

[10]   http://www.docs.yahoo.com/info/terms/, at 18.; also http://pages.ebay.com/help/community/png-user.html, at 12.

Under most of the private international law systems, the parties may choose the applicable law only in circumstances where there is a foreign element in the contract. If the participants in the auction on a Japanese website are Japanese nationals living in Japan, Japanese law would be automatically applied to any issues between them and the auctioneer. On the other hand, when a Japanese citizen living abroad, or a foreigner living in Japan, participate in the auction and problems arise, the law referred to in the choice of law clause will apply. If an auctioneer chooses the law of a country where its liability can easily be waived and it calculates its fees and the premium of insurance based on this law, he would clearly prefer that the same law should also apply where there is no foreign element, but this would only be possible where this does not violate Japanese law.

II.   The Legal Relationship Between Seller And Auction Buyer

(1)   At the traditional auction, many bidders make offers and the highest bidder is determined by the fall of the hammer. This whole process usually takes no more than 40-50 seconds. The appropriate legal analysis is that declarations of intent are made by many possible buyers, and the seller accepts only one of them. The German law explains this situation very clearly. If a higher bid is made, other lower bids become void and the sales contract is effected by the fall of hammer (art. 156 BGB). Without such a provision, the legal basis on which the contractual relationship does or does not come into effect is a matter of interpretation of the intention of the parties, something which will involve establishing what the offer and the acceptance were and how definite was the intention of the parties. If, for example, the offer were to be interpreted as insufficiently definite, it would fall into the category of being an invitation to treat and, therefore, not the basis on which an acceptance could conclude a binding contract. In the case of an auction based contract, given that competition is the unique characteristic of the auction, it may also be necessary to investigate how competitive the sale was.

One might classify the auction into the following groups:

The bidder can see the bids of other participants (known as the "competitive conclusion of contract in the narrower sense"). This can be further divided into two groups, that where the highest bidder wins, while the price goes up, and that where the price goes down, and the first bidder wins. In the case where the highest bidder wins there is yet a further sub-division, namely that where the seller does not express his or her minimum selling price, and that where he or she does. The seller's silence means that no definite intent to sell can be inferred, in effect, implying that the seller has simply made an invitation to treat and not an offer. The highest bid is, therefore, the offer in the legal sense and not an acceptance. A binding contract will only come into existence if and when the seller agrees to sell at the price of the highest bid. On the other hand, where the minimum selling price is expressed, a firm intent to sell the item is clearly shown. Here, there is an offer – to sell at the minimum price or higher – and the highest bid does constitute an acceptance (and therefore concludes a binding contract) provided it is at or above the minimum price. At the auction whereby the first bidder wins, while the price is going down, the seller's intent to sell is firm. The seller has made an offer by putting up the item for sale and the first bid is the acceptance of that offer.

A similar, but different form of transaction is "conclusive bidding", whereby the bidding conditions of other bidders are not shown. Therefore the bidder has no chance to rethink if he should change his or her bid, taking other bids into consideration. Here the bid is the offer in the legal sense and the fall of hammer is the acceptance. The seller is therefore not bound necessarily to accept the highest bid. He may, for example, choose another less advantageous bid: theoretically, all bids remain valid. Thus, the seller might take other factors, like the buyer's paying power, into consideration in deciding not to select the highest bid.[11]

(2)   In the light of this description of the traditional auction bidding systems, how should the Internet auction be classified? How does it differ, legally from the traditional auction? Since there are two types of Internet auctions, the auction where the bids of other bidders are not shown (for example eBay Japan) and where they are shown (for example, Yahoo), it may at first sight appear that the former is an example of "conclusive bidding" and the latter of the "competitive conclusion of contract in the narrower sense". However, one common service at Internet auction sites is automated bidding through inputting the maximum bid. When this service is used, the maximum bid is not shown to other bidders. Here the most important element of the "competitive conclusion of contract in the narrower sense" is lacking; the latest information on the bidding price is not available for the bidder to decide whether he should continue or withdraw, in the light of other bids. In fact, owing to the automated system, the bidder often does not know until the last date if other bidders have exceeded his or her bid. In addition to that, owing to excessive access to the server at the same time, there is always a gap between the inputted price and the price shown on the website. This kind of gap is technically unavoidable. Therefore the Internet auction cannot be understood as the "competitive conclusion of contract in the narrower sense", but rather "conclusive bidding".

(3)   Therefore at the Internet auction, the bidding is the offer in the legal sense and the fall of hammer is the acceptance. As a result, the seller is not bound to accept the highest bid. At the traditional auction, if the seller establishes a minimum bid, as above mentioned, this is likely to be interpreted as the seller's definite intent to sell to somebody who offers a higher price than the minimum bid. This minimum bid is equivalent to the "start price" at the Internet auction. But at the Internet auction, the start price is usually nominal (often 1Yen or 10cents) and should not, therefore, be interpreted as conveying a firm intention by the seller to sell. Instead to glean the definite intent of the seller, one should focus on the "reserve price", which is the equivalent to the minimum hammer price at a traditional auction. In short, the bidding is usually the offer in the legal sense,

---

[11]   Vgl. Sakae Wagatsuma, Saiken Kakuron jo (Law of Obligation, part 1) (1954), at 68., Masao Miyake, Keiyakuho Soron (Contract Law, General Rules) (1978), at 20.

but presenting items on an auction site can be interpreted as the offer, where the seller provides a so-called reserve price.

This conclusion could lead to uncertainty, since the reserve price should be given item by item, and this may affect the character of bidding on each different item. Without this, arguments between sellers and buyers are likely after closing the bid: the seller may assert that there was no reserve price and refuse to deliver the item to the highest bidder, on the basis that the bid was the offer, which left him free to choose any one of the bids. A similar contractual issue was recently raised in a case in Germany.[12] If Internet auctioneers want to avoid trouble in the future, they will need to clarify in their terms and conditions how the offer and the acceptance are defined and that this is the basis on which any participation will be assessed.

Since it is the auctioneer that makes and uses the terms and conditions, the clause concerning the offer and the acceptance cannot automatically be a part of the agreement between the seller and the buyer. For countries which do not have legislation concerning the terms and conditions, like Japan, it must be determined what is necessary in order to ensure the integration within the contract of the clause as to what constitutes the offer and the acceptance. In my view, the fact that the terms and conditions contain not only clauses concerning the relationship between the auctioneer and the participants, but also concerning the relationship among the participants, should be properly notified to all the participants, and the participants should signify their agree to be bound by these clauses through mouse-clicking, before participating in the auction.

(4)   According to major contract law systems such as those in Germany, France or Japan, a sales contract comes into effect when a buyer receives an offer expressing the seller's definite intent and the seller receives the buyer's acceptance of that offer indicating his or her definite intent, and where both these intents are in accord on the price, quantity and quality of goods, the delivery date and so on. Each party must receive the other's serious expression of intent to be legally bound. However, at the Internet auction, it is only after the fall of hammer that the seller and the buyer begin to contact each other. Until that point, the seller signifies his intent to sell by mouse clicking to the server of the auctioneer and this information is stored in the server. The intent of bidders is also sent to the server of the auctioneer. This is technically unavoidable producing the effect that the contract may come into existence without the parties being aware of the intent of the other.

If we wish to remedy this, we either have to abandon the traditional structure of contract and accept the idea that a contract may come into effect without communication of the parties' respective intent, or we need to ensure the appointment of an agent, who receives the respective intents on behalf of the seller and bidders. Since the first alternative seems

---

[12]   LG Muenster, NJW-CoR, 3/00, S.168ff., OLG Hamm, NJW 2001, S.1142ff.

unrealistic, we would have to adopt the second alternative and find an agent. Realistically the auctioneer is the only possibility for this position and it must, therefore, be clearly stated in the terms and conditions that the auctioneer acts as the agent of both seller and bidders to receive their intents. Otherwise no contractual basis cannot be established for the sale through the Internet auction.

But this would, in effect be the appointment of an agent which cannot be cancelled by the buyer, thus a one-sided appointment of the agent which would be unlawful[13] However, if one makes too much of a classic dogma, it would kill a new born baby who might grow as a giant in the field of transaction. It should be sufficient to ensure the contractual validity of internet auction transactions, that the participants are well informed of the appointment of the auctioneer as the agent of both parties before they join transactions through the Internet.

If the auctioneer is the agent of the participants in this way it is no longer possible to maintain the concept that the Internet auction is a "venue, since to maintain this concept, the auctioneer must have nothing to do with the conclusion of the sales contract between the seller and the buyer. Yahoo!Auctions, for example, state in their terms and conditions that "Yahoo! Auctions is a platform for our users to connect with one another. Yahoo! does not participate in, nor is it a party to, auction transactions.....Sellers and buyers are completely responsible for working out the sale and exchange of goods."[14] This is clearly untenable given – as analyzed above – that the parties have no direct contact until the fall of hammer and if the auctioneer indeed, has no connection with the sales contract, no contract can come into existence.

(5)   A further problem arises as to the compatibility of the "venue" concept, with clause to be found in the terms and conditions, which states that the cancellation of selling or bidding is not possible. EBay, for example, has the following clause:

> "Bids are not retractable except in exceptional circumstances such as when the seller materially changes the item's description after you bid, a clear typographical error is made, or you cannot authenticate the seller's identity."[15]

If the Internet auction is just a venue and the auctioneer has nothing to do with the sales contract, surely the participants might be entitled to agree to the cancellation of their contract? We have to re-think the concept of cancellation in relation to internet auctions.

---

[13]   Johannes Hager, JZ 2001, 786-791, at 791.

[14]   http://user.auctions.yahoo.com/html/guidelines.html

[15]   http://pages.ebay.com/help/community/png-user.html, at 4.

The problem is that a cancellation would disturb the order on an Internet auction site and violate an obligation included in the contract between the auctioneer and participants, namely the contract between the auctioneer and the bidder as to the use of the software. A cancellation violates the contract with the auctioneer and the limitation of the seller's right to cancel should be understood the same way. The point is that the last minute cancellation of bidding might cause problems to this system which requires that in order to determine who the highest bidder is, all bids must remain valid until the closing day.

(6)   One of the characteristics of Internet transactions is anonymity and dual-direction. At an Internet auction, the following cannot be known to the participants, namely whether

the seller is offering for sale goods bought for the purpose of resale,

if it is the first participation of the other party or he or she has experience of having sold at the Internet auction (although it can be found out to some extent through referring to the feedback profile of the seller),

the seller is a natural person or a corporation.

Under the Japanese law, for example, if one buys something in order to resell it later, it is an "absolute commercial transaction" within the terms of art. 501 of the Japanese Commercial Code), which, in turn, leads to the application of the Commercial Code, irrespective of the nature of the subject. The consequence is that the seller gives no warranty for hidden defects in the sale article, unless the buyer investigates the article immediately and notifies the seller of the defect (art. 526, Commercial Code). And the buyer is obliged to store the article, even if he or she cancels the sales contract due to the hidden defect (art. 527, Commercial Code). Notification of such cancellation is not necessary where the sale item cannot be delivered by a certain date, and as a result, the purpose of the contract would be lost (where, for example the sale item is a concert ticket art. 525, Commercial Code).

These are special provisions of the Civil Code and while often unsuitable to the majority of Internet auction participants, it is also undeniable that there are plenty of people as participants to whom these rules would apply. In other words, the apparently separate territories for the application of the Civil and Commercial Codes are indistinguishably mingled at an Internet auction. With the development of the Internet transaction, the typical model of transactions in the civil law system may be changing and the significance of the law for Commercial Transactions may have to be revised. The same would also apply to French and German law, which also know this distinction.

(7)   In international transactions through the Internet auction, the seller and the buyer could, in theory, choose the applicable law. If the applicable law does not acknowledge the difference between merchants and non-merchants, (such as English law or Swiss Law), warranty and liability issues will apply equally to both these categories of participants. Obviously a different result might obtain where the legal system does

recognize this distinction. A further possibility is that, again in theory, the applicable law could be chosen for each bid with the result that the seller's liability at one session could differ from the seller's liability at another session. This could lead to chaos.

Even at the traditional auction, it is desirable to apply the law of the place of the auction rather than applying different laws to each bid. At the Internet auction the necessity to achieve clear solutions must be even greater, since far more and diversified players will sell and buy at far more various items within a short period. However the place of the location of the Internet auction is not readily determinable and a further alternative would be the application of the law of the principal office of the auctioneer. But this will not always be fair to all participants (Californian law is more advantageous to residents in California as opposed to non-residents). The better solution would be to assume the intent of all participants to apply the law of the country, for which the portal is designed. When, therefore, someone participates in the auction through a portal site of an auctioneer, for example Yahoo!Germany, it should be assumed that he agrees that German law should apply to his transactions. The best solution, however, would be to draft model general terms and conditions, which both parties would adopt as their rules. The Hague Conference of Private International Law would be an adequate institution for this project.

C.   B2B

(1)   Suppose that a PC manufacturer decided to open its purchasing process to many parts suppliers. If this purchasing system were digitized, it would be a simple type of B2B. Suppose that a supplier, Y, makes an offer. The contents of this offer are usually not recognized by other competing suppliers. Therefore, legally speaking, it is not the "competitive conclusion of a contract", but rather the "conclusive bidding". The announcement of X calling for offers from various suppliers is a mere invitation to treat. Y's bidding is an offer and X can determine which supplier's offer to accept. It is not bound to accept the highest bid, and may take other factors into consideration. Legally speaking this raises no contractual problems. However, there must be persuasive reasons for this decision. For example, at the "conclusive bidding" for the public authorities, as the procedure for awarding public contracts, art.26-6 of the Japanese Fiscal Law requires reasonableness if the highest bidder is not chosen. This should also apply to "private" conclusive bidding mutatis mutandis in order to prevent abuse.

(2)   In practice, transactions through the Internet are usually carried on with suppliers with which a business relationship has been already established, since starting a business with a foreign partner is too risky for secured payment and delivery of goods. In this sense, the fully opened B2B transactions through the Internet would not be feasible. Perhaps only transactions whereby every element of the transaction, from order to delivery and payment, can be made digitally (e.g. to sell music, images, digitized literature) can be fully open through the Internet.

When the above-cited system is developed as a new system, in which several buyers and many suppliers join, it resembles the B2C platform. Once, for example, the RosettaNet[16] is further developed, it will be a good example. Its legal structure should be the same as the system of "conclusive bidding", so long as the contents of bidding are not known to the other participants.

The important thing here is to keep the conditions of participation, and the outcome as fair as possible. It would be unrealistic to let all participate in this scheme without any conditions, but if these conditions are so strict that they hamper the participation of other suppliers, this may raise problems of antitrust law, depending upon the market share of the existing members. In addition, if the highest bidder does not win, the fairness of the system itself would be questioned.

Once the system is established, the operation of the platform could be taken over by a particular institution. If so, this institution must pay attention to the provisions on commercial brokerage, for example, Japanese Commercial Code, art. 543 et seq. At present, art. 546 requires the broker to make and deliver paper documents and this will, therefore need to be reformed so that a digital file and e-mail may satisfy these requirements. In addition, the obligation imposed on a broker by art. 549 to perform the contract even when not informed of the name or trade name of the other party would raise difficult questions, since in the automated system, the names of bidding companies (suppliers) are usually not known to the buyer. The application of this provision to Internet transactions should be excluded and it would follow that legal systems that resemble this aspect of the Japanese system should also be modified.

D.   SUMMARY

The concept of the Internet auction as a venue is legally unsustainable. The analysis of the terms and conditions of several Internet auctioneers show that amendments are necessary in order to prevent problems in the future. Moreover, there are other issues

---

[16]   http://www.rosettanet.org/rosettanet/Rooms/DisplayPages/LayoutInitial

such as the *raison d'etre* of the Commercial Code, a review of the functions of Private International Law and the applicability of anti-trust law.

THE INVISIBLE BORDERLINES OF TORT ON THE INTERNET

Antony J. Sebok[*]

Contents

[*] Professor of Law, Brooklyn Law School, Brooklyn, NY, USA.

TOSHIYUI KONO/ CHRISTOPH G. PAULUS/ HARRY RAJAK (eds.); THE LEGAL ISSUES OF E-COMMERCE
© 2002 Kluwer Law International. Printed in the Netherlands, pp. 57-77.

T. Kono et al. (eds.), Selected Legal Issues of E-Commerce, 57–77.
© 2002 *Kluwer Law International. Printed in the Netherlands.*

A. INTRODUCTION

Technology drives change in tort law. This is because tort law deals primarily with compensation for injury, and technology, in addition to improving life, also can rapidly accelerate and multiply the speed and rate of injuries in a society. This fact leads to an interesting question, however: When do new technological facts become legal facts? At what point does a change in technology produce such widespread changes in the kinds of injuries or the modes or injuring that we can say that the technology has created (or has created the demand for) a new form of tort law?

One might argue that all technology does is multiply the number of existing torts the system has to handle. This, arguably, how we might view the development of the airplane. Airplane accidents are catastrophic when they occur, but it is not obvious that they raise issues that are not present in car accidents. On the other hand, a case can be made that the development of the steam engine and certainly the internal combustion engine changed tort law in England and America. As Morton Horwitz and other have demonstrated, the Industrial Revolution created not only new opportunities for physical injury, but whole new classes of injuries and whole new classes of injured. As a result of the rapid industrialization during the 19th Century, tort law shifted its focus from land and strict liability to personal injury and negligence. Thus, in the mid-19th Century, technology "changed" tort law.

It is still too early to tell which way the Internet will affect tort law. There have been rash predictions about the Internet's uniquely powerful effect on antitrust law, communications law, and even constitutional law, but tort law, so far, has escaped much of the hyperbolic claiming that these other fields have seen. This is partially because one of the areas of tort law where the Internet poses its most serious challenge--the protection of personal data--has been treated as a separate field by lawmakers and scholars. But other areas--such as the intentional interference with large numbers of computers through a virus--have curiously escaped almost all attention by either scholars or lawmakers.[1] This lecture is an attempt to address this lack by clearly and carefully organizing the various ways in which tort law and the Internet intersect.

At the outset I want to make clear that this paper is about *substantive* tort law and the causes of action that come out of interactions on the Internet. It is not, therefore, about questions of procedure. Torts resulting from interactions on the Internet, like contracts struck between parties connected by the Internet, raise problems of jurisdiction and

---

The reason why there is little or no litigation relating to torts resulting from computer viruses may be that the wrongdoers are difficult to find and have almost no assets to warrant a private lawsuit. *See* Christopher J. McGurie, "Old Torts Never Die – They Just Adapt to the Internet," NAT. L.J., September 25, 2000, B15.

conflict of laws that are very complex.[2] My contribution to this conference is limited to the initial question of when and how parties in a typical United States jurisdiction could characterize another's act a tortious. The further question of whether a party, injured under the law of their home jurisdiction or the jurisdiction of the party who injured them, could successfully bring an action and which law they would have to use, is very difficult and deserves separate consideration. I would simply observe that my impression is that scholars have been looking at the question of civil procedure and the Internet with some energy and interest, as a search through the current literature will reveal.

B.   WHAT IS AN INTERNET TORT?

The first thing which must be clarified in any discussion about the Internet and torts is that the field of inquiry is not coextensive with the field of computers and tort law. Computers have been around a lot longer than the Internet, and the tort issues involving computer hardware and the software designed to run computers are by now well known. At the risk of making a too-simple generalization, most of the tort litigation relating to computers is products liability. While fascinating from a technical point of view, products liability litigation for defects in computer hardware follows the same legal principles as products liability for automobiles.[3] The question might have gotten interesting if there had been, as predicted, widespread failure of software on January 1, 2000. There was such a significant fear of litigation in response to the physical and consequential economic harms that would have ensued if "Y2K" had proved to be a real problem, that the United States Congress, at the urging of the high tech industry, passed a special law limiting the right to sue in products liability.[4]

---

[2] *See, e.g.*, Black, Vaughan, & Deturbide, Mike, *Commentary* – Braintech, Inc. v. Kostiuk: *Adjudicatory Jurisdiction for Internet Torts*, 33 CAN. BUS. L.J. 427 (2000).

[3] In both cases, state law, as reflected in either the Restatement of Torts (Second) §402A and Restatement of Torts (Third), Products Liability. Fraud has also become a potential cause of action in certain design defect cases. Recently Toshiba agreed to settle for $2.1 billion a class-action fraud claim based on the allegation that they had knowingly sold laptops with a flaw that could result in the loss of some data on floppy drives. The complaint did not allege that any customer had lost data or was physically or economically injured by the loss of data. The complaint alleged that Toshiba knew that the laptop could lose data and did not inform the buyer of this fact. *See* Pasztor, Andy and Landers, Peter, *Toshiba Agrees to a Settlement On Laptops in $2.1 Billion Pact*, WALL ST. J., November1, 1999, at http://interactive.wsj.com/articles/ SB941169193142159945.htm.

[4] Congress enacted broad legislation covering virtually all civil actions (including product liability claims) involving Year 2000 date-related device or computer system failures. See Y2K Act, Pub. L. 106-37, 113 Stat. 135 (1999). The most important doctrinal limitation on computers in products liability is that § 402A allows for strict liability for defective products in the case of physical injury and consequential economic loss caused by physical impact onto either the victim's body or property by the defective product. Thus, liability for Y2K problems in products liability would have to come through physical accidents caused by faulty software–such as the failure of equipment in hospitals or on assembly lines.

The capacity of the Internet to facilitate communication means that the salient feature of the Internet, from a torts perspective, is very different from that of computer hardware or software. The Internet is not a collection of computers, although it is in part; nor is it a collection of programs, although it is in part, too; nor is it a collection of voice and data transmitters, although it is in part that too. It is a combination of computers and programs and telephonic equipment, and as such, it carries forward all of these different technologies risks as injurious devices and combines them in interesting ways. In fact, as I will demonstrate below, the most salient feature of the Internet as an injurious device in tort is not its capacity to wreak damage as the result of an unnoticed defect suddenly manifesting itself, which is the archetypical products liability story. It is, rather, that individuals will use the Internet to intentionally injure other, either by using the Internet to invade others' intellectual property or to interfere with others' future economic advantage. In this sense the Internet's closest neighbor in tort is the postmarked letter or the completed phone call, not the automobile or chemical factory.

Traditionally speaking, there are at least three ways to divide up the causes of action in common law tort. First, one might divide up tort law by the *grounds of liability*: absolute liability, strict liability, negligence, and intentional tort. Second, one might divide up tort law by the *injury suffered*: unpermitted physical contact with the body, unpermitted physical contact with chattel; invasion of real property, invasion of intellectual property, economic loss, emotional distress, and dignitary harm. Third, one could divide up tort law by the *means of injury*: physical contact; harmful linguistic expressions or images; omissions in professional duties; and fraud and misrepresentation. I shall approach torts that occur through the Internet from the second perspective–the injury suffered. As I think will becomes apparent, most torts that occur through the Internet are some version of intentional tort, and the means of injury in most Internet torts is either through some form of linguistic expression, usually written language injures another's protected interest. Where the torts are quite diverse and difficult to categorize is the kinds of protected interests at stakes–namely the range of injuries that can be suffered through Internet torts.

C.   A BRIEF TOUR OF THE WORLD OF INTERNET TORTS

I.   Invasion Of Intellectual Property

1.   Trademark

Trademark cases are predominately statutory, with a focus upon the Lanham Act, 15 U.S.C. §1125, in particular. Thus, when trademark issues arise on the Internet, one must turn to federal law. The Lanham Act encompasses unfair competition, which in turn encompasses such elements as trademark infringement, trademark dilution and false designation of origin. While the tort of unfair competition is traditionally a common law tort, the Lanham Act provides a more effective federal statutory tort. As a federal law, the

Lanham Act invokes federal question jurisdiction, alleviating some of the problems associated with finding proper jurisdiction in Internet cases.

The Federal Trademark Dilution Act ("FTDA") became effective on January 16, 1996. The new provision added section "(c)" to U.S.C. 1125. Under section (c) the owner of a famous and distinctive mark can obtain an injunction and has the possibility of obtaining damages as determined by the court and equity, for the commercial use of a mark that "causes dilution of the distinctive quality of the mark." In order to obtain injunctive relief, intent need not be shown. This particular element may be seen as strict liability offense in that a plaintiff need only show that a mark was famous, it was associated with a certain product or entity, and that it was being used for a commercial purpose by the infringing party. False designation of origin, included in the causes of action stated under §1125(a) does not even require the mark infringed upon to be federally registered and is thus used to protect against improper use of unregistered trademarks. Intent is, however, a necessary element that must be proven in order to obtain monetary remedy.

The Internet has produced a set of novel complaints under the Lanham Act that result from the fact that the it is designed to allow the viewer to move rapidly between sites on the Internet. The very thing that makes the Internet-published content superior to conventional, printed content–the ease with which one can move from one author's content to another–is its Achilles heel from the point of view of the Lanham Act. If a user can move himself to a new page, or can simultaneously bring up images from multiple pages, so can a publisher, thus "hijacking" other people's content, and presenting it as his own, or in some other way profiting from it. This problem can be seen in the following sets of issues.

1)   *Framing*

Framing was introduced in 1996 as a proprietary feature of the Netscape Navigator web browser. Framing technology allows a web site designer to "frame" an independently scrollable window within its own border. As the name implies, a "frame" is a bordered area of a web page that acts as an independent browser window. This independent browser window then usually "frames" the contents of a secondary "target" web page or web site, hiding the secondary page's Universal Resource Locator ("URL") and domain name. The framed site thus appears to be a part of the original page's content. This illusion is furthered when a user attempts to bookmark the web page, as the bookmark will save the URL of the framer rather than the targeted, framed, site.

By framing, any company or person can freely utilize another company's or person's web site content, making their own site appear much more rich in content than in actuality. Web sites, especially news sites, attract visitors based on the quality and quantity of their content. With an increase in visitors to a page due to a perceived greater quality of the page, the page owner's have a greater possibility of selling advertisements on their site, increasing revenue. Thus, framing allows a method to increase site "stickiness," the attraction and retention of viewers, at little to no cost to the site owner.

The chief complaint in tort against framing (and related actions such as linking) is unfair competition under the Lanham Act. Plaintiffs usually claim a combination of trademark infringement, trademark dilution and misappropriation.[5] Injunction is granted after a showing of the use of a registered (or unregistered, if the complaint is false designation of origin (dilution)) mark or copyrighted content being used for commercial purposes, the minimal requirements posited by the Lanham Act for injunctive relief. If the mark or content is being used with the *intent* to commercially gain from its use, monetary damages, defendant's profits and attorney's fees may be obtained. The showing of intent to profit is thus key in achieving real damages.[6]

b)   Linking

HREF Links are a form of "hyperlink". A hyperlink is a piece of text that is usually differentiated from regular text by a special color, usually blue, or special formatting, such as underlining. A hyperlink, when activated by clicking, directs the user's browser to establish contact with a new web address. The new site for which contact was established either takes over the browser window of the original site or opens in a new browser window. HREF hyperlinks allow the viewing of content from only one site at a time. These are standard, most utilized form of hyperlink. HREF links are used on all web sites. They may be used to point a user to another site of interest, or simply to navigate through the original web site. HREF links are the basis of the Internet as interconnected web pages.

IMG Links make use of "in-lined" images and do not share the HREF link limitation that only content from one site can be viewed at a time. In-lined images are graphics that are visible on screen as part of a Web document's main body (as opposed to being within a separate window), but which originate at a source other than the site that stores the document being viewed.

IMG links were designed to allow a web page builder to create a single repository of images, saving web space, i.e., no matter what page in a designer's site a viewer was

---

5   *See* Wilson, Jr., Clyde H. & Wilson, Susan M., *Cyberspace Litigation: Chasing the Information Highway Bandits*, TRIAL, Oct. 1, 2000, at 48, *and* Tucker, Robert L., *Information Superhighway Robbery: The Tortious Misuse of Links, Frames, Metatags, and Domain Names*, 4 VA. J.L. & TECH. 8 (1999).

6   The primary method of calculating damages is lost advertising revenues. A chief method web sites utilize to generate revenue is from "click-through" advertising. "Banners," specific-sized advertisements placed on web sites, pay web sites a certain amount (usually 5-15 cents) each time a banner located on their site is "clicked" by a visitor, an action that launches an advertisement in a separate window, or leads the visitor to a new site. Another method of generating advertising revenue is by impression. In this method, rates for advertisers are determined by number of visitors to a site; counters exist on a site that can tell a web site proprietor how many times a site has been visited, and by how many different visitors.

currently on, he would be looking at the same picture, the builder didn't need to upload the same picture to reside as a resource for each page. As the IMG link allowed specifications as to where to find the image, however, designers found that they could link to a picture on another site, and make this stolen image appear, without credit, on their own page.

Actions in tort in linking cases use the same statutory basis as in framing. In HREF cases, the wrongdoer directs visitors to his page to another's page through a hyperlink with no indication that the visitor is being directed to the intellectual property of another. Thus, the visitor to Defendant D's page will believe after clicking the offending hyperlink that she is viewing D's content when in fact she is viewing Plaintiff P's content.[7] So far, the courts have found for plaintiffs where there was a clear risk that the viewer would be confused as to the actual author of the page to which they were directed by clicking the HREF. In IMG cases, Defendant D is not sending the viewer to a new page, he is allowing Plaintiff P's image to "float" on his own page. Since the viewer is actually connected to P, there is not copy being made of P's image.[8] In addition to he obvious intellectual property issues, there is a question of trademark dilution, since IMG linking allows the designer of a webpage to place a trademarked image in a context that might be damaging to that mark, without copying it.[9]

c)   *Metatags*

Metatags are key words used by search engines (Google, Yahoo!, AltaVista, Web Crawler, and InfoSeek among others) to find sites relevant to a user's query. Metatags are embedded in the computer code of web sites, or may be invisible text on the face of the site itself. When a search term is submitted by a search engine user, the search engine scans all web pages that it has indexed, looking for the term in the pages metatags or text. Upon finding the metatags, the search engine includes the Web site in its search results. The search engine then ranks the relevant sites according to the relative frequency that the key words appear within the metatags and in the text of the site.

While most companies use their own trademarks and other appropriate descriptive words within their site's metatags, tort issues arise when companies also use trademarks owned

---

[7]   *See Shetland Times Ltd. v. Wills*, Scot. Sess-Cas., (Oct. 24, 1996), 1 E.I.P.L.R. 723 (Nov. 1, 1996); *Ticketmaster Corp. v. Tickets.com*, 2000 U.S. Dist. LEXIS 12987, 2000 WL 1887522 (C.D.Cal. 2000); *and House of Blues, Inc. v. Streambox, Inc.*, (complaint filed 9/13/2000, C.D. Cal.; *as described in* Fausett, Bret A., *Linking Legalities*, WEB TECHNIQUES, February 1, 2001.

[8]   *See* discussion on the "Dilbert Hack" Case in Tucker, *Information Superhighway, supra* n.5. (Defendant, a fan of plaintiff's cartoon strip created own web page and used IMG links to call up images (cartoon strips) from plaintiffs server on is own page.)

[9]   *See Playboy Enterprises, Inc. v. Universal Tel-A-Talk*, CIV. A. 96-6961 (E.D. Pa. 1998) (court held that intentional linking of defendant's site to image of plaintiff's "bunny logo" was a trademark infringement).

by others in the metatags on their site in the hope that Internet users searching for the competition will instead be led to their own site. Innocent appropriation of metatags is hard to imagine; if one sells sporting supplies, and one specifically instructs one's webpage designer to embed "NBA" on one's page, the courts are likely to find that this conduct was willful and calculated to lead consumers to somehow believe that the website is connected with the NBA. Thus, where violations of the Lanham Act because of metagging have been found, statutory damages are often awarded.[10]

d)   Cybersquatting

Cybersquatting (or cyberpiracy) refers to the deliberate, bad-faith, and abusive registration of Internet domain names in violation of the rights of trademark owners Generally, there are four variations:

(i)   The traditional cybersquatter registers domain names based or trademarks and tries to sell the domain names to the mark owners for profit.

(ii)   A related practice is "cyberpiracy." A cyberpirate registers a domair name incorporating a variation of a trademarked term and uses it for a website that lures traffic intended for the mark owner's site. "Web-jacking" is similar to this practice, though in web-jacking the site is actually hacked so that when a searcher enters one name they are directed to the web-jacker's site instead.

(iii)   Another variation is "typo-squatting." A typo-squatter registers domair names that incorporate variations of well known marks such as misspellings or missing characters (e.g., yafoo.com) to take advantage of unsuspecting web surfers.

(iv)   Finally, some people register domain names that resemble trademarks bu never use them. These passive holders or "pseudo-cybersquatters" do no construct active websites, make no offers to sell the domain names, and are often very difficult to contact.

The primary motivation in cybersquatting is money. At the inception of the Internet's widespread use, many companies were hesitant or slow in establishing an online presence. Cybersquatters took advantage of this fact and registered the large corporations' names and variations thereof, in the hopes that these companies would find it more cost efficient to simply buy the names from the cybersquatters rather than litigate

---

10   *See Playboy Enterprises, Inc. v. Asiafocus Int'l, Inc.*, CIV. 97-734-A (E.D. Va. 1998) (court held tha intentional embedding of word "playboy" and "playmate" as metatags was illegal and, in addition t issuing an injunction to desist, awarded $1 million per infringement), *and see Playboy Enterprises, Inc v. Calvin Designer Label*, 985 F. Supp. 1220 (1997) (same; no damages requested).

to reclaim the name.[11] The Anti-Cybersquatting Consumer Protection Act ("ACPA"), 15 U.S.C. 1125(d), has become the primary cause of action in the reclaiming of domain names from cyber-squatters.[12] The ACPA was signed into law on November 29, 1999 and created a statutory cause of action against "bad faith" registration of domain names. In summary, a cybersquatter is liable to a trademark owner if the cybersquatter, in bad faith, intends to profit by registering or using a domain name that is identical or confusingly similar to a trademark. The ACPA allows trademark owners to sue anyone who engages in cybersquatting for the higher of actual damages or statutory damages of $1,000 to $100,000 for each infringement, and in the case of pseudo-cybersquatters, the Act allows for suit against the domain name itself, allowing the reclamation of a trademark without the response of the owner.[13]

2. Copyright

In regard to sheer publicity, the area of copyright and the Internet is the area receives the most attention. The case of *A&M Records, Inc. v. Napster*[14], in which A&M Records, Interscope, Sony Music, Motown Records, MCA, Atlantic Recording, Island Records an Capitol Records sued and won a case against Napster for contributory and vicarious copyright infringement, is a prime example of this publicity. Napster is as of this writing instigating digital fingerprinting technology which allows a song to be "fingerprinted" and stopped from illegally being copied through the Napster servers.

Another example is the recently decided *N.Y. Times v. Tasini*[15], in which the Supreme Court of the U.S. decreed that freelance writers have the right to obtain remuneration for the publication of their works in electronic databases. This means that in the absence of a specific contract with the freelance writers, publishers must either pay for the use of the writer's work on an electronic database or remove the work from the database. As a result, publishers such as the NY Times have announced the removal of thousands of works written by freelance writers from their online databases, a removal based on fear of additional lawsuits.

---

[11] *But see Panavision International v. Toeppen*, 131 F.3d 1316 (1998), in which plaintiff successfully enjoined cybersquatter's use of trademark.

[12] Currently, ICANN (Internet Corporation for Assigned Names and Numbers) has set up an alternative to litigation for domain name disputes which reflect the requirements for an action set out under the APCA. To prevail, a complainant must assert and prove that: (1) the domain name is identical or confusingly similar to the Complainant's trademark or service mark; (2) the domain name holder has no rights or legitimate interests in the domain name; and (3) the domain name was registered and is being used in bad faith. Remedies include only the cancellation or transfer of domain name registration; monetary damages are not available.

[13] *See Sporty's Farm L.L.C. v. Sportman's Market, Inc.*, 202 F.3d (2nd Cir. 2000); *Electronics Boutique Holding Corp. v. Zuccarini*, CIV. 00-4055 (E.D. Pa. 2000).

[14] 239 F.3d 1004 (9th Cir. 2001).

[15] 2001 U.S. LEXIS 4667; 69 U.S.L.W. 4567 (2001).

Two schools of thought exist in the issue of copyrights and their pertinence to the digital Internet. One school fights for the freedom of such publishers as the NY Times and companies such as Napster, calling for the free dissemination of information, exhibiting a fierce belief in complete freedom of information. The other school believes more in traditional copyright regulation, and that an artist, writer or everyday person has the right to create, to be protected in that right, and to be able to profit if they are so able.

Regardless of theoretical beliefs behind the use of the Internet in providing a forum for information, rulings such as *Napster* and the *Tasini* aptly illustrate that statutes and court rulings are catching up to the technology of the Internet, and that traditional copyright regulations now are being applied to online technology. Indeed, as *Tasini* in particular illustrates, in copyright law the Internet has, at most, merely posed a technological challenge to the old rules, but the old rules are not changing. At this point in the law and the Internet, it appears that through the Digital Millennium Copyright Act, which sets standards for ISP's and their procedures for ridding pages under their control of copyrighted works, all standard copyright rules now are able to be applied to the Internet.

II.   Unpermitted Physical Contact With Chattel

1.   Intentional Injury

As strange as it may sound, there is no reason why the Internet cannot be treated as a medium through which intentional *physical* touchings occur. One might want to think of the Internet as a series of channels which allow one user of the Internet to cause very small changes in the hard drives and memory chips of computers owned by other users of the Internet. The threshold question of whether the transmission of electronic data and instructions to another computer is a physical touching is one which modern tort law seems content to approach functionally. Certainly an instruction sent by phone to by Defendant D's computer to Plaintiff P's computer that is intended to cause P's computer to short circuit, spark, and catch fire would satisfy the Restatement of Torts (Second)'s definition of Trespass to Chattels at §217. But the consequences of the phone transmission need not be so dramatic. Current doctrine seems to suggest that *any* intentional physical touching, no matter how slight, may be a trespass. In the context of trespass to land, intentional touching of another's property with microscopic particles is sufficient.[16] There is no reason to presume that an intentional invasion of another's computer by sending harmful data into its physical apparatus could not be trespass either.[17]

---

[16]   *See Bradley v. American Smelting & Refining Co.*, 709 P.2d 782 (Wash. 1985).
[17]   *See* Robins, Mark. D., *Electronic Trespass: An Old Theory In a New Context*, 15 COMP. L. 1 (1998).

In *Thrifty-Tel, Inc. v. Bezenek*[18] the plaintiff, a provider of long distance services, sued the defendant, whose children had used a computer to "hack" into their database, and stole confidential codes. The lawsuit was not for the monetary value of the codes, since the children did not use them to steal anything of value, but for damages incurred as a result of the 'break-in'. This case seems to have established that, to the extent that they can be identified and have assets, hackers may be pursued in trespass to chattels.

The much more likely target of trespass to chattels claims are "spammers"–marketers who send vast numbers of unwanted advertising to the subscribers of an on-line provider who maintains the mailboxes for clients. In *Compuserve v. CyberPromotions, Inc.*[19] the court cited *Thrifty-Tel* for the proposition that a low-level of intrusion, such as electronic signals, could constitute physical intrusion, where it the intrusion was intentional and knowing. This case has been followed by the federal court in the Eastern District of Virginia, which, coincidentally, is where America Online is based.[20]

Based on this logic, hackers who create programs like the "ILOVEYOU" virus that struck 45 million computers and caused an estimated $10 billion in damage in May 2000 could also be sued in trespass to chattels.[21] Perhaps an even greater threat are Distributed Denial of Service (DDOS) viruses. DDOS attacks are accomplished when a person or group of people exploit weaknesses in other computers, and force the other computers, known then as "slaves," to concurrently transmit requests for information to a specified web site. The targeted web site becomes inundated and inoperable. Both Yahoo! and Amazon.com have been victims of these attacks. As mentioned earlier, there are two reasons why tort law is unlikely to play an important role in these cases: the defendants are very hard to find and they are almost certainly judgement-proof.

2.   Unintentional Injury

The logic of tort law suggests that plaintiffs and litigation flows towards those defendants with assets to compensate for the injuries suffered by the plaintiffs. Thus, if hackers and DDOS attacks continue, one might expect to see plaintiffs choosing to sue the manufacturers of the email programs that allowed the injurious programs into their computers, as well as the manufacturers of security programs that were marketed to protect against unwanted intrusions by others through the Internet. As a threshold matter, it may be the case that most programs that connect up to the Internet would be found by a

---

[18]   46 Cal. App. 4th 1559 (1996).
[19]   962 F. Supp. 1015 (S.D. Ohio 1997).
[20]   *See America Online, Inc. v. IMS*, 24 F. Supp. 2d 548 (E.D. Va. 1998) *and America Online, Inc. v. LCGM, Inc.*, 46 F. Supp. 2d. 444 (E.D. Va. 1998). The federal courts in Virginia, in addition to common law, also applied the state's "Computer Crimes Act," which prohibits the use of "a computer or computer network without authority … with the intent to [c]onvert the property of another," since it authorizes a private right of action for violations of the Act.
[21]   *See McGuire, Old Torts, supra* at note 1 at B16.

jury to be nondefective even if they were unable to provide 100% protection. But even if a program were in fact defective, there remains a further question whether computer programs are products (as opposed to services) and therefore fall under conventional products liability doctrine.

Email, for example, is simply a piece of software which, as other software, may be customized or sold as a turnkey product. While no specific case law is settled, there does seem to be a test in the issue of customization versus mass-market sale. Mass-market software appears to place software in the category of a "product" as per the UCC, and place it in the realm of strict liability in tort as per § 402A.[22]

The question of whether products liability can apply to pure economic losses might be finessed under the logic used in the trespass to chattels cases discussed above. If the courts are willing to consider small changes in the molecular structure of computer hard drives to be physical touchings, than it seems that the physical injury requirement under § 402A would be satisfied whenever a computer's memory and or capacities were affected by a virus transmitted through the Internet which was permitted to enter the plaintiff's computer because of a defect in an email or security program.

The purchaser of a defective email or security program, even if she could convince a court to consider the program a property and her injury to be "physical", would face one last hurdle: almost all software programs are protected by "shrinkwrap" licenses which limits damages. The controlling case in this area is *ProCD, Inc. v. Zeidenberg*.[23] This case defines shrinkwrap licenses, those that become effective once the packaging of a piece of software is opened, as valid, stating "Shrinkwrap licenses are enforceable unless their terms are objectionable on grounds applicable to contracts in general (for example, if they violate a rule of positive law, or if they are unconscionable)."[24] The Court stated that even if the terms of the contract/warranty were later found to be disadvantageous, they were still valid.

III.   Unpermitted Physical Contact With The Body

The most likely way that the Internet could facilitate injuries of the body is through negligence. It is unlikely that the Internet will ever become a useful tool for battery or

---

[22]   As per the Restatement of Torts (Third), Products Liability, § 19, cmt. a, "History," "it is for the court to determine as a matter of law whether something is, or is not, a product." The Reporters' Note, cmt. d, "Intangible Personal Property," analogizes to the UCC in that under the Code, mass-market software is considered a good, while customized software "developed specifically for the customer" is considered a service.

[23]   86 F.3d 147 (7th Cir. 1996).

[24]   Id. at 1449. The case analogized shrinkwrap licenses to the limitations found on such things as tickets, and cited *Carnival Cruise Lines, Inc. v. Shute*, 499 U.S. 585 (1991) for authority.

assault. However, it is worth remembering that tort law in America is concerned, for the most part, with the compensation of *negligently* caused physical injury. In this regard, most important form of "Internet negligence" will probably occur as a result of the provision of medical care by services that offer to interview, diagnose, and treat patients via the Internet.

There are no medical malpractice lawsuits currently pending regarding misdiagnosis by a "cyberdoctor." This is not to say that such suits won't become prevalent, given the rise of "cyberdoc" websites on the Internet such as www.cyberdocs.com. Though email is usually reliable, the reliance on such a medium may provide interesting cases of medical malpractice, i.e., a diagnosis is transferred via an email that is never received. Online medical care stands to bring to litigation matters in the area of levels of confidentiality maintained by a website and the subsequent control over consumers' personal health information; the reliability of online information; and deceptive and/or fraudulent medical practices.

A more immediate concern seems to be the ability of people to obtain prescription drugs from online pharmacies and cyberdoctors. Consumers tend to be using these online pharmacy's for obtaining "embarrassing" drugs like Viagra. This use of the Internet has the possibility of becoming litigious, as online pharmacy's may be lax in verifying prescriptions or obtaining a patient's overall drug history (leading to possibly negative drug interactions).

Prompted by the ease in the ability to buy prescription drugs over the Internet, Congress has proposed the Pharmaceutical Freedom Act of 2000, (the Internet Pharmacy Consumer Protection Act ("IPCPA").[25] This act would require that the sale comply with restrictions imposed by the act, with all applicable state laws and that the web site post accurate information regarding compliance with the FDA. The IPCPA is still before the House of Representatives Subcommittee on Commerce. Specifically, the bill seeks to provide the FDA the ability to prohibit web sites from the introduction or delivery of a prescription drug into interstate commerce if the purchaser of the drug submitted the purchase order for the drug, or conducted any other part of the sales transaction for the drug, through an Internet site, or if the site fails to meet certain specified requirements.

IV. Dignitary Harm

The Internet has the capacity to transmit information much more quickly than the print media, and the information it carries can be custom-designed with greater precision than radio or television. In addition, the Internet is now a familiar part of the workplace, which

---

[25] *See* Carlini, Joanna M., *Liability On The Internet: Prescription Drugs And The Virtual Pharmacy,* 22 WHITTIER L. REV. 157 (2000), which validates the online sale of prescription drugs.

means that it can bring offensive content to individuals who not only do not expect it, but who are, to some extent, unable to avoid it. There seem to be three types of dignitary torts caused by the intentional transmission of harmful linguistic expressions and images over the Internet.

1.   Defamation

a)   Defamation And The Common Law

To maintain an action for defamation, a plaintiff must show a communication with three elements: (1) defamatory imputation, (2) publication, (3) without privilege. Communications sent over the Internet concerning employee evaluations have produced some litigation. For example, in *Hassler v. Raytheon Technical Services Co.*[26], defamation was alleged by a plaintiff against her former employer for an alleged defamatory email that was sent around the company. However, the email, though sent intentionally, was not found to be defamatory, as it was found to be true; the case was dismissed for failure to state a claim.

Another promising area of litigation relates to "chat rooms" on the Internet. These discussion forums are designed to be frank and open, and for that reason speakers usually have "screen names" which both protect their identity and encourage candid language. According to Restatement of Torts (Second) § 564, statements of a defamatory nature must be understood as being directed at a certain person. In the arena of bulletin boards and suits by people who were defamed on bulletin boards or chat rooms, this is a difficult standard to meet, because the defamatory statement about them may have identified them only through their screen names.[27]

On the other hand, where the speaker on a chat room or a bulletin board remains anonymous but uses the real name of the person or company they defame, then a defamation lawsuit may be effective. Since most companies that host chat rooms or bulletin boards maintain records that allow a court to determine the identity of the holder of a screen name, discovery in a defamation suit usually involves the unmasking of anonymous posters.[28] In the case of anonymous postings on investment bulletin boards

---

[26]   2000 WL 33309587 (S.D.Ind. 2000).

[27]   This is illustrated in *Marczeski v. Law*, 122 F. Supp.2d 315 (Conn. 2000), in which a case brought for defamation in a chat room was dismissed, the Court finding that it is necessary that the recipient of the defamatory communication understand it as intended to refer to the plaintiff. As the plaintiff in the case used screen names, and several of those, the plaintiff was unable to show intentional defamation directed at her. In addition, she was unable to show a pecuniary loss or other special damage caused by the defamatory statements, largely due to the vagueness of the screen name. As such, summary judgment was granted for the defendant.

[28]   *See* Collins, Tom, *Cyberslander Suits Multiplying Rapidly but Victories Harder to Come By*, MIAMI DAILY BUS. REV., June 29, 2001, *reprinted at* http://www.law.com.

who attempt to manipulate stock prices, the power to unmask libelous posters is a key piece of contemporary securities regulation. In the case of anonymous postings about events occurring in a company written by "whistle-blowing" employees, one might argue that the real goal of such libel suits is not the possibility of recovering damages, but to discover the identity of the whistle-blower so that the company can fire him or her.[29]

b)   Defamation, ISPs, And Statutory Immunity

As with other media, there is no reason why the "publisher" of a defamatory statement may not be held liable as well as its author, as long as the other criteria of common law defamation are satisfied. With particular regard to Internets Service Providers ("ISP's"), this posed a significant litigation risk until the Communications Decency Act ("CDA"), 47 U.S.C. § 230(c), was enacted. The CDA gave ISP's immunity from liability for the common law civil publishing torts of libel and slander. The CDA provides protection for an ISP for the private blocking and screening of offensive material on their web sites. The CDA was enacted to minimize state regulation of Internet speech by encouraging private content providers to self-regulate against offensive material.

The CDA was passed by Congress in response to two New York cases, *Stratton Oakmont, Inc. v. Prodigy Services Co.*[30], and *Cubby, Inc. v. Compuserve, Inc.*[31] In *Stratton*, an ISP was found to be liable for offensive postings upon the company's self-maintained bulletin boards/chat rooms. The ISP, Prodigy, held itself out to the public as a family-friendly online environment, and Prodigy itself retained control over the editorial content of the postings, using its own staff to moderate the bulletin boards on its service. By retaining control, Prodigy was found to be akin to an original publisher, and therefore liable for the posted offensive material. In contrast, in the 1991 case of *Cubby*, an ISP was found not liable for offensive material posted on its member bulletin boards. The ISP, Compuserve was found to be merely a distributor of information, and not an original publisher. Compuserve's bulletin boards were maintained by a third party, and Compuserve made no advertisement of retaining editorial control.

Seen in combination, the two cases led to the predicament that an ISP had no liability when no attempt was made to self-regulate content of their proprietary bulletin boards, but an ISP could be held liable when they attempted to self regulate for a family-friendly environment. The Communications Decency Act was the solution to this predicament,

---

29   *Id.*
30   24 Media L. Rep. 1196, 1995 N.Y. Misc. LEXIS 712 (1995).
31   776 F. Supp. 135 (S.D.N.Y. 1991).

forbidding an ISP publisher liability for the exercise of editorial and self-regulatory functions.[32]

2.   Privacy

There is a large amount of information collected online. This includes click-stream data, the recording of where a person has been, either through transmittal (used by companies such as Double Click) or when a person re-visits a page a cookie placed on the persons hard drive will tell the site where the person has been in the intervals between their visits This collection of information makes detailed information easily available. The information may then be used to create detailed profiles of a web user to target advertising to them to sell more effectively.

Perhaps nowhere are the differences between the United States and other tort systems more apparent than in the way injury in this area are described. In most European systems, the tort system protects "personality interests".[33] In the United States, a person's "personality" is protected by different common law torts that fall under the rubric of "privacy". This difference between structures and approaches is important to the extent that the common law protects the public disclosure of personal information to a lesser degree than the civil law.

There are four main cause of action under Invasion of Privacy. These are:

(i)   the unreasonable intrusion upon the seclusion of another;
(ii)   the unreasonable publicity given to another's private life;
(iii)   the publicity that unreasonably places another in a false light before the public; and
(iv)   the appropriation of another's name or likeness.

There have also been efforts to allege that the placing of cookies onto an Internet user's hard drive is a trespass onto their chattel, but these have been unsuccessful.[34]

---

[32]   The CDA specifically states "No provider or user of an interactive computer service shall be treated as the publisher or speaker of any information provided by another information content provider." 47 U.S.C. § 230(c)(1). *Zeran v. America Online, Inc.* 129 F.3d 327, (4th Cir. 2000), *cert denied* 524 U.S. 937 (1998) reiterated this, holding the CDA "creates a federal immunity to any cause of action that would make service providers liable for information originating with a third party user of the service....Thus, lawsuits seeking to hold a service provider liable for its exercise of a publisher's traditional editorial functions--such as deciding whether to publish, withdraw, postpone or alter content--are barred." *Id.* at 330.

[33]   *See* Schwartz, Paul M., *European Data Protection Law and Restrictions on International Data Flows,* 80 IOWA L. REV. 471 (1995).

[34]   *See, e.g., In re Double Click, Inc. Privacy Litigation,* 60 CIV. 0641, 2001 U.S. Dist. LEXIS 3498 (S.D.N.Y. 2001). The Court dismissed the case on the grounds that the placing of cookies was not

The Internet may have the greatest potential to produce torts involving the publicity of private life, through the unreasonable disclosure of personal information. To be sure, most persons who disclose personal information on the Internet are aware that they are providing that data. But there are still questions of knowing consent and reasonable use, and these questions cannot always be handled by contract, since there may be no contract between the user and the data-gatherer (as there is when one buys a book at Amazon.com).[35] For example, in *Dennis v. Metromail Corporation*[36], the suit was initiated by a woman who had given her name, address, sex, age, medical condition, and buying habits to a Metromail survey in exchange for the promise of discount coupons and free products. The survey response was processed by a prison inmate who then sent the plaintiff an offensive, sexually graphic, and threatening letter.[37]

The Internet is also a fertile source of claims by individuals, famous or otherwise, for the tort of the appropriation of name or likeness. Just as a soap company cannot use the face of a woman to advertise soap without her permission[38], an Internet company may not use images placed on the Internet for one purpose (a homepage of a college student) to advertise a product or illustrate its content.[39]

Finally, celebrities are discovering that the Internet is a double-edged sword. On the one hand, for those seeking to develop an audience, the Internet's cost-advantage over print and broadcast media makes it possible for marginal figures to reach a large audience. On the other hand, the ease and lack of expense with which images may be appropriated on the Internet means that the images of celebrities may be associated with contexts with

---

unauthorized access, as a visit to a site constituted authorization to place the cookies. Further, Double Click was found to have no tortious intent, which was necessary for a successful tort claim, nor was damage suffered by the user.

[35] Koster, Erika S., *Zero Privacy: Personal Data on the Internet*, 16 THE COMPUTER LAWYER 7 (1999).

[36] No. 9604451 (D. Tex., Travis County, filed April 18, 1996),

[37] This case was initiated in April 1996 and was later expanded to a class action including plaintiffs from California, Illinois, and New York who also responded to Metromail surveys processed by prison inmates. The complaint was amended to add a claim for breach of contract. In addition, the fraud claim was expanded to include Metromail's "deceptive acquisition" of information by promising to provide coupons, and then selling the information to telemarketers, bill collectors and others, while also making the information available over a 1-900 number "people locator" service for $3 a minute.

[38] *Flores v. Mosler Safe Co.*, 7 N.Y.2d 276, 164 N.E.2d 853 (1959).

[39] *See, e.g., Stern v. Delphi Internet Services Corp.* 165 Misc. 2d 21; 626 N.Y.S.2d 694 (1995). Radio celebrity Howard Stern brought suit against Delphi Internet Services Corporation for appropriation of name and likeness (based on NY civil law) after Delphi used Stern's photograph without his consent in an advertisement. Stern had announced his candidacy for governor of New York, and Delphi used Stern's photograph to advertise an online bulletin board service set up to debate Stern's candidacy. The court found that, although Delphi had used Stern's name and photograph for a commercial purpose without Stern's consent, Delphi's use was permissible because Stern's candidacy was a matter of public interest.

which they disapprove.[40]. This suit was brought under a California statute, which awards $750 for each right to publicity violated, a relatively minor recovery. By posting the pictures of the models on its website, along with the names of the models in the case of Violetta Kolek, Ashley Degenford, and Vanessa Norris, defendant violated the models' rights of publicity, both statutory (California Civil Code § 3344) and common law, which has been assigned to the plaintiff, Perfect 10. In this sense, the tort of the "right to publicity" is like trademark. Unlike trademark, a celebrity's name or physical features are not intellectual property, but like trademark, a celebrity had a right to control how their name or image is used.[41] Websites are privileged by the First Amendment to freely use images in the context of commenting on issues of public importance.[42]

3.   Intentional Infliction Of Emotional Distress ("IIED")

Although the use of the Internet requires deliberation and choice, outrageous material may be intentionally sent to users through email. In this sense, however, the role of the Internet in IIED is not too different from that of the phone or the postal system, each of which provides the opportunity for surprise and shock. Where the Internet seems to have added a new dimension to IIED claims is in the context of the workplace, where the ubiquity of the computer provides a novel problem: to what extent are employers responsible for the outrage experienced by a co-worker who inadvertently and involuntarily observes material viewed by another co-worker?

In such cases, IIED is usually filed in conjunction with a charges of harassment and defamation, either libel or slander. Several cases have been filed in which plaintiff sues for IIED damages resulting from fellow workers viewing pornography in the office in sight of the plaintiff. The IIED claims were filed in these cases in conjunction with harassment and creating an uncomfortable work environment. The main block in these cases is in reaching the level of outrageousness needed to validate a charge of IIED.[43] So far, research had revealed no cases where a workplace Internet IIED claim has succeeded,

---

[40]   This has become an issue with regard to unauthorized "fan" sites and sites that collect together the photographs of models. *See, e.g. Perfect 10, Inc. v. Talisman Communications Inc.*, 2000 WL 364813 (C.D.Cal. 2000).

[41]   "The right of publicity may be defined as a celebrity's right to the exclusive use of his or her name and likeness." *Martin Luther King, Jr. Center for Social Change, Inc. v. American Heritage Products, Inc.*, 694 F.2d 674, 676 (11th Cir.1983).

[42]   *Gridiron.com, Inc. v. National Football League Player's Ass'n, Inc.*, 106 F.Supp.2d 1309 (S.D. Fla. 2000).

[43]   *See, e.g. Gur v. Nemeth-Martin Personnel Consulting, Inc.*, 2001 WL 357356 (Conn.Super. 2001) (plaintiff sued employer, alleging that viewing of Internet porn in open view of all employees caused her extreme emotional distress; court ruled that while the viewing of porn in the office was without taste, it does not rise to the level of outrageousness needed for a claim of IIED); *Coniglio v. City of Berwyn, Ill.*, 2000 WL 967989 (N.D.Ill. 2000) (same). The proving of intent of an email to harm has also prevented a finding of IIED. *See, e.g., Hassler v. Raytheon Technical Services Co.*, 2000 WL 33309587 (S.D.Ind. 2000).

although there is a good chance that such claims add pressure to settle the outstanding sexual harassment claim.

D.   CONCLUSION

The tour of Internet torts above suggests that there is no single critical element that binds together torts that occur on the Internet. A cynic might suggest therefore, that it makes as much sense to classify torts under the rubric of "The Internet" as it did for the Legal Realists to produce torts casebooks with chapters titled "Telegraph Torts" and "Railroad Torts." Nonetheless, I think a closer examination of the results above reveals three interesting trends which bear closer scrutiny.

I.   The Rise Of Statutes

One salient feature of the development of the law relating to the Internet and torts is the significance of statutes in identifying, controlling and even creating the causes of action. The causes of action under which trademark and copyright actions are brought are statutes, albeit older than the Internet itself. But new statutes were also created when needed very quickly to deal with cybersquatting (the APCA), cyber-conversion (for example, Virginia's Computer Crimes Act), cyber-malpractice (the IPCPA), and cyber-libel (the CDA). The response by legislatures to new liability challenges posed by the Internet is remarkable not only for its swiftness, but for the degree to which it has escaped the traditional "tort reform" debate that has paralyzed the American Congress in asbestos and wracked so many state legislatures. One might even suggest that the Internet has pushed American tort law a step closer to a civil law approach to the definition of tort liability. That is, rather than depend on common law evolution through the somewhat random litigation patterns of lawyers who take cases on for contingency fees, the federal and state governments in the U.S. have acted proactively and sought to define, in advance, new causes of action in order to protect interests that did not even exist ten years ago.

II.   The Rise Of Intent

Another salient feature of the torts described in this paper is that the ground of liability upon which they rely is usually some form of intentional torts. The torts that defend dignity, chattel, and emotional well-being require proof of some desire to bring about an injury to the protected interest, or at least knowledge that the injury is substantially and proximately certain to follow from the use of the Internet. Even the torts protecting intellectual property, which famously follow a simpler model of trespass and therefore allegedly do not require proof of improper motive, in fact do require just that. Except in the case of "pseudo-cybersquatters," the group of rules described above are clearly designed to punish bad actors who know that they are acting in violation of a protected interest. The fact that Internet torts are predominantly *intentional* torts is worth noting, if for no other reason than the history of modern tort law was 'supposed' to be a march away from intent to negligence and then ultimately to strict liability. Ever since Holmes, and certainly throughout the work of Fleming James and Guido Calabresi, the modern tendency of tort law has been to be suspicious of intent as a useful category of analysis. I have elsewhere talked about what I call the "remoralization" of tort law.[44] Despite rumors of the demise of intent, intent has become a crucially important factor mass tort litigation relating to tobacco, products liability, and business torts. I will merely note that the rise of Internet torts, as a category, seems to be of a piece with the tenor of the times in America, which is to expand the role of tort law as a response to intentional anti-social conduct.

III.   The Disappearance Of Borders Between Doctrinal Categories

The commonplace metaphor to use when discussing the Internet is to describe the disappearance of borders in space and time – to capture the insight that the Internet has "globalized" law, since it takes place in cyberspace. I have deliberately avoided adopting this line of analysis because I am not sure that it is the most promising way to understand tort law as it relates to the Internet. The torts described above take place on the cusp of different kinds of borders – doctrinal borders that have helped organize English and American common law since the 16th Century.

The category of intellectual property, for example, loses its physical essence on the Internet. When an image is "hijacked" by IMG framing, the violation does not involve the physical copying of the image, and yet the courts have rightly held that the injury is the same as if the defendant had copied a drawing or reprinted a book or mark. Similarly, when someone invades millions of hard drives with unwanted email, there is an trespass to chattel that is not, technically, trespass in the 16th Century meaning of the word. Only a very stubborn metaphysician would insist that the disturbance of magnetized particles on a hard drive is a "touching" in the same way that one touches another's furniture or clothing. And courts have rightly held that the wrong involved when a defendant disturbs another's control and repose of their email programs is a form of trespass to chattel, and that the courts can use the traditional categories to invoke the traditional remedies.

The Internet is not the only technological advance that has forced tort law to confront the rigidity of its formal categories. It is the latest among a series of challenges that include toxic torts that "touch" the body years before they manifest health effects, and 'mass' fraud in which reliance must be hypothesized over thousands of people, since it would be impossible to actually determine to what extent any individual person was motivated by

---

[44]   "The Remoralization of Tort Law and Mass Torts," Section on Torts and Compensation Systems, American Association of Law Schools Annual Meeting, January 5, 2001, San Francisco, CA..

the defendants false utterances. The Internet pushes across so many doctrinal borders, however, than we may see that it will force tort law to reorder its doctrinal architecture in dramatic way, just as the development of the internal combustion engine did in the Nineteenth Century.

USE OF ELECTRONIC MEDIA AND JAPANESE COMPANY LAW

*Hideki Kanda**

Contents

---

*   Professor of Law, University of Tokyo, Japan.

TOSHIYUI KONO/ CHRISTOPH G. PAULUS/ HARRY RAJAK (eds.); THE LEGAL ISSUES OF E-COMMERCE
© 2002 Kluwer Law International. Printed in the Netherlands, pp. 79-86.

T. Kono et al. (eds.), Selected Legal Issues of E-Commerce, 79–86.
© 2002 *Kluwer Law International. Printed in the Netherlands.*

A.   INTRODUCTION

This paper discusses company law reform in Japan, particularly reform efforts in response to rapidly changing information and communications technology. Company law is only one area in which such reform efforts are necessary and in fact being made in Japan. Other areas of Japanese law have already responded or are expected to respond in the near future. Section 2 of this paper describes general legal issues concerning the use of electronic means in commercial transactions, and some of the responses thereto that have already taken place in Japan. Section 3 describes the current efforts of company law reform in Japan in this area. Section 4 takes up some of the issues that I think have important implications for future company practice in Japan. Section 5 is my preliminary conclusion.

B.   THE USE OF ELECTRONIC MEANS AND JAPANESE LAW

In Japan, as in other countries, the use of electronic means has become popular, and corresponding legal issues have been identified, discussed, and resolved, though not completely as of this date. While this paper is not the place for full discussion of this topic, a brief overview concerning the legal issues and corresponding responses may be worthwhile.

Generally, the use of electronic means has two dimensions. One is substitution for paper-based actions, the other is as a substitution for signatures and/or seals or name-stamps (known as "inkan" in Japanese). At the outset, I must emphasize that the use of name-stamps (hereafter called "stamps") has been very popular in Japanese practice, while the use of hand-written signatures has been rare.

First, with regard to paper-based actions, Japanese law does not, generally, require that contracts be in writing in order to be valid and enforceable. There are, however, certain contexts in which law requires that transactions be in writing, for example, bills of exchange and cheques must be paper documents. "Accounting records" that must be prepared by joint stock companies under the Commercial Code, on the other hand, do not have to be written on paper. Thus, the pre-reform Commercial Code can be interpreted as allowing such records to be prepared and maintained in electronic form, and this means that a change of company law would not be necessary to permit the use of such electronic means.

Special legislation regarding this matter was passed in November 2000 and became effective on 1 April 2001. This Act (the Omnibus Act for the Use of Information and Communication Technology relating to the Delivery of Papers, Act No. 126 of 2000) has had a material effect on 50 statutes and made possible the use of electronic means in lieu of the written documents previously required by these statutes for various transactions, provided that the interested parties to the relevant transactions agree. Company law (the main part of which is codified in the Commercial Code) was not included in this legislation on the ground that reform of company law would be better dealt with in connection with other reform matters. And company law reform was, in fact, enacted in November 2001.

Second, the matter of signatures or stamps appears to be more complicated. Many jurisdictions have enacted electronic signature legislation that, in general, gives the same legal effect to electronic signatures (as defined in the legislation) as to hand-written signatures. In Japan, legislation of this sort is relatively unimportant, because hand-written signatures are rarely used in practice. As already mentioned, stamps are commonly used in Japan. Thus, it is legislation that will give "electronic stamps" the same legal effect as actual stamps which is called for.

Generally, there are three sets of situations where stamps matter in Japanese law. (1) As a general principle, if the signature or the name of a person and its stamp are found on a document, there is a presumption that the document was in fact written by that person (Civil Procedure Code art. 228(4)). A name and its stamp are not required for a contract to be valid, but if they are on a document, the evidential value of the document increases in litigation. (2) Some laws require names and stamps (or signatures) in certain contexts. AS already mentioned, a bill of exchange and a cheque would be invalid unless it has the signature or the name and stamp of the maker. Also, under the pre-reform Commercial Code, the signature or the name and its stamp of one of the representative directors of the company must be affixed to the minutes of shareholders' meetings and board of directors meetings in joint-stock companies. (3) Finally, in practice, signatures or names and stamps play an important role when a debtor obtains a discharge. Thus, when a depositor withdraws money from his or her deposit account with a bank, the traditional practice in Japan is for the bank to ensure that the deposit book is marked with the stamp of the depositor (although now, of course, the use of ATM cards is very popular). In fact, if someone steals the stamp (and the deposit book) of a depositor, the bank would usually be discharged if it were to pay to such thief after recording the stamp. This is the generally recognized effect of art. 478 of the Civil Code.

Of the three situations identified in the last paragraph where stamps matter in Japanese law, the third will not need special legislation to ensure the legality of the conversion to electronic means, but can instead be resolved by proper interpretation of the current law; in particular, art. 478 of the Civil Code. The first and second such situations do, however, call for special legislation in order to permit the use of electronic means in lieu of stamps. In response to the first, special legislation was adopted in 2000 and became effective on 1 April 2001. This Act (the Act for Electronic Signature and Authentication Business, Act No. 102 of 2000) recognizes electronic signatures, as defined in the Act, as having the same effect as hand-written signatures and names and stamps; that is, as having the presumptive effect under the Civil Procedure Code art. 228(4) described above. For the areas in which laws require signatures or names and stamps, one must wait for amendments to each statute that will permit the use of electronic means in lieu thereof. Thus, for example, company law needed amendments to permit the use of electronic means in substitution for signatures or stamps of representative directors on minutes of shareholders' meetings and board of directors meetings.

C.   REFORM EFFORTS IN COMPANY LAW

A wide-range reform program of Japanese company law is now underway. Matters concerning the use of electronic means were included in this reform program. The Ministry of Justice released on 18 April 2001, for public comment, an interim draft proposal of amendments to the current company law (hereinafter "the Interim Draft"), and the amendments to the Commercial Code were finally passed in November 2001, with effective from 1 April 2002. In this article, I refer to the legal scheme which incorporates these amendments as "the new scheme."

I.   Documents

Under the new scheme, documents that must be maintained in written form for joint-stock companies and other companies under the Commercial Code and related statutes may be maintained by electronic means, if they are prepared by using electronic means. Where the law requires signatures or names and stamps in connection with such documents, electronic signatures, as defined under the Electronic Signature and Authentication Business Act, may be substituted. When documents are maintained by electronic means, shareholders and others who have the right to see and inspect such documents may ask the company to print out the documents in a legible form. It is important to note that this proposal permits the maintenance of documents by electronic means only if they are prepared electronically. According to the explanatory notes of the Ministry of Justice, the reason is that, if they are prepared as written papers and then changed into electronic form there might be a risk of unauthorized changes or other abuse, and that a signature or a name and stamp on a paper, by definition, cannot be converted into an electronic signature. The exceptions to this rule include certificates of shares and bonds, which are expected to be dematerialized in separate legislation relating to the securities settlement system reform.

II.   Public Notices

Company law requires joint-stock companies and other companies to make public notices on various occasions. Thus, for example, when a company issues new shares, the content of such issuance must be announced by public notice two weeks in advance of when the issuance becomes effective. The current law requires companies to specify in the company charter, the method of making public notices, and such method must be to publish notices either in the state official gazette or in a daily newspaper. The Interim Draft permitted substitution of these paper-based public notices by those in electronic form. However, this amendment was not accepted in November 2001 and this matter will be resolved in the future, together with the issue of introducing the electronic state official gazette.

III.   Notices To Shareholders

Company law requires joint-stock companies and other companies to send notices to shareholders on various occasions, for example, when a company issues new shares, such company must notify existing shareholders, individually, of such issuance two weeks in advance of when such issuance becomes effective. The current law does not specify the method of this notice, but is understood to require that the notice be made in written form. The new scheme permits companies to provide this notice by electronic means if individual shareholders, as the recipients of such notice, agree to this in advance. Additionally, shareholders who have agreed to receive notices from the company in electronic form may send their communications to the company or its directors using electronic means. Some notices are required to be accompanied by documents: for example, a notice of a shareholders' meeting must be accompanied by the company's financial statements and the auditor's report. Thus, when such notice is sent using electronic means, there is a question of whether accompanying documents may be sent electronically, for example, as file attachments to an email message. An alternative option may be to send the notice only and identify a website, for example, that shareholders can visit to view the accompanying documents.

IV.   Voting At Shareholders' Meetings

The new scheme permits companies, upon resolution of the board of directors, to use proxy voting and for this purpose shareholders may, by electronic means, provide the company with evidence of their delegation of their voting power to their agent.

Voting at shareholders' meetings in large public companies in Japan prior to the new scheme required that large companies having 1,000 or more shareholders send the voting cards with other documents (including not only the firm's financial statements and the audit report but also explanatory materials and the counterparts of proxy statements in other jurisdictions) to shareholders when calling a shareholders' meeting. This is known as the mail voting system. Large companies are defined under Japanese law as joint-stock companies having legal capital of 500 million yen or more or debts of 20 billion yen or more on the date of their most recent balance sheet. There are currently about 9,700 large companies in Japan. The new scheme permits the above-mentioned documents of large companies having 1,000 or more shareholders to be prepared by electronic means. As a result, electronic voting by shareholders not attending the shareholders' meetings will now be permitted. The details of the mechanism of such electronic voting, including the method of transmitting explanatory materials and other documents, are expected to be specified in regulations promulgated by the Ministry of Justice after the amendment to the law is made.

It is important to note that companies may adopt electronic voting without shareholder consent. This is because shareholders may always attend meetings in person, and they also have the right, under the law, to vote by mailing their voting cards. In other words, even though the proposal does not require shareholder consent, shareholders always have the option to act by the use of non-electronic methods.

The pre-reform law restricted mail voting to certain large public companies only (as defined above), while the new scheme provides that electronic voting may be permitted to the shareholders of all companies. Those companies that do not fall into the category for mandated mail voting but which want to employ electronic voting methods must make appropriate provision in their company charters. For such companies, shareholders can attend meetings in person, but cannot vote by using voting cards.

Finally, it should be noted that unlike some jurisdictions, notably Delaware, which permit electronic shareholders' meetings, that is to say that shareholders' meetings *themselves* to be held on the Internet, the new scheme does not make this change in Japanese law. In Japan, even after the enactment of the new scheme, shareholders' meetings must be held at a physical place.

D.   MAJOR ISSUES

At first glance, permitting the use of electronic means on various occasions in relation to various activities of companies, may appear to be a matter of course given the growth and the popularity of information and communications technology. Indeed, the new scheme may be said to have been driven by this line of this thinking. However, the use of electronic means may have somewhat unexpected effects in practice, and, if so, certain technical issues will need to be carefully considered. Here I make a few comments relating to the consent of recipients of shareholder notices, and list a few points regarding shareholders' meetings.

The new scheme correctly requires the advance consent of a shareholder if the company wishes to send notices by electronic means. A number of questions arise in connection with this advance consent. First, is consent necessary each time a notice is made or may consent be granted generally? Another possibility might be that consent may be treated as applicable for the future but limited to that activity of the company for which the consent was originally given. Secondly, may a shareholder withdraw a consent given, and, if so, when would such withdrawal become valid? Thirdly, should any such withdrawal of consent be by a specific method (or example the method by which it was first granted)? Thirdly, who would bear the burden of proof concerning the sending and receipt of any notice sent by electronic means? Fourthly, when shareholders provide the company with email addresses, are they then obliged to keep the company informed of all changes of email addresses even when such changes are due to changes of the provider's domain names? Fifthly, can a shareholder provide more than one email address? Sixthly, is there a limit to the number of times a shareholder might change his or her email address? Finally, until what moment can shareholders consent to electronic delivery? Might consent, for example, be granted for delivery right up to the last moment before the shareholders' meeting?

Many issues also arise with the use of electronic means in connection with shareholders' meetings. The first such issue concerns the register of shareholders. Prior to the new scheme, the law required companies to maintain a register of shareholders in which the names and addresses of all shareholders had to be recorded in writing, and any shareholder had the right to inspect the register, thus being able to learn the names and addresses of all shareholders. The issue arose whether, if notices were to be made via email to shareholders who agree and who submit their email addresses, these email addresses should be recorded in the shareholders' register, and, if so, whether all shareholders should have the right to see such email addresses. On the one hand, this would certainly have made it easier, for instance, for minority shareholders to communicate with each other and to coordinate their strategy and tactics; on the other hand, there would have been a risk of abusive practices such as spam mailing to such email addresses. In fact, the latter was considered (correctly in my view) to be the determining factor and the new scheme adopted the position that there be no requirement for the recording of all shareholders' email addresses.

The second issue concerned the date by which notices of shareholders' meetings had to be dispatched. Pre-reform company law requires that such notices be dispatched at least two weeks in advance of the date of the meeting. Under this regime, companies are discharged from their duty to so notify if they dispatch such notices to the addresses in the shareholders record, even if such notices do not in fact reach their intended recipients. This scheme has two bases, one being the shareholders' record, and the other the postal delivery system, which is run by the government in Japan. What should be the position under the electronic regime? If electronic notice is permitted and email is used (with shareholder consent), what should be the rule if the email does not reach a shareholder? Neither of the premises on which the pre-reform rule is based apply and there is, therefore, doubt whether the same rule should continue to apply to electronic notices . It is also significant that the infrastructure of email delivery is, in my view, far less reliable than the postal system in Japan.

The third issue concerns the fact of the shareholders' meeting. Should the requirement of having shareholders' meetings at a physical place continue unaffected by the new scheme? As described above, the new scheme has not yet gone this far. The current practice, however, sometimes results in the situation that the physical place prepared by the company is not large enough because too many shareholders present themselves in person. In such a situation, the practice is for the company to prepare another room, usually in the same building as the "primary" room for the meeting, and to connect the two rooms through the use of a video-television system. This method has been considered legally valid provided that communications between the two rooms are not disrupted. This suggests that current law could be interpreted as allowing shareholders' meetings in which one physical room is prepared and shareholders attend such meeting by "connecting" themselves to such room via the Internet or other telecommunication devices or methods. Such an interpretation would imply that shareholders would be treated as attending the meeting in person.

Finally, it is expected that if electronic means for voting and attending meetings are recognized, the number of shareholders who exercise voting rights may increase because the method of voting will become easier. Currently, in large public companies about 30% of shareholders (the dispersed shareholders as opposed to the so-called stable shareholders) send voting cards back to companies, but this voting rate may increase significantly if electronic voting is introduced. While this should be a welcome result from the perspective of company law, its practical effect would not be negligible. Shareholders' meetings, which have been regarded as "sleeping beauties", may suddenly awaken and begin to play an important role in corporate governance.

E.   CONCLUSION

Information and communications technology have been and are changing our lives. Company activities are no exception. Laws have been and are responding to this new environment by introducing necessary amendments to existing statutes and new legislation. Reform efforts of company law in Japan include such responses. The basic idea in Japan is to permit the use of electronic means in all aspects of company activities under minimum necessary conditions. While such reform should incorporate the advantages of modern technology within company practice and thus be welcomed in general, the impact of permitting the use of such technology in company law may have unexpected hidden effects on company practice.

Note

I owe some of the points in this paper to Souichirou Kozuka's work, The Reformation of Corporate Law and the Use of Information and Communication Technology (Draft, May 2001).

Legal Issues Concerning The Use Of The Internet In Securities Markets: The Japanese Case

*Sadakazu Osaki**

Content

---

*   Nomura Research Institute, Tokyo, Japan.

TOSHIYUI KONO/ CHRISTOPH G. PAULUS/ HARRY RAJAK (eds.); THE LEGAL ISSUES OF E-COMMERCE
© 2002 Kluwer Law International. Printed in the Netherlands, pp. 87-97.

T. Kono et al. (eds.), Selected Legal Issues of E-Commerce, 87–97.
© 2002 *Kluwer Law International. Printed in the Netherlands.*

A.   INTRODUCTION

In recent years, advances in information and communications technology have led to a rapid growth in online securities trading and other uses of the Internet in securities markets.

At the retail end of the securities business, individual investors have been making increasing use of online trading services provided by brokerage firms and mutual fund companies which enable investors to place orders to buy and sell equities and mutual funds via the Internet. On the other hand, at the wholesale end, the emergence of online trading systems called "proprietary trading systems" (PTSs) or "alternative trading systems" (ATSs) has led to fierce inter-market competition.

Although the United States has led the way in the development of online securities trading, Japan is catching up—especially since the "Big Bang" program of financial reform began in November 1996. Taking this as our starting point, this paper looks at related developments—especially in the Japanese legal system—and outstanding issues.

B.   PROBLEMS RELATED TO ONLINE SECURITIES TRADING BY RETAIL INVESTORS

Online securities trading is not something that has emerged overnight. The world's first proprietary trading system, Instinet, was launched in 1969, and the NASDAQ, where shares are traded on computer terminals rather than on a trading floor, began life in 1971. In the late 1980s, institutional investors and securities companies began to make extensive use of online systems to route orders to stock exchanges as well as in their back offices.

However, with the exception of the rules which the US Securities and Exchange Commission (SEC) was quick to draw up for proprietary trading systems (see below), the development of such systems generally did not have much of an impact on legislation governing securities trading. This situation changed significantly in the late 1990s when growing use of the Internet led to retail investors joining the list of those who traded online.

National legislation and regulation governing securities trading is basically designed to protect retail investors. The use of online systems, such as Instinet, in trading by institutions did not raise much concern from the regulator's point of view. However, the arrival online of retail investors brought home the need to review securities regulation in order to ensure that small investors would be reasonably protected in the new world of cyber-space.

Internet trading of securities by retail investors has created a number of problems not covered by existing legislation. These include the following.

First, there is the risk that client orders may not be processed properly because the host computer of the securities company concerned may not be working or may be overloaded because of a temporary surge in orders. Also, the fact that the manner of how messages are routed on the Internet cannot be decided in advance means that it is not clear whether it is the investor himself, his Internet service provider, the telecoms company or the securities company that is responsible if a problem occurs.

Second, there is the possibility that an incorrect order may be accepted because an investor has misunderstood something or input the wrong data. A simple mistake that would have been spotted by a live broker if an order had been received either orally at a branch of a securities company or by telephone may be assumed to be correct by a computer if received online.

Third, unlike the situation where a client decides to buy or sell securities after talking to a broker, there is a risk in online trading that a client may not have understood fully the information upon which he is acting. There is therefore a need for rules to oblige a securities company to provide information in a way that takes into account the specific nature of online trading. However, online trading does eliminate the possibility of the kind of fraudulent sales talk that has been known to occur when a client talks to a broker before buying or selling securities.

Fourth, there is a risk that the number of unregistered or unauthorized persons offering false or misleading investment advice or services could increase. It is difficult for investors to tell which online securities traders are acting within the law and which are not. There is also a risk that unscrupulous operators could use the anonymity of the Internet and the low cost of sending information to a large number of people simultaneously to spread rumors (e.g., on investor bulletin boards or by e-mail) and to try to manipulate markets.

Fifth, there is the risk of impersonation (if Internet users' IDs and passwords are stolen) and electronic eavesdropping.

Some of these problems can be solved (at least in part) if securities companies improve their system security, while others, (such as market manipulation) should be solved by applying the Securities and Exchange Law more rigorously. It is also often unclear (1) whose responsibility it is for implementing rules and monitoring whether they are being implemented or (2) what standards apply.

The guidelines ("Points to Beware of When Trading Securities on the Internet") issued by the Japan Securities Dealers Association (JASDA, the body responsible in Japan for self-regulation under the Securities and Exchange Law) in September 1999 are an attempt by the securities industry to regulate online trading services targeted at retail investors and to take into account some of these risks.

The guidelines set out the various issues that face securities companies offering online trading on the Internet as a result of the fact that such trading lacks any personal contact and there is no written record.

As well as pointing out a number of general points (e.g., the fact that online trading is subject to the same rules and regulations as conventional trading and that there has to be a proper compliance system with its own rules and regulations), the guidelines describe in detail the following: (1) general matters concerning the type of financial products that can be traded online and how they may be traded; (2) matters concerning compliance and transactional security; (3) matters concerning the provision of information to clients and trading procedures; and (4) matters concerning adherence to rules and regulations.

Unlike the Association's rules, the guidelines are not legally binding. However, they do deal in detail with many of the issues that are likely to arise in the course of online securities trading and should be a valuable source of advice for all those involved in the securities industry. Recently, the guidelines were reviewed by a working group of practitioners. In April 2001, a revised version of the guidelines was finally adopted.

C.   NEED TO REVIEW EXISTING REGULATIONS

Existing regulations on securities trading presuppose that investment advice is given and investment instructions received orally (either face to face or by telephone), and confirmed in writing. With the growth of online trading, however, this presupposition no longer necessarily applies.

In particular, the very rules and regulations that were intended to protect investors (especially retail investors, who have traditionally been at a disadvantage to professionals and institutions in terms of access to information and knowledge) are actually making it more difficult for retail investors to enjoy the efficiency benefits of online trading.

It was this realization that led the Securities and Exchange Commission in the United States to carry out an extensive review of US securities rules and regulations several years ago. Twice (in October 1995 and May 1996) the SEC published interpretative releases and revised some of the existing rules in order to encourage issuers and securities companies to use the Internet and other electronic media.[1]

The release issued in October 1995 allowed prospectuses and proxy documents to be sent to shareholders electronically. More specifically, issuers and broker-dealers were allowed to send investors electronic prospectuses provided the following three conditions were met: (1) investors had to be notified of this separately (e.g., by telephone, fax, conventional mail or e-mail); (2) electronic documents had to be just as convenient as paper documents and investors had to be able to access information; and (3) hard copies of prospectuses and other documents had to be provided if investors requested.

This has enabled (1) issuers to post prospectuses on their Web sites and invite investors to subscribe to new securities (a new method of raising capital that might well be called "Internet finance") and (2) online securities companies to market initial public offerings (IPOs) aggressively.

Meanwhile, the release issued in May 1996 allowed broker-dealers and investment advisors to use electronic media to send investors the various documents they are legally required to send them (e.g., execution confirmations, statements of account, and performance reports). The conditions that had to be met are virtually the same as those that apply to sending prospectuses: (1) an electronic version of a document had to contain the same information as a hard copy; (2) investors had to be notified separately that they had been sent an electronic document and there had to be a means of checking that it had been sent properly and that investors could access it; and (3) hard copies of documents had to be provided if investors requested.

Given the confidential nature of much of the information contained in such documents, the 1996 release stressed the importance of system security and the need for informed consent by investors.

In Japan, following the complete liberalization of brokerage commissions in October 1999 and the appearance of online brokers charging very low rates, retail investors have also begun to make increasing use of online securities trading. Given that low cost is one of the main selling points of online brokers, the cost of having to send investors documents such as prospectuses and transaction reports by conventional mail is not insignificant, and the need to find a solution has increased since December 1998, when the revised Securities and Exchange Law added prospectuses for mutual funds to the list of documents that have to be sent to investors.

---

[1] Use of Electronic Media for Delivery Purposes, SEC Release, No. 33-7233; 34-36345; IC-21399 (October 6, 1995), Use of Electronic Media by Broker-Dealers, Transfer Agents, and Investment Advisers for Delivery of Information, SEC, Release No. 33-7288; 34-37182; IC-21945; IA-1562 (May 9, 1996).

Since then, the May 2000 revision to the Securities and Exchange Law has allowed information contained in prospectuses to be sent as an electronic file via the Internet by adding the following: "Where a prospectus has to be sent to an investor, the information contained in the prospectus may be sent instead using an electronic communications network, provided this is stipulated in a Cabinet order, or by any other means stipulated in a Cabinet order" (Securities and Exchange Law, 27-30-9). This is regarded as equivalent to sending the prospectus itself.[2]

Moreover, the enactment in November 2000 of the Law for the Provision of Laws on the Use of Information Technology to Send Documents made it possible to send execution confirmations and mutual fund performance reports in the same way from this April. In January of this year the corresponding government orders, which stipulate that clients must give their consent before this can be done, were enacted. In April 2001, the corresponding Cabinet order was enacted, but most Japanese securities firms still do not send prospectuses electronically. This is because the Cabinet order effectively provides that "delivery" of a prospectus will only be completed when a customer actually downloads an electronic file containing the information in a prospectus to his own computer. Currently, Japan's Financial Services Agency is trying to amend the Cabinet order in order to make it possible for securities firms to send prospectuses electronically without taking unnecessary legal risks.

D.   CROSS-BORDER NATURE OF THE INTERNET

The growth of online securities trading (especially the increasing use of the Internet) has not only produced the kind of technical amendments to rules and regulations we saw above, but also raises a more fundamental question about the Internet related to it distinctive characteristics. This is the question: which country (or region) has jurisdiction over financial promotion or public offerings of securities given the Internet's stateless status that makes it possible to access the same information from anywhere in the world.

In the United States and the United Kingdom the regulators have sought to provide partial answer by clarifying the law.

In the United States, the SEC made it clear in a March 1998 release that (1) a company offering investment advisory services on the Internet would be exempted from the registration requirement of the Investment Advisers Act, provided it had taken measures reasonably designed to limit the number of its US clients to no more than 15 (e.g., by posting a disclaimer stating that it was not offering a service for US persons) and that (2

---

2   A detailed discussion of Japanese regulations on electronic prospectuses can be found in Sadakazu Osaki "The Lifting of Restrictions on the Use of Electronic Media for the Delivery of Prospectuses: A Unfinished Job," Capital Research Journal, Summer 2001.

a foreign broker-dealer operating a Web site would not be required to register under the Securities Exchange Act provided it had taken measures reasonably designed to make it clear that its service was not intended for US persons or that it would not enter into any transactions with such persons.[3]

Meanwhile, in the United Kingdom in May 1998 the Financial Services Authority published a guidance release to the effect that it would not regard investment advertising on the Internet that did not appear to be targeted at UK residents as being subject to the Financial Services Act.[4] Similarly, the Financial Services and Markets Act of June 2000 (a complete revision of the 1986 Financial Services Act) states that, even if a communication originating outside the United Kingdom can be construed as financial promotion, it will be subject to regulation only if the communication is capable of having an effect in the United Kingdom (Section 21(3)), thereby clarifying the treatment of financial services offered on the Internet.

The approaches of the United States and the United Kingdom are basically supported by the International Organization of Securities Commissions (IOSCO). A report published by IOSCO's Technical Committee in September 1998 ("Securities Activity on the Internet") gives the following three conditions as examples of the kind of criteria for deciding whether a particular country (or region) should have jurisdiction over Internet securities trading services or public offerings of securities on the Internet: (1) the information provided is clearly targeted at residents of the regulator's area of jurisdiction; (2) the service provider or issuer has already entered into transactions with residents of the regulator's area of jurisdiction; and (3) the information provided has been targeted at residents of the regulator's area of jurisdiction using e-mail and other such methods.[5]

In Japan, an overseas-based broker-dealer is not required to register if it has simply received an unsolicited order from a Japanese resident (Law on Foreign Securities Firms, 3-2 and Cabinet Order for the Enforcement of the Law on Foreign Securities Firms, 2-2). Indeed, there appears to be a significant level of such cross-border transactions by Japanese retail investors, and there is no denying that a number of Web sites operated by overseas-based broker-dealers appear to be targeted at Japanese residents.

The response of Japan's Financial Services Agency was to issue a revised set of administrative guidelines on this issue in December 2000 in order to clarify the status of

---

[3] Use of Internet Web Sites to Offer Securities, Solicit Securities Transactions, or Advertise Investment Services Offshore, SEC, Release No. 33-7516; 34-39779, IA-1710, IC-23071, International Series Release No. 1125 (March 23, 1998).

[4] Treatment of material on overseas Internet World Wide Web sites accessible in the UK but not intended for investors in the UK, FSA, Guidance Release 2/98 (28 May 1998).

[5] Technical Committee of the International Organization of Securities Commissions, Securities Activity on the Internet, September 1998. As a Special Research Staff of the Japan Securities Dealers Association, the author took part in the discussions by the IOSCO taskforce that produced the report.

cross-border transactions entered into by Japanese residents with overseas-based broker-dealers via the Internet (Regulatory Issues Involving Foreign Securities Firms, 1-4-4). The guidelines make it clear that (as in the United States) advertisements posted on such a broker-dealer's Web site will not be regarded as targeting Japanese residents provided there is a disclaimer on the site that the service is not available to such investors and there is a mechanism to prevent any such transactions from taking place. The next issue will be what exactly the Japanese authorities should do if a Japanese investor does enter into such a transaction in apparent ignorance of these rules.

E. RULES GOVERNING ONLINE SECURITIES TRADING SYSTEMS

I. Lifting Of Restrictions On Proprietary Trading Systems As Part Of Big Bang

Another issue connected with online securities trading—but slightly different from the issues mentioned so far, which have mainly been about online securities trading targeted at retail investors—is that of how proprietary trading systems (PTSs, also known as "alternative trading systems") should be regulated.

The first of these systems, which are similar to stock exchanges, was the US system Instinet, which began operation in 1969. PTSs have become a force to reckon with since the late 1980s, when trading volume began to increase by allowing broker-dealers to participate. Particularly noteworthy has been the growth of so-called "electronic communications networks" (ECNs), which appeared soon after the SEC introduced its Order Handling Rules in 1997 and now account for 30%-40% of trading in NASDAQ shares.

In the United States, PTSs have basically been subject to the regulations governing broker-dealers since Instinet began its operation. In Japan, on the other hand, PTSs were effectively banned by the Securities and Exchange Law, which (until its 1998 revision) prohibited the formation of an organized market for securities other than a stock exchange (Securities and Exchange Law, 87-2).

This situation changed completely when, as part of the Big Bang program of financial reform, the government decided to encourage competition between securities markets as a means of improving their efficiency and quality. Operating a PTS was designated as one of the licensed activities of a securities company. The Securities and Exchange Law was revised so that the rule prohibiting the formation of alternatives to stock exchanges would not be applied to anyone who had received permission to operate a PTS (Securities and Exchange Law, 2-8-7; 167-2-3 prior to the 2000 revision). In June 2000 the first approvals under the new regime were granted to Japan Bond Trading Company and E-Bond Securities.[6]

II.   Shortcomings Of Original Rules For Proprietary Trading Systems

The lifting of the restrictions on proprietary trading systems as part of the Big Bang reforms was epoch-making insofar as it gave broker-dealers the right to match orders to buy and sell securities, which had previously been the monopoly of the stock exchanges, and encouraged competition between markets. However, proprietary trading systems were still subject to considerable restrictions, and it was thought unlikely that the Japanese authorities would permit electronic communications networks similar to those in the United States.

This is because, under Japanese law, proprietary trading systems were severely restricted in the type of price discovery mechanism they could use. More specifically, the Securities and Exchange Law limited this to the following three types: (1) in the case of listed securities, the same price as that at which the securities traded on a stock exchange; (2) in the case of securities quoted on the OTC market operated by the Japan Securities Dealers Association, the same price as that at which the securities traded on the OTC market; and (3) in other cases, at a price negotiated between the clients concerned (Securities and Exchange Law, 2-8-7). Although the Law also allowed "any other mechanism stipulated in a Cabinet or Ministry of Finance order," no such order was enacted.

As a result, two PTSs that were granted approval by the Financial Supervisory Agency (as it then was) were required to use prices negotiated between clients. However, in order to maintain this pretence, one of the systems was even obliged to adopt an absurd procedure that prevented it from matching orders automatically even when price and quantity did match.

III.   Financial Services Agency's Revised Guidelines

In December 2000 a set of Financial Services Agency guidelines on operating PTSs was enacted together with a related Cabinet order and a set of administrative guidelines, thereby enabling PTSs to use two price discovery mechanisms in addition to those that

---

[6]   See S. Osaki, "Legal Revisions Allow Exchanges to Be Formed as Joint-Stock Companies," Capital Research Journal, Autumn 2000. E-Bond Securities stopped its operation and was dissolved in May 2001.

had already been statutorily approved: (1) using client limit orders to match transactions and (2) using multiple price quotations by securities companies (Prime Minister's Office Order on Definitions of the Wordings in the Securities and Exchange Law, 8-2).

In addition, in response to public comment on the administrative guidelines, it was made clear that the following should not be regarded as PTSs: (1) an arrangement whereby a securities company, that makes the only market in a security, enters into a transaction with a client via an online system and (2) information vendors.

Since January 2001, six additional PTSs for trading bonds and equities have been approved under the new guidelines.

IV.   Unresolved Issues Facing Proprietary Trading Systems

Although considerable progress on the issue of how PTSs should be regulated has therefore been achieved in a short time, a number of major issues remain unresolved.

First, it is difficult to justify why a PTS should be regarded as an inferior means of price discovery to an organized securities market operated by a stock exchange or a securities dealers' association. While the more public status of stock exchanges and the need to protect investors may well require that they be subject to rigorous regulation, there is no good reason why particular price discovery mechanisms should be the preserve of stock exchanges or an organized OTC market operated by the Japan Securities Dealers' Association.

In the United States, trading systems with a similar function to stock exchanges are regarded as alternative trading systems (ATSs), and the degree of regulation to which they are subject depends on the level of trading volume rather than the particular price discovery mechanism used. Also, even a stock exchange (with its obligation to meet certain self-regulatory standards) may be exempted from the need to register with the SEC in order to lighten its regulatory burden, if trading volume is exceptionally low.

In Japan, the December 2000 revision to the Securities and Exchange Law, which permits the demutualization of stock exchanges, can also be interpreted as restricting competition. The fact that demutualized stock exchanges are subject to more restrictions than PTSs (e.g., restrictions on diversification of business and a 5% limit on shareholdings) makes it very difficult for PTSs to become stock exchanges. As a result, Japanese law makes it difficult for trading systems, that use the same price discovery mechanisms as existing stock exchanges, to compete and can be said to shield the latter from competition.

Second, as intermarket competition increases and more PTSs trade the same security, the need to prevent market fragmentation by consolidating trading information and quotation information will also increase. In the United States, a "National Market System" (NMS) has been proposed as a means of providing the necessary infrastructure for this, and a number of sub-systems, including a "consolidated quotation system" (CQS), are up and running. Similarly, the NASDAQ consolidates and reports quotation data from ECNs trading mainly NASDAQ shares.

In its guidelines the Financial Services Agency permits PTS operators to report trading information on their Web sites until it is possible to do this centrally. In the medium to long term, however, some system solution is required.

Third, as it becomes possible to execute orders on more than one market (stock exchange, proprietary trading system, etc.), it will become necessary to impose certain requirements on how securities companies deal with client orders (especially those from retail investors) to ensure that investors' rights are protected. In the United States, broker-dealers are, in principle, subject to a "best execution obligation," which is understood to oblige them to execute a client order on the best terms if the order can be executed on a number of markets or systems.

In Japan, on the other hand, this notion is not very well established. Until recently, the Securities and Exchange Law protected investors' rights by prohibiting activities such as "bucketing." However, these rules assumed that client orders would normally be routed to a stock exchange, and are not really suitable for a situation where several proprietary trading systems exist. Rules will therefore have to be devised for handling client orders and explaining the situation to clients (drawing, for example, on US experience of the SEC's order-handling rules).

Technological Innovation As A Challenge To Exchange Regulation: First Electronic Trading, Then Alternative Trading Systems And Now "Virtual" (Internet) Exchanges?

Harald Baum[*]

Contents

This paper is composed of three parts. Part A deals with the far-reaching structural changes in the market for exchange services which have happened within a surprisingly short period of time over the last few years. Part B discusses some major regulatory concerns raised by these changes. Part C briefly summarizes the findings.

---

[*]   Senior Research Fellow, Max Planck Institute for Foreign Private and Private International Law, Lecturer in Law, University of Hamburg, Germany.

Toshiyui Kono/ Christoph G. Paulus/ Harry Rajak (eds.); The Legal Issues Of E-Commerce
© 2002 Kluwer Law International. Printed in the Netherlands, pp. 99–125.

T. Kono et al. (eds.), Selected Legal Issues of E-Commerce, 99–125.
© 2002 *Kluwer Law International. Printed in the Netherlands.*

A.   STRUCTURAL CHANGES

I.   Exchange Services On The Internet As Part Of A Broader Trend

The main purpose of a stock exchange has been traditionally, and still is, to organize a market for financial instruments. Thus, exchanges are mostly regarded as organized markets. Over the last couple of years technical innovations have, together with other factors, led to fierce competition between those markets and the proliferation of a "market for markets"[1]. It is becoming increasingly accepted to see markets as firms selling the organization of a marketplace for financial instruments rather than as markets themselves,[2] and technical innovations have created an active market for exchange services - at the moment probably the most rapidly changing part of the general market for financial services.[3]

Internet technology has played an increasingly important part in this. However, it would be misleading to link the revolution in the market for exchange services to the arrival of the Internet. Instead, the fundamental changes started earlier with the innovations in information and communication technology that made the electronic trading platform possible.[4] This has been the magician's wand, pulling the exchanges out of their cozy institutional slumber that lasted nearly a century. Thus the use of the Internet as a means to facilitate exchange services should be viewed as part of this broader development rather than something unique, even though it will probably only be a matter of a comparatively short time until we see the arrival of a full-fledged "virtual" exchange based entirely on the web, encompassing retail investors and functioning with little or no intermediation.[5]

For a better understanding of the regulatory issues raised by the structural upheaval in the market for exchange services, it is necessary to start with a look at what actually happened there on an institutional and organizational level.

---

[1]   PRIGGE (2000).

[2]   MUESS (1999); KÖNDGEN (1998); RUDOLPH/RÖHRL (1997); FERRARINI (1997); MACEY/KANDA (1990).

[3]   A discussion of the term 'exchange services' (Börsendienstleistungen) can be found in KLENKE (1998) 108 et seq.; see also HOPT/BAUM (1997) 372 et seq.

[4]   NOBEL (1999).

[5]   So far, there seems to be no internet-based exchange in operation in the true meaning of the term; for further details see *infra* IV.

II. From State-owned Monopolies To Web-based Trading Platforms

Until fairly recently, stock exchanges could be characterized by specific organizational features, and an understanding of their legal nature and economic functions did not change much over the last century. Some exchanges operated as state-owned enterprises until as recently as 1998.[6] In Germany stock exchanges are still defined as public law institutions.[7] Under the German stock exchange law,[8] a competent state authority must approve the formation of an exchange, and supervision is delegated to a state exchange commissioner.[9] Sworn-in official brokers, who enjoy public status, are entrusted with price determination, thus adding an additional layer of intermediation. However, a major reform of the exchange law of 1896 is expected for 2002.[10]

If not state-owned outright, exchanges have predominantly been organized as institutions owned by the exchange's members who are also responsible for the self-regulation by which these exchanges are governed. Member-owned exchanges can be regarded as some kind of cooperatives, which are acting as non-profit organizations in the interest of their members and at the same time are fulfilling a public service. Accordingly, they are regarded as public utilities in the U.S. and elsewhere. Under the Austrian or German concept, exchanges are seen as fulfilling a public task. Exchanges have traditionally operated with heavy (and costly) layers of intermediation, which generated profits for their members. Economically, they were regarded as natural monopolies; in any case, most of them were regional monopolies. Major exchanges were often seen as "national champions".

This concept of the stock exchange – which was valid for the greater part of the last century – has started to change dramatically within a very short span of time. Many of the features just described have already disappeared or at least have been fundamentally

---

[6] OPPITZ (1998); KALSS (1997).

[7] After some organizational reforms in the early 1990s, at present we see a mixture between a private company (Deutsche Börse AG) acting as an operator and owner of the exchange's technical infrastructure, and the public body, acting as an organizer of the trading platform; cf. BREITKREUZ (2000); KÖNDGEN (1998); HOPT/BAUM (1997); for an comprehensive analysis of the development of stock exchange organization and regulation in Germany cf. MERKT (1997).

[8] Börsengesetz, Law of 22 June 1896, revised version of 17 July 1996 (BGBl. I 1030).

[9] Actually, at present there are three layers of supervision: at the level of the exchange (Handelsüberwachungsstellen), at the state level (Börsenaufsichtsbehörden) and the federal level (Bundesaufsichtsamt für den Wertpapierhandel). Foreign market participants sometimes regard the complexity of this structure as outlandish; at least reforms have now been proposed, cf. HOPT/BAUM (1997) 449-453 pleading for a centralized supervision.

[10] The reform will be part of the so called 'Fourth Financial Markets Promotion Act' currently under preparation. The comprehensive reports and recommendations in HOPT/RUDOLPH/BAUM (1997) were compiled as part of this undertaking.

altered. Of course, this is an ongoing process that has not yet been completed; on the contrary, its outcome is more open than ever. The emerging picture is far more colourful than before:

> Instead of exchanges being natural monopolies we see fierce competition between traditional exchanges and a plethora of newly developed electronic facilities offering various exchanges services. These platforms that are increasingly making use of Internet technology will be described in greater detail later.[11]

Regional monopolies are also challenged by competition as electronic trading has led to a far-reaching delocalization of trade.

Instead of "national champions" we see international exchange *alliances* as the first steps towards an *international* exchange.[12] An example is *Euronext*, a merger of the Paris, Amsterdam and Brussels exchanges in September 2000 that provides a single integrated trading platform with a single set of trading rules. Legally, however, *Euronext* is not yet a harmonized exchange but is operating by means of three local exchanges subject to their own local regulations in three jurisdictions.[13] An earlier example was the launch of *Eurex* in 1998, a joint undertaking of Deutsche Börse AG and the Swiss Stock Exchange (SWX), which in only three years, has become the world's most successful derivative exchange, although legally Eurex Zürich and Eurex Frankfurt remain two separate entities.[14] Most recently, *Virt-X*, a merger of SWX and Tradepoint, a small electronic exchange already recognized as an investment exchange under British law, has started its business as a pan-European exchange in London with the result, *inter alia*, that it will be there that Swiss Banks will do their principle trading in Swiss blue chips in the future.[15] This has – together with the rise of multiple listings – led to a denationalization of trading.

As a result of these trends we see markets that are no longer structured along national borders but along sectorial lines. The markets for exchange services are becoming increasingly segmented and thus – contrary to long lasting assumptions[16] – it is *competition* and *structural diversity* and not centralization that characterize the

---

11   Cf. *infra* IV.
12   For an overview over trends and different strategies cf. NOBEL (2000); PRIGGE (2000).
13   Cf. BECKERS/RIJCKMANS/STAM/STORM (2001); PRIGGE (2000) 6.
14   Their staff, members and rulebooks, however, are identical; for details of the rather complex structure cf. HOPT (1999).
15   Cf. THE ECONOMIST, 30 June 2001, 68.
16   Mostly promoted by the large exchanges and their supervisory and regulatory entourage to keep competition at bay; for an early critic of the monopoly assumption cf. MACEY/KANDA (1990); GIERSCH/SCHMIDT (1986).

present situation.[17] As this segmentation is accompanied by regional concentration within the different segments, there is no harmful loss of liquidity.[18]

Instead of state ownership and member ownership in the form of so-called "club-exchanges", private ownership is on the rise. In a comprehensive demutualization, chair holders are making room for shareholders.

Most exchanges are now owned by stock companies. The majority of these are still privately held but some are on their way to going public. Sweden's Exchange paved the way some years ago with demutualization and flotation. Deutsche Börse AG listed a minority stake of its shares early in 2001, Euronext and the London Stock Exchange followed half a year later. As a result we see exchanges listed *on* themselves, and their ownership, at least in part, is shifting towards the investing public.

Going public, of course, only makes sense if the company stops acting as a non-profit organization and is no longer run in the interests only of the exchange's members but for profit. Thus stock exchanges are increasingly behaving like normal firms and are even confronted with the risk of being taken over, as the LSE discovered last year when the Swedish OM Group, which is running the Stockholm Exchange, launched a hostile take-over bid.[19]

Traditional exchange floors with open-outcry trading and located in pompous buildings have mostly vanished to be replaced by electronic trading platforms supplemented by electronic trading facilities. The latest example is the New York Stock Exchange (NYSE), which recently introduced an electronic wholesale as well as retail trading system as separate from the floor.[20]

The alternative trading systems mentioned above, without exception offer only electronic communication and/or trading facilities.

Even if there seem to be no full-fledged "virtual" exchanges in operation at present that are based entirely on the Internet and allow for direct access of retail investors, it seems a safe guess that their arrival is only a matter of time.[21] Such a "light" exchange, possibly being a publicly held listed corporation, without members and lacking self-regulation, operating for profit and offering an intermediation-free access to trading, would indeed differ significantly from the stately institutions that dominated the financial centres for much of the last century.

What are the driving forces behind these changes?

---

[17]   SCHMIDT ET AL. (2001).
[18]   KÖNDGEN (2000) 1407; for a recent overview of the controversial discussion of order flow fragmentation vs. liquidity and efficiency cf. BENY (2001).
[19]   It may not have been a takeover attempt but only a clever – and successful - device to derail the envisaged merger of the LSE and Deutsche Börse.
[20]   BUDIMIR (2001).
[21]   See *infra* IV.

III. Driving Forces For Change

The structural upheaval in the way exchanges are organized, governed and owned as well as the way in which exchange services are offered can be traced back to various mutually reinforcing and partly inter-dependent developments.[22] Major driving forces of this change have been:

> innovation in information and communication technologies,
>
> institutionalization (and professionalization) of market participants,
>
> the increasing importance of equity financing accompanied by securitization and the development of new financial products,
>
> globalization of markets,
>
> government policies easing cross-border capital flows, market access and innovation in exchange services by deregulation.

All of these forces are interrelated. Professional market participants had the means to use both the technical possibilities as well as the regulatory freedom. In turn, they are creating the demand for more sophisticated trading possibilities and they are pushing for further deregulation. However, the most important single factor with respect to securities exchanges has been technical innovation, i.e., the increase of computing capacities and the proliferation of information and communication technologies. These innovations have made it possible to offer cheaper and quicker exchange services by means of electronic communication and trading platforms. The spread of electronic trading has resulted in the proliferation of a competitive market for exchange services that has in turn unleashed increasingly dynamic forces of structural changes.

IV. Variety Of Systems

It all began with telephone-based trading in the over-the-counter (OTC) markets and computer assistance for floor trading back in the late 1960s and early 1970s. Then gradually fully electronic trading facilities were developed during the 1980s. European exchanges have been rather quick to integrate this technique,[23] whereas in the U.S. exchanges, especially the NYSE have been slow to adapt. A number of so-called 'proprietary trading systems' (PTS) started offering more cost-efficient services to

---

[22]   For a detailed analysis cf., e.g., SEC (1994); RUDOLPH/RÖHRL (1997) 146-161.

[23]   Although regulators have been somewhat slow to respond to these new developments. In Germany e.g. only in 1994, after an amendment to the exchange law was the price created in an electronic trading system fully accepted as an alternative to the price determined by the official brokers (§ 11 I 2 BörsG); cf. SCHWARK (1997) 297.

institutional investors there first. The first and most important of these is *Instinet*, run since 1987 by *Reuters*, and which went into business as early as 1969 and which now has been admitted to seventeen exchanges worldwide.[24] Today we see an astonishing variety of so-called 'electronic communication networks' (ECNs) or 'alternative trading systems' (ATSs) as these facilities are commonly referred to in regulatory terms. (Depending on the country and the time of research or publication, the terms ECN and ATS are sometimes used as synonyms; sometimes ECNs are regarded as one specific group of ATSs.[25])

According to some new studies, the cost of fully automated trading – where computers match buyers and sellers – is about one-third lower than traditional trading on the NYSE and even NASDAQ[26]. Small wonder that today ECNs account for approximately 30% of total share volume and 40% of the dollar volume traded in Nasdaq securities,[27] and are thus creating a kind of parallel market in such securities.[28] What makes the competition of ECNs especially worrying for the conventional exchanges is their ownership structure. Most of the ECNs are wholly or largely owned by the major investment banks which are, or used to be, members of various exchanges.[29] At present, the question of how to regulate ATSs is probably internationally the most controversial and intensely discussed issue in exchange regulation.[30]

What are an ECN and/or an ATS? No generally accepted definitions exist. Put simply, an ECN brings together buyers and sellers for an electronic execution of trades. The U.S. *Securities and Exchange Commission* (SEC) defines as an ECN, any electronic system that disseminates widely to third parties orders entered into by a market maker (whether operating on an exchange or OTC), and which permits such orders to be executed.[31] In a consultative paper published in June 2001, the *Forum of European Securities*

---

[24]   GRUBER/GRÜNBICHLER (2000) 771.

[25]   Equally unclear is the use of the term PTS with respect to ECN and/or ATS.

[26]   National Association of Securities Dealers Automated Quotation System; cf. THE ECONOMIST, 10 February 2001, 85 with further references.

[27]   Cf. SEC (2000) 4.

[28]   If a market maker chooses a specific ECN, his order is routed first to that platform. If it cannot be matched within a certain period it is automatically transferred to NASDAQ; cf. GRUBER/GRÜNBICHLER (2000) 771.

[29]   PRIGGE (2000) gives an overview of investment banks' stakes in ECNs (at 10). A recent example is Deutsche Bank. In spite of being the biggest shareholder of Deutsche Börse, it announced plans to build an ECN that is expected to handle some 400,000 orders per day - mostly of retail investors - by 2004. That volume corresponds with some 25% of all orders at present executed on all German exchanges and Xetra. The bank will act as a market maker and be counterparty to all trades and hopes to avoid making use of the exchange altogether by offering its own clearing and settlement facilities; cf. Börsen-Zeitung Online, Editions Nos. 249 and 250, 23 and 30 December 2000, respectively, at 'Finanzmärkte'.

[30]   This question is addressed *infra* at B.I.

[31]   Cf. SEC (2000) 4/5.

Commissions (FESCO[32]) defines an ATS rather broadly as an entity which, without being regulated as an exchange, operates an automated system that brings together buying and selling interests in that system and according to rules set by the system's operator in a way that forms, or results in, an irrevocable contract.[33] As a rule, the securities traded here are principally traded on securities exchanges or other organized markets. Some ATSs have price discovery functions; others serve as matching systems using only prices already established on organized markets.[34]

All this leaves much room for interpretation. As the European Commission has recently stated, ATSs do not constitute a homogenous group.[35] Depending on the product they offer – as a rule, some selective aspect of the comprehensive kind of services being offered by the exchanges[36] – various types of electronic facilities can be distinguished, namely[37]

- passive electronic bulletin boards,[38]
- active electronic bulletin boards,[39]
- order-routing systems,[40]
- day trading centers,[41]
- crossing systems,[42]
- proprietary trading systems,[43]
- electronic communication networks.[44]

---

[32] Established in December of 1997 in Paris by the 15 supervisory agencies of the Member States plus those of Iceland and Norway, following the model of the *International Organization of Securities Commissions* (IOSCO) and pursuing similar goals within the EU, namely close cooperation and the development of joint supervisory standards.

[33] FESCO (2001) 6.

[34] IOSCO (1998) Part II. B.(3).

[35] COMMISSION (2000) 13.

[36] Typical exchange services are: dissemination of pre-trade information, order routing, price determination, matching and confirmation, reporting and documentation, dissemination of post-trade information, clearing and settlement; cf. KLENKE (1998) 108 et seq.

[37] There are some recent official studies into the nature of these facilities, cf. e.g. FESCO (2001); BÖRSENSACHVERSTÄNDIGENKOMMISSION (2001); POSITIONSPAPIER (no date); SEC (2000), (1998), (1994) Appendix IV; IOSCO (1998) Part II. B.; the most comprehensive work in the literature so far is LEE (1998); see also OPPITZ (2000); MACEY/O'HARA (1999); DOMOWITZ (1996); DE BELL (1993).

[38] Only offers are posted; trading takes place between the parties and the system is not involved.

[39] The system matches offers, acting as an agent for one party.

[40] Orders are collected and passed for profit to a specific trading platform.

[41] This function is similar to that of an introducing broker: Rooms and PCs linked to exchange members are provided for trading by private investors.

[42] Matching of orders within the system in accordance with fixed rules; price import and often active in after-hour trading.

[43] Definitions differ, mostly understood as screen based trading systems, typically sponsored by broker-dealers; independent, for-profit business; no self-regulatory organization; cf. SEC (1994) Appendix IV.

Depending on the pertinent definition of an ATS, some of these can be classified as ATSs while others are clearly not.[44] Using its own definition of an ECN – i.e., excluding internal broker-dealer order-routing systems and crossing systems – the SEC at present counts nine ECNs that are active in the U.S. securities market.[46] On a worldwide scale, in 2000 the number of ECNs engaged in trading bonds was estimated to total 73 systems.[47]

V.   Role Of The Internet

What role does the Internet play in this? In its 1998 survey 'Securities Activities on the Internet', the *International Organization of Securities Commissions* (IOSCO) found that traditional exchanges with conventional closed membership structures have so far been relying on their own sophisticated closed trading systems, using dedicated lines for their operations.[48] The Internet has only been used as a means for the dissemination of information and advertising. IOSCO has further found that broker-dealers, active in the organized OTC-markets that are using electronic communication system, were also relying predominantly on their proprietary trading networks, rather than the Internet, to conduct their trading.[49] Even the ATSs[50] existing at that stage were obviously closed systems and not generally accessible to the public through the Internet. However, IOSCO expects emerging ATSs to make use of the Internet to increase order flow by providing new participants with easier access to their trading systems.[51] Indeed, this has already happened.

In 2000 the Swedish *OM-Gruppen* and the investment firm *Morgan Stanley Dean Witter* surprisingly launched their joint Internet-based trading platform *'Jiway'.*[52] Jiway aims at the retail investor and claims to be the "first online-exchange in Europe". However, it is only accessible for brokers and does *not* offer direct access for the public. Thus private investors have first to address their bank or broker, but once they have opened a deposit

---

[44]   As mentioned above, definitions differ, cf. text accompanying note 31 *supra*.
[45]   See also *infra* at B.I. for further discussion *inter alia* of the position recently taken by the German Exchange Expert Commission (BÖRSENSACHVERSTÄNDIGENKOMMISSION (2001)).
[46]   These are: Instinet, Island, Bloomberg Tradebook, Archipelago, REDIBook, Strike, Attain, NexTrade, Market XT, and GFI Securities; cf. SEC (2000) Part II., I.B. Two ECNs had formerly filed applications to register as an exchange. The others are registered as broker-dealers and are subject to the Regulation ATS issued in 1998; this regulation is described in greater detail *infra* at B.I.
[47]   SCHERFF (2001).
[48]   IOSCO (1998) Part II. B. (1).
[49]   IOSCO (1998) Part II. B. (2).
[50]   IOSCO is referring to ATSs rather than ECNs and did include PTSs in its survey.
[51]   IOSCO (1998) Part II. B. (3).
[52]   Cf. PRIGGE (2000) 6; reports in: Zeitschrift für das Gesamte Kreditwesen 5/2000, 249/250; Frankfurter Allgemeine Zeitung, 17 November 2000.

with them, their orders are executed online in real time. Jiway plans to offer a central counterparty and netting, and intends eventually to offer online cross-border transactions in some 6,000 European and American shares listed on the major European exchanges as well as on NYSE and Nasdaq. Execution at the best price is offered. The British Financial Service Authority has recognized Jiway as an investment exchange.

Another example of an Internet-based trading platform is the German *'Quotrix'* system that will start its operations this autumn.[53] This quote-driven ECN, where a market maker supplies liquidity, is a joint venture of the regional Düsseldorf exchange, the private trading platform *TradeLink*, (so far the biggest ECN in Germany), and the German broker *Lang & Schwarz*.[54] Qoutrix is regarded as a trading system of the Düsseldorf exchange and thus supervised in the same way. The system imports prices: only securities listed somewhere else are traded; it has none of its own listings. The market maker promises to offer at least the price quoted at the reference market at the time of the order. Again, private investors have no direct access but must have an Internet link with their online-bank or online-broker. Once this has been installed, the investor can contact Quotrix from his own PC, demand a quote for a specific security, and, if he agrees with the price, accept it directly. The order will then be transferred to the market maker and executed via the exchange.

Although some initial securities offerings have been successfully placed over the Internet with private investors,[55] and online-broking is all the rage,[56] so far there seems to be no "virtual" or Internet-based exchange in operation in the true meaning of the term, that is to say which would allow *direct* access, i.e., intermediation-free access to securities trading.[57] A major obstacle is the counterparty risk: an investor has to be sure that his order is actually cleared and settled and that the counterparty will not default on his obligations after matching but before settlement of the order. However, this risk can be neutralized if the system provider acts as or provides for a clearinghouse acting as a central counterparty.[58] This practice is becoming increasingly common with new trading systems (e.g., Eurex, Euronext). An alternative might be if each customer has to submit a security deposit or a bank guarantee and his or her orders are restricted in volume

---

[53]   Press release of 13 June 2001.

[54]   Cf. Börsen-Zeitung , 20 February 2001, 1 et seq.; information given on the homepage of Quotrix at <www.quotrix.de>.

[55]   Cf. e.g. VAUPEL (2000).

[56]   In the U.S. some 170 online-brokers were offering their services in 2000, cf. Frankfurter Allgemeine Zeitung, 22 July 2000, 25.

[57]   As KÖNDGEN (1998) 228, 245, points out, such an organizational structure *did* already exist some time ago: In the 18th century, the Vienna exchange was organized by an issuer and open to intermediation-free trading by a scarcely restricted public. However, this "modern" state of affairs lasted only till 1811.

[58]   KÖNDGEN (2000) 1417/18; WASTL/SCHLITT (2000) 393.

accordingly.[59] Another option for the operator of the exchange might be to insure the counterparty at comparatively low cost.[60]

A specific obstacle exists at present under German exchange regulation, where so far § 7 II of the Börsengesetz does not permit private investors to participate directly in exchange trading. However, it seems unlikely that this restriction will last. Already, the discussion of the legal implications of establishing an Internet-based exchange are already in full swing,[61] and some Internet-based trading platforms, open for all kind of investors, are claimed to be under "construction".[62]

As the remaining legal and structural obstacles do not appear insurmountable, most probably it will be only a matter of time before we see the arrival of a fully fledged online-exchange.

B. REGULATORY CONCERNS

The fundamental technological and structural changes described in Part A have some far-reaching institutional consequences that in turn challenge traditional exchange regulation. Three issues will be addressed in this part. The first concerns the systemic challenge. The unbundling of exchange services resulted in a plethora of different financial intermediaries performing customized functions and offering specific services. These trends have increasingly blurred the conventional distinction between markets and market participants and raise a central regulatory question: What constitutes an exchange? (I). Disintermediation and profit-orientation may lead to conflict of interests and put the functionality of self-regulation into question. Also the relationship between rules of consumer protection and exchange regulation appears to be uncertain with respect to retail investors executing online-trading without intermediation (II). Finally, delocalization and ubiquity of electronic and especially online-trading cause difficult jurisdictional and supervisory problems (III).

---

[59]   RIEHMER/HEUSER (2001) 386.

[60]   KÖNDGEN (1998) 246.

[61]   For the German discussion cf. e.g. RIEHMER/HEUSER (2001); PFÜLLER/WESTERWELLE (2001) at Nos. 122 et seq.; WASTL/SCHLITT (2000); KÖNDGEN (2000) 1415 et seq.

[62]   Cf. e.g. the home pages of the U.S. Wit Capital Corporation <www.witcap.com> or the German Webstock AG <www.webstock.de>; the later claiming to be first European securities trading platform based on the internet (last visit for both sites 15 June 2001).

I.   The Systemic Challenge: What Constitutes An Exchange?

The German Börsengesetz of 1896 does not define the term "exchange". Even then it was regarded as too difficult to formulate a definition that would be open enough to incorporate future developments. On the other hand, at the same time the lawmakers were optimistic that it would be fairly easy to decide in a given situation whether an organized trading facility should be legally regarded as an exchange or not.[63] The difficulty in defining what constitutes an exchange, or put differently, what distinguishes exchange services from other financial services, is now bigger than ever. The idea that it is possible to recognize an exchange "when one sees it" seems today rather outlandish given the multitude of new dealing facilities offering *some* of the services conventional exchanges usually provide and thus competing *selectively* with them.[64]

It is beyond the scope of this article to find an answer to this question that is puzzling regulators all over the world wherever exchange services are offered.[65] However, it may be possible and worth trying to formulate some basic policy considerations and, using those as a background, to give an overview of current legislative activities and proposals.

Policy considerations:

> The unbundling of exchange services can be viewed from two different perspectives, namely the supply side and the demand side.[66] As mentioned before, technological innovation, namely automated trading, allows for a selective offering of exchange services at competitive costs. These varying offers correspond with different preferences of consumers. Preferences may be immediacy, liquidity, low trading costs, anonymity, or transparency depending on the kind of trade to be executed and the type of investor involved. In policy terms, regulation should allow these specific demands to be satisfied and should not hinder the supply of selective exchange services by forcing the service provider to comply with regulations designed for a broader range of services.

> Furthermore, whatever form of regulation is adopted, it must not hinder new developments. If there is a tradeoff between innovation and comprehensive protection of market participants, innovation should have priority – at least in the initial stages.[67] As far as the given constitutional framework allows, regulation of ATSs should be

---

[63]   Cf. HOPT/BAUM (1997) 377/78 with further references.

[64]   LEE (1998) 4.

[65]   There is an intense discussion about a proper definition of an exchange that cannot be taken up here; cf. e.g. LEE (1998) especially 279 et seq.; HOPT/BAUM (1997) 377-391; DOMOWITZ (1996).

[66]   For details see PRIGGE (2000) at II.

[67]   The SEC, e.g., decided in the mid 1990s *not* to regulate PTSs in any substantive way but to watch developments closely so as not to hinder further innovation in trading. The pertinent regulation was only adopted in 1998; cf. *infra*.

undertaken at the level of ordinances or releases rather than at the legislative level, for the sake of greater adaptability and flexibility.

In order to find a workable trade-off between sufficient legality and adaptability for future technological developments, it may be useful to try to define the term 'exchange' as precisely as possible – the known difficulties notwithstanding[68] – and to use a rather wide description of the term ATS.[69]

As already indicated, technological innovation has unleashed fierce competition in the market for exchange services. As always, contestability is the best way to "regulate" a market. Thus the intensity of conventional exchange regulation can be reduced. In other words, in various aspects, deregulation is feasible. Furthermore, as established exchanges have stopped being natural monopolies which enjoyed network externalities because of their control of liquidity, no specific 'exchange' regulation is necessary to secure access and proper market behaviour. Rather, competition policy and law should regulate the structure of the market for exchange services as it does with other markets.[70]

As the conventional boundaries between exchanges perceived as markets and financial intermediaries as market participants are disintegrating, a functional approach to the regulation of ATSs is probably the only workable solution. The organizer of an ECN/ATS should be free to choose what kind of services he wants to offer and be regulated accordingly, *independently* of the technology used or the volume of its business.[71] Different roles are possible: the ECN can act only as an agent (broker) for the customer or it can act also as a dealer and/or market maker; alternatively it can add further elements of exchange services like offering liquidity and reputational services usually associated with an exchange.[72]

Furthermore, there should be the possibility for an ECN/ATS to *opt up* into a stricter regulatory framework if it wants to in order to be attractive to a certain group of customers or to qualify as a regulated market in the sense of Art. 1 No. 13 of the Investment Services Directive (ISD[73]) given that it would then fulfil the pertinent requirements.[74]

---

[68]   Cf. *supra*, note 66.

[69]   This is e.g. the Swiss approach, where the term 'exchange' is defined in Art. 2 lit of the Swiss Exchange Law (BEHG) but not the term 'börsenähnliche Einrichtung' (alternative trading system); cf. NOBEL (2000) 1490. A similar approach is used in the U.S. by the SEC in a newly adopted Rule 3b-16 intended to expand the Commission's interpretation of the term 'exchange'; cf. text *infra*.

[70]   LEE (1998) 308/09; HOPT/BAUM (1997) 362-364, 435/6.

[71]   MACEY/O'HARA (1999) 49 et seq.

[72]   MACEY/O'HARA (1999) 49.

[73]   Directive 93/22/EEC of 10 May 1993, Official Journal L 141, p. 27.

[74]   HOPT/BAUM (1997) 399.

Notwithstanding the functional approach, if a regulator wants to create a specific regulation for ECNs that offer *some* selective exchanges services without being fullyfledged exchanges, the question arises as to how to regulate and where to locate that regulation. This can be done in two ways: either as some kind of exchange regulation "light" or as part of the general regulation of financial services. The first solution is preferable as organizing a market is inherently different from offering services in a bilateral relationship.[75] If viewed as a firm, with the product being the organization of a *market* in financial instruments, exchange regulation should aim at securing the quality of that service and differentiate this from regulation guiding the behavior of intermediaries as, e.g., the ISD does.[76]

Current regulatory activities:

(1) The most recent and most comprehensive regulation of ATSs can be found in the U.S. In December 1998, after lengthy preparations the SEC adopted new rules to allow most alternative trading systems to *choose* whether to register as securities exchanges, or to register as broker-dealers and comply with additional requirements under the so called 'Regulation ATS'.[77] Most of the release went into force in April 1998, with the remainder in December 2000. The regulatory framework is supposed to "encourage market innovation while ensuring basic investor protection" and to recognize the fact that advancing technology has increasingly blurred the distinction between broker-dealers and exchanges which has been the regulatory cornerstone so far.[78]

The new regulations follow a two-step approach. A new Rule 3b-16(a) clarifies that any organization, association, or group of persons will qualify as an exchange within the terms of Section 3(a)(1) of the Securities and Exchange Act of 1934[79] if it (1) brings together the orders for securities of multiple buyers and sellers, *and* (2) uses established, non-discretionary methods under which such orders interact with each other, and the buyers and sellers entering such orders agree to the terms of a trade.[80] Rule 3b-16(b) expressively exempts systems that merely route orders to other trading facilities, or are operated by a single registered market maker, or that allow persons to enter orders for execution against the bids and offers of a single dealer.[81]

---

[75]   KÖNDGEN (2000) 1418; HOPT/BAUM (1997) 398.

[76]   KÖNDGEN (1998) 241.

[77]   "Regulation of Alternative Trading Systems", Exchange Act Rel. No. 34-40760 (Dec. 8, 1998), 63 Fed. Reg. 70,843; 17 CFR 242.300-303; <www.sec.gov/rules/final/34-40760.txt>.

[78]   *Id* at Executive Summary, at II.

[79]   "...... market place or facilities for bringing together purchasers and sellers of securities or for otherwise performing with respect to securities the functions commonly performed by a stock exchange"; 15 U.S.C. 78c(a)(1).

[80]   17 CFR 240.3b-16(a).

[81]   17 CFR 240.3b-16(b).

In a second step, most alternative trading systems are *exempted*, even if they perform the same function as an exchange as defined above, as long as they do *not* undertake any *self-regulatory* activities, i.e. set rules governing the conduct of subscribers or discipline them (other than exclusion from trading). However, the SEC might determine that an exemption is not available if a certain (high) trading volume of a given security is achieved by the ATS. An exempt ATS has to register as a broker-dealer, become a member of a SRO, and – depending on the trading volume – fulfil a couple of other obligations under the new ATS Regulation.[82]

With ATS regulation, the SEC has recognized the evolving role of alternative trading systems and by giving them a choice to register either as a market or as market participant, the Commission has adopted a flexible regulatory system. Currently the discussion has moved on to new challenges posed by the activities of ECNs in after-hour trading.[83]

(2) Within the European Union two complementary proposals are currently under discussion:[84]

The *European Commission* issued a communication called "Upgrading the Investment Services Directive" in November 2000.[85] The release of the revised directive has been announced for early 2002. The communication states four priorities for the revision of the ISD: an improvement of the so called 'European Passport' for securities firms doing business in different member states,[86] a consolidation of cross-border clearing and settlement, the introduction of common safety standards for ATSs and other new electronic service facilities, and – most relevant in this context – the facilitation of competition between conventional exchanges and ATSs.

The Commission expresses doubts to whether the traditional strict separation between securities firms and regulated markets is still functional in the light of new technological developments in trading.[87] Although ATSs are basically regarded as securities firms, in their business activities they face increasingly the same challenges as exchanges and regulated markets. So far the term 'regulated market' as defined in Art. 1 No. 13 requires the market to offer - for all securities traded - the possibility also to acquire a listing there.[88] As this requirement is an impediment to competition, the Commission proposes

---

[82] The whole regulatory context is rather complex, the pertinent rules together with explanations and examples cover some 250 pages.

[83] Cf. SEC (2000).

[84] For the recent reforms in Japan see the contribution of OSAKI in this volume.

[85] Communication from the Commission to the European Parliament and the Council: "Upgrading the Investment Services Directive", 16 November 2000 (93/22/EC).

[86] Cf. LOMNICKA (2000) 325 et seq.

[87] Also skeptical SCHWARK (1997) 300/01.

[88] The concept of the regulated market is discussed with HOPT (1999).

to differentiate between an admission for listing and one for trading.[89] This change would be a precondition for ATSs to register as a regulated market, as these do not list companies. On the other hand, the Commission is concerned that exchanges may give up cost intensive listing activities with their resulting transparency duties. In general, the Commission sees a danger, that demutualization and the shift of exchanges towards profit oriented firms – although welcome in principle – might lead to restrictions of access and other anti-competitive behavior. A solution is seen in a strict application of competition law by the pertinent authorities (and *not* the agencies supervising the capital markets).[90]

The Forum of European Securities Commissions published a consultative paper in June, entitled "Proposed Standards for Alternative Trading Systems", asking for comments.[91] The issue of a communication on the final standards is envisaged for late 2001. The FESCO paper contains a useful table where its own "Standards", organized by risks, are compared with the proposals of the Commission for the revised ISD[92] and is meant as complementary to the latter proposals.

The proposed standards focus on potential risks posed by ATSs for investor protection and market integrity. According to FESCO, the existing conduct of business rules do *not* address these risk properly.[93] The proposed standards concentrate on registration, transparency, reporting rules, and the prevention of market abuse.[94] They may vary depending on the specific activities of an ATS. The standards are formulated in rather general terms and mix elements of conduct of business rules with conventional exchange regulation.

(3) In Germany, as mentioned before, a major revision of the Exchange Law of 1896 is under preparation for 2002.[95] There is no doubt that the reform will deal with the question of how to regulate ATSs.[96] In this context, the *German Exchange Expert Commission*, an advisory body of the Ministry of Finance, recently issued

---

[89]   *Id.* at 15.

[90]   *Id.* at 16.

[91]   "Proposed Standards for Alternative Trading Systems", Consultative Paper, Paris, 11 June 2001, at <www.europefesco.org>.

[92]   Cf. *id*, at Annex A.

[93]   *Id.* at 4.

[94]   *Id.* at 5.

[95]   A comprehensive review of recent developments and the current discussion can be found with WEBER (2000).

[96]   Those few that are active at the moment are licensed at present as financial services firms. However, it is not clear whether at least in some cases de facto material exchange trading is given that is forbidden without a proper license as an exchange; cf. DREYLING (2000) 20; for a general discussion see HAMMEN (2001); for the Austrian discussion see OPPITZ (2000).

recommendations for the regulation of ATS.[97] The report proposes a *dual* categorization of trading system[98]s that differs from other approaches: (1) those with a multilateral functionality ("Marktplätze") matching orders of different market participants, and (2) systems with a bilateral functionality ("Kontrahentensysteme"), e.g., quote-driven systems that display a dealer's price (acting as a market maker) and enable customers to trade at those prices against the dealer's principal book. Among systems with multilateral functionality, a further differentiation is made between recognized exchanges and those trading facilities, that function as a market place but have no formal license as an exchange ("Wertpapierhandelssysteme"). The first distinction is drawn from a functional perspective, the second from a regulatory one.[99]

Basically, systems with a bilateral functionality are *not* classified as ATS and no specific need for regulation is seen for those other than (existing) conduct of business rules and the obligation to inform private investors using the system that they are not doing business with a "Wertpapierhandelssystem".[100] As these systems are not regarded as marketplaces the Commission accordingly sees no need to give them the status of a regulated market in the sense of Art. 1 No. 13 ISD. FESCO, on the other hand, *does* include bilateral systems in its definition of an ATS.[101]

As elsewhere, the Commission states that the traditional distinction between Exchanges and financial services firms (broker-dealers) is no longer sufficient. The proposed regulations contain elements of conventional exchange regulation, but are far less restrictive than those. Emphasis is laid on transparency with respect to price and traded volumes.[102] Another central aspect is the security of the system. Refreshingly, questions of liquidity, price building mechanism, or market access are expressively *excluded* from regulation, rather competition and openness for innovation is stressed instead.[103]

Different from other proposals, it recommends a definition of the two different systems.[104] Quite surprisingly, a preference is expressed for a regulation in the Securities Trading Act (WpHG) rather than in the Exchange Law.[105]

---

[97]   BÖRSENSACHVERSTÄNDIGENKOMMISSION (2001); for a similar undertaking of the Bundes-Wertpapieraufsicht, the Austrian supervisory agency, that comes to some different results, see POSITIONSPAPIER (no date).

[98]   E.g. a regulation depending on the volume traded – like the U.S. Regulation ATS – is rejected.

[99]   The Commission deems it impossible to distinguish on functional grounds between exchanges and trading facilities with a market function; cf. *id.* at 8 et seq.

[100]   *Id.* at 11-13.

[101]   Cf. FESCO (2001) 7 (note 3).

[102]   BÖRSENSACHVERSTÄNDIGENKOMMISSION (2001) 9.

[103]   *Id.* at 10/11.

[104]   *Id.* at 15.

[105]   *Id.* at 14.

II.   Demutualization And Self-regulation, Disintermediation And Consumer Protection

The parallel, though not necessarily linked, developments of demutualization and disintermediation are reaching an extreme point in the hypothetical but no longer fantastic case of an Internet-based trading platform with direct access for retail-investors. Let us assume that one institution, an international investment bank, owns the platform. Let us further assume that the bank is not acting as a central counterparty – (it might thus be a bilateral system) – but grants access to all its worldwide interested preferred customers (who either put down a safety deposit or have their trading obligations up to a certain volume guaranteed by the bank). A final assumption is that the system matches orders. Then we see a trading system with a multilateral functionality, in other words, we see an exchange or its functional equivalent, an ATS. However, there are no members any longer, but only a genuine business enterprise as a profit-interested owner. Neither are there any intermediaries acting as brokers, dealers or market makers any longer, only a server automatically matching orders according to programmed priorities. This scenario gives rise to at least two different sets of regulatory questions:

First, what are the consequences for the governance of such a system? Is there still room for self-regulation and self-supervision that traditionally played a major part in exchange governance? The conventional system of self-regulation worked because standards were agreed collectively, and violations led to disgrace among the group of exchange members. As members earned their living at the exchange and the valuable membership (seat) was held as a kind of collateral by the exchange against possible future liabilities, they had great incentives to play by the rules. Our assumed Internet exchange lacks all of these foundations of self-regulation. This suggests that conventional governance will not work any longer.[106] Other ways and means have to be found. Again, it is beyond the scope of this article to try to do so. In any case, the discussion about possible solutions has already begun elsewhere.[107]

Secondly, intermediation-free trading with direct access of retail investors to the trading platform raises a bundle of complicated questions with respect to consumer protection laws. These too shall be only addressed summarily here.[108] The private investor is

---

[106]   The fact that internet-based trading systems are not wholly compatible with classical exchange regulation and governance is, of course, no reason to ban these platforms, cf. SCHWARK (1997) 300; on the contrary, this fact has recently been regarded as a specific incentive for a reform of the "antiquated" exchange law by two German authors; cf. WASTL/SCHLITT (2000) 396.

[107]   Cf. e.g. IOSCO (2000); MCBRIDE JOHNSON (2000); also PRIGGE (2000) at II.3; PFÜLLER/ WESTERWELLE (2001) at No.147.

[108]   For an excellent comprehensive discussion from the perspective of German/European law see RIEHMER/HEUSER (2001).

(normally) regarded as a 'consumer' in the legal sense of the term.[109] If so, from the present German perspective the following directive and laws might be applicable:

- the Directive on E-Commerce,[110]
- the Law on Long Distance Selling,[111]
- the Law on Standard Contract Terms.[112]

The Directive on E-Commerce – the future provisions of the corresponding German regulation[113] – is applicable if a service of the information society is offered. This, in turn, will be the case if a service is delivered electronically in the way of long distance selling and on the individual request of the consumer. The services offered by an Internet-based trading platform are offered electronically on demand of the investor if he places an order. Thus the Directive is applicable for services by an Internet-exchange/ATS located within the Common Market.[114] This has far reaching consequences for the question which law decides whether a given exchange service is permitted.[115]

With respect to the Law on Long Distance Selling, the situation is less clear.[116] It is probably applicable only in relation to the Internet-exchange/ATS but not as between the individual buyers and sellers of securities. The later is obvious if the consumer is *selling* shares, but the same must be true if he is *buying* them, as the seller is only using the facilities of the exchange/ATS and is not running distribution facilities of his own. To be applicable, the law requires just that. If one applies the law with respect to the contractual relationship between the exchange/ATS and the consumer/investor, the thrilling question arises as to whether the latter has the right to revoke his orders in accordance with § 3 of the Law. He might be tempted to do so if the price of the share moves in an unexpected direction after he has placed the order.

The Law on Standard Contract Terms is not applicable with respect to the rules of an exchange if that exchange has a *public* law status – as is the case in Germany at

---

[109] At least as long as he is not making use of the exchange services in connection with his professional (business) activities; cf. SPINDLER (2001) 341 et seq.

[110] Directive 2000/31/EC of the European Parliament and of the Council of 8 June 2000 on certain legal aspects of information society services, in particular electronic commerce, in the Internal Market ('Directive on electronic commerce'), Official Journal L 178, 17 July 2000, p.1-16.

[111] Fernabsatzgesetz, Law of 27 June / 21 July 2000; BGBl I 887, 1139.

[112] Gesetz zur Regelung des Rechts der Allgemeinen Geschäftsbedingungen (AGB-Gesetz), Law of 9 December 1976; BGBl I 3317.

[113] The Directive will be transformed into German law in the near future; for a discussion of the transformation cf. TETTERBORN (2000).

[114] RIEHMER/HEUSER (2001) 388.

[115] Cf. *infra* at III.

[116] For the rather complicated reasoning and the intriguing interplay of various directives concerned with financial services see RIEHMER/HEUSER (2001) 389/90 with further references.

present.[117] However, if it is a *private* undertaking, like an ATS, its rules and regulations are subject to that law. Whether that difference in evaluating exchange services is still justified in the light of the new developments appears to be doubtful.

III. Delocalization And Supervision Of Trade

Denationalization of exchanges and delocalization of electronic and especially online-trading with its ubiquity as a network facility cause difficult jurisdictional and supervisory problems. However, these are not fundamentally different from the questions commonly addressed with respect to services offered over the net. As always, the first distinction is whether the cross-border services are offered within the Common Market or whether the exchange/ATS is located outside this area.

Even at the European level things are complicated but far less so than from the international perspective.[118] If an Internet-exchange/ATS is accepted as a regulated market in the sense of Art. 1 ISD, according to the principle of 'home country control' the supervisory authorities of the state where it is located are competent.[119] If, on the other hand, the Directive on E-Commerce is applicable, according to its Art. 3 I & II, the principle of control by the 'country of origin' has to be observed.[120] As a result, authorities of the market place where exchanges services are accepted by investors, may not interfere under their national laws as long as the services offered cross-border from a member state are consistent with the pertinent regulation in that member state. That latter state has the sole supervisory competence. The two principles appear to be somewhat different as, clearly, there are varying technical approaches to the definitions. The practical consequences of these differences, if any, are not clear yet. However, the central inquiry in both cases seems to be "where is the principal place of business of the Internet-exchange/ATS located?" As a rule this is the place where its matching server is located and where accordingly trades are matched.[121] The matching of trades is the core function and the central business activity of such a trading platform.

Things are more complex if we turn to the international level. Again, we are confronted less with an exchange specific problem but rather with the general question of possible

---

117   Cf. RIEHMER/HEUSER (2001) 390/91.

118   For a general overview the regulation of cross-border financial services in the EU Internal Market see
        CORCORAN/HART (2001).

119   For a short explanation of the principle see e.g. LOMNICKA (2000); for a detailed analysis with respect
        to its implications on national conflict laws see e.g. CARBONE/MUNARI (1998).

120   The rather complex conflict of law questions raised by this principle are discussed in great detail with
        MANKOWSKI (2001) and SPINDLER (2001).

121   PFÜLLER/WESTERWELLE (2001) at No. 164; RIEHMER/HEUSER (2001) 388/89; WASTL/SCHLITT (2000)
        394/95.

regulatory responses to globalizing capital markets.[122] To the extent that capital markets become globalized, policymakers are challenged to "regulate" such international markets with national laws. From a technical point of view, delocalized screen-based securities trading poses the greatest challenge to securities regulators who are trying to allocate jurisdiction based on a territorial approach. The server of an Internet-based exchange/ATS is practically accessible from all over the world and thus regarded by some as omnipresent. Theoretically, this could lead to the need to comply with countless different exchange regulations if those – as is still common – are based on a territorial approach.

Taking the U.S. with its stringent securities regulation as an example, securities offerings and sales on the Internet are potentially subject to the Securities Acts as long as they could be viewed from the U.S., regardless of where in the world they are placed on the Internet. As the Commission realized that this approach is untenable, it has clarified its position in an interpretive release issued in 1998 with respect to securities offerings and sales on the Internet.[123] According to that release, Internet postings as such do not result in a registration obligation under the U.S. securities laws, provided the issuer has implemented measures reasonably designed to prevent sales into the U.S.[124] The relevant test is whether offers are *targeted* to the U.S. market.

This targeting-approach has been taken up by IOSCO in its 1998 report on "Securities Activities on the Internet".[125] The German Federal Supervisory Office for Securities Trading (BAWe) has adopted this for Internet-based public offerings as well.[126] The same is true for Japan[127] and others. As an interim solution the targeting-approach may work not only for public offerings but also for other Internet-based exchange activities in lieu of any other practical international solution at present available. In any case, compared to the untenable and counterproductive view that claims an omnipresence of the Internet with corresponding extensive legal obligations, this is a step in the right direction. Most of the relevant discussion is focused on the rather technical question when an offer is targeted and what the offerer can do to disclaim responsibility.[128]

---

[122] This topic will only be briefly taken up as it was extensively discussed in a contribution to a conference organized in Kyushu two years ago; cf. BAUM (2000) an overview of the different approaches taken and the international discussion.

[123] Statement of the Commission Regarding Use of Internet Web Sites to Offer Securities, Solicit Securities Transactions or Advertise Investment Services Offshore, Release Nos. 33-7516, 34-39779 (March, 1998), text available at <www.sec.gov/rules/concept/33-6516.htm>.

[124] Cf. Release at p. 2-4. A reasonable measure could be a disclaimer posted on the Web site making it clear that the offer is directed only to countries other than the U.S.

[125] Cf. IOSCO (1998) at Part III.A.(4).

[126] Bekanntmachung des Bundesaufsichtsamtes für den Wertpapierhandel zum Verkaufsprospektgesetz, as amended of 9 September 1998 (BGBl. I 2701).

[127] Cf. the contribution of OSAKI in this volume.

[128] For the relevant German discussion cf. BORGES (2001).

However, the crucial question is an entirely different one: By forcing foreign exchanges (and other providers of financial services) either to comply with one's own national regulations or alternatively to deny access to one's citizens the targeting-approach neutralizes most of the advantages of a globalized capital market.[129] Domestic investors are deprived of lucrative investment opportunities abroad and the restrictions of access hinders world savings to look for their most productive uses by means of new and cheap trading technology. Basically, the targeting-approach re-creates separate markets along the geopolitical boundaries and thus impedes a healthy regulatory competition.

A better solution would be to abandon this still inherently territorial approach for a closer look at the systems architecture of the foreign exchanges to see whether those are acceptable from the point of investor protection.[130] This would correspond with what has been labeled a "truly cooperative strategy".[131] In the end it might lead to some kind of mutual recognition as is known from the integrated market of the EU. Of course, this approach will take time and may not be feasible with the present regulatory status and governance structure of various exchanges, but it would supply a strong *incentive* for good exchange regulation and governance. As virtually all trading platforms, including Internet-based ones, are interested in acquiring as much liquidity as possible, this may well turn out as a surprisingly strong incentive leading to a race to the *top* rather then the habitually bemoaned race to the bottom used as a standard pretext for impeding regulatory competition.[132]

C.   OUTLOOK

The last two decades have seen a revolution in the market for exchanges services sparked by technological innovations that made the electronic trading platform possible. Electronic trading has given rise to a plethora of new trading facilities (PTSs, ATSs, ECNs and the like) that dramatically increased competition and rather abruptly pulled the traditional exchanges out of their cozy institutional slumber. Internet technology was not crucial at the beginning but has rapidly started to play a more important role in this development. We will probably see the arrival of a fullyfledged "virtual" exchange based entirely on the web, encompassing retail investors and functioning with more or less no intermediation in a comparatively short time. It seems unlikely that remaining structural and legal obstacles will prevent this from happening.

The far reaching institutional changes challenge most of the time honoured assumptions about exchange regulation and governance. Regulators and supervisors all over the world

---

129   For a harsh but convincing critic see MOON (2000).
130   Cf. MOON (2000).
131   BAUM (2000) 99 et seq.
132   For a critical review of this pretext cf. BAUM (2000).

are having a hard time catching up with these developments. As always, change and innovation can be seen either as a chance or as a threat. Globalized markets lead to regulatory competition that in turn hurts vested interests of national regulatory and supervisory agencies. Technological innovation allows the dismantling of layers of intermediation and thus sends profits tumbling and endangers jobs in parts of the securities industry. The winners are firms looking for cheaper ways to raise capital and investors who are offered an ever increasing variety of investment opportunities at low trading costs.

Actually, almost all areas of exchange regulation are tested. As exchanges are increasingly regarded as firms run for profit – which is true for ATSs/ECNs anyway – competition law rather than specific exchange regulation will play a growing role to secure basic market functions. The conventional distinction between markets and market participants no longer works as the traditional cornerstone it used to be for regulating exchanges on the one hand side and financial intermediaries on the other. New approaches are tested a present. With disintermediation reduced, the basis for self-regulation has become shaky. Either new ways are found or state regulation will increase. If private investors, mostly regarded as consumers, enter a direct contractual relationship with an Internet-based exchange or ATS, consumer protection laws will apply despite not being tailored to cope with the specific features of securities trading.

Delocalized screen-based securities trading and especially online-trading challenge securities regulators who are trying to allocate jurisdiction based on a territorial approach. The internationally adopted so-called targeting-approach as a possible regulatory response can be nothing more than an intermediate step as it neutralizes most of the advantages of globalized capital markets. Here, too, new and better ways, not based on a territorial approach, have to be found. If anything, the future systemic and regulatory architecture of securities trading facilities will become more colourful.

References

BAUM, HARALD (2000), "Globalizing Capital Markets and Possible Regulatory Responses", in: Basedow/Kono (eds.), Legal Aspects of Globalization. Conflict of Law, Internet, Capital Markets and Insolvency in a Global Economy, The Hague 2000, 77-132.

BECKERS, STAN H.A.J. / RIJCKMANS, LUCAS J.L. / STAM, YVONNE T. M. / STORM, STEVEN E. (2001), "Euronext: A Dutch Perspective", Butterworths Journal of International Banking and Financial Law, 2001, 323-328.

BENY, LAURA N. (2001), "U.S. Secondary Stock Markets: A Survey of Current Regulatory and Structural Issues and a Reform Proposal to Enhance Competition"; The Harvard John M. Olin Center for Law, Economics, and Business, Discussion Paper No. 331 (7/2001) <www.law.harvard.edu./programs/olin_center/>.

BÖRSENSACHVERSTÄNDIGENKOMMISSION (2001), "Empfehlungen der Börsensach-verständigenkommission zur Regulierung alternativer Handelssysteme", Frankfurt/Main, May 16, 2001, at <www.finanzplatz.de>.

BREITKREUZ, TILMAN (2000), "Die Ordnung der Börse. Verwaltungsrechtliche Zentralfragen des Wertpapierbörsenwesens", Berlin 2000.

BORGES, GEORG (2001), "Lokalisierung von Angeboten beim Electronic Banking", 55 Wertpapier Mitteilungen, 2001, 1542-1553.

BUDIMIR, MIROSLAV (2001), "NYSE startet elektronischen Handel", Die Bank, No. 1/2001, 25-29.

CARBONE, SERGIO M./MUNARI, FRANCESCO (1998), "The Enforcement of the European Regime for Investment Services in the Member States and Its Impact on National Conflict of Laws", in: Ferrarini (ed.), European Securities Markets – The Investment Services Directive and Beyond, London 1998, 317-361.

COMMISSION (2000), "Communication from the Commission to the European Parliament and the Council: Upgrading the Investment Services Directive", November 16, 2000 (93/22/EC).

CORCORAN, ANDREA M./HART, TERRY L. (2001), "The Regulation of Cross-Border Financial Services in the EU Internal Market: A Primer for Third Countries", Working Paper, SSRN Electronic Paper Collection, 7/2001, <http://papers.ssrn.com/sol3/paper.cfm?abstract_id=274849>.

DE BELL, JAN (1993), "Automated Trading System and the Concept of an 'Exchange' in an International Context. Proprietary Systems: A Regulatory Headache", 14 University of Pennsylvania Journal of International Business Law, 1993, 169-211.

DOMOWITZ, IAN (1996), "An Exchange Is a Many-Splendored Thing: The Classification and Regulation of Automated Trading Systems", in: Lo (ed.), The Industrial Organization and Regulation of the Securities Industry, Chicago 1996, 93-123.

DREYLING, GEORG (2000), "Aufsichtsrecht im europäischen Wertpapiermarkt und Internet-Problematiken", Paper presented at the WM Seminar "Internet-Börse und außerbörsliche Handelssysteme", Wiesbaden, Oktober 24, 2000.

FERRARINI, GUIDO (1997), "Exchange Governments and Regulation in the European Union: An Overview", in: Ferrarini (ed.), European Investment Markets: Implementations of the Investment Services Directive and National Law Reforms, The Hague 1997, 245-268.

FERRARINI, GUIDO (1999), "The European Regulation of Stock Exchanges: New Perspectives", 36 Capital Markets Law Review, 1999, 569.

FESCO (2001), The Forum of European Securities Commissions, "Proposed Standards for Alternative Trading Systems", Consultative Paper, Paris, June 11, 2001, at <www.europefesco.org>.

GIERSCH, HERBERT/SCHMIDT, HARTMUT (1986), Offene Märkte für Beteiligungskapital: USA-Großbritannien -Bundesrepublik Deutschland, Stuttgart 1986.

GRUBER, ALFRED/GRÜNBICHLER, ANDREAS (2000), "Electronic Communication Networks - Börsen der Zukunft?", 48 Österreichisches Bank-Archiv, 2000, 769-774.

HAMMEN, HORST (2001), "Börsen- und kreditwesengesetzliche Aufsicht über börsenähnliche Handelssysteme, Wertpapierbörsen und Börsenträger", 55 Wertpapier Mitteilungen, 2001, 929-940.

HOPT, KLAUS J. (1999), "Zum Begriff des geregelten Marktes nach der Wertpapierdienst-leistungsrichtlinie - am Beispiel von Eurex -", in: Horn/Lwowski/Nobbe (eds.), Bankrecht - Schwerpunkte und Perspektiven, Festschrift für Herbert Schimanski, Köln 1999, 631-652.

HOPT, KLAUS J./RUDOLPH, BERND/BAUM, HARALD (eds.) (1997), "Börsenreform. Eine ökonomische rechtsvergleichende und rechtspolitische Untersuchung", Stuttgart 1997.

HOPT, KLAUS J./BAUM, HARALD (1997), "Börsenrechtsreform in Deutschland", in: Hopt/Rudolph/Baum (eds.), Börsenreform. Eine ökonomische rechtsvergleichende und rechtspolitische Untersuchung, Stuttgart 1997, 287-467.

IOSCO (1998), International Organization of Securities Commissions, "Securities Activities on the Internet Report", Paper at <www.iosco.org/docs-public/1998/internet_security.html>.

IOSCO (2000), International Organization of Securities Commissions, Technical Committee, "Discussion Paper on Stock Exchange Demutualization", December 2000, at <www.iosco.org/docs-public/2000>.

KALSS, SUSANNE (1997), "Österreichisches Börsen- und Kapitalmarktrecht", in: Hopt/Rudolph/Baum (eds.), Börsenreform. Eine ökonomische rechtsvergleichende und rechtspolitische Untersuchung, Stuttgart 1997, 1167-1264.

MACEY, JONATHAN/KANDA, HIDEKI (1990), The Stock Exchange as a Firm : The Emergence of Close Substitutes for the New York and Tokyo Stock Exchanges: 75 Cornell Law Review 1990, 1008-1052.

KLENKE, HILMAR (1998), "Börsendienstleistungen im europäischen Binnenmarkt. Die Marktkonzeption der Wertpapierdienstleistungsrichtlinie am Beispiel der Aktienmärkte", Berlin 1998.

KÖNDGEN, JOHANNES (1998), "Ownership and Corporate Governance of Stock Exchanges", 154 Journal of Institutional and Theoretical Economics (JITE), 1998, 324-251.

KÖNDGEN, JOHANNES (2000), "Mutmaßungen über die Zukunft der europäischen Börsen", in: Schneider/Hommelhoff/Schmidt/Timm/Grunewald/Drygalla (eds.), Festschrift für Marcus Lutter zum 70. Geburtstag, Deutsches und europäisches Gesellschafts-, Konzern- und Kapitalmarktrecht, Köln 2000, 1401-1420.

LEE, RUBEN (1998), "What is an Exchange? The Automation, Management and Regulation of Financial Markets", Oxford 1998.

LOMNICKA, EVA (2000), "The Home Country Control Principle in the Financial Services Directives and the Case Law", European Business Law Review, 2000, 324-336.

MACEY, JONATHAN R./O'HARA, MAUREEN (1999), "Regulating Exchanges and Alternative Trading Systems: A Law and Economics Perspectives", 28 Journal of Legal Studies, 1999, 17-54.

MANKOWSKI, PETER (2001), "Das Herkunftslandprinzip als Internationales Privatrecht der e-commerce-Richtlinie", 100 Zeitschrift für Vergleichende Rechtswissenschaft, 2001, 137-181.

MCBRIDE JOHNSON, PHILIP (2000), "Getting to grips with self-regulation in the new e-markets", International Financial Law Review, 2000 (June), 41-46.

MERKT, HANNO (1997), "Zur Entwicklung des deutschen Börsenrechts von den Anfängen bis zum Zweiten Finanzmarktförderungsgesetz", in: Hopt/Rudolph/ Baum (eds.), Börsenreform. Eine ökonomische rechtsvergleichende und rechtspolitische Untersuchung, Stuttgart 1997, 17-142.

MOON, JOHN G. (2000), "The Dangerous Territoriality of American Securities Law: A Proposal for an Integrated Global Securities Market", 21 Northwestern Journal of International Law & Business, 2000, cited after the draft from the SSRN paper collection, kindly supplied by the author.

MUESS, JOCHEN (1999), "Die Börse als Unternehmen. Modell einer privatrechtlichen Börsenorganisation", Baden-Baden 1999.

NOBEL, PETER (2000), "Börsenallianzen und -fusionen", in: Schneider/Hommelhoff/ Schmidt/Timm/Grunewald/Drygalla (eds.), Festschrift für Marcus Lutter zum 70. Geburtstag, Deutsches und europäisches Gesellschafts-, Konzern- und Kapitalmarktrecht, Köln 2000, 1485-1511.

OPPITZ, MARTIN (1998), "Grundfragen der Börseorganisation in Österreich – Rechtsdogmatische und rechtspolitische Überlegungen", in: Aicher/Kalss/Oppitz (eds.), Grundfragen des neuen Börserechts, Wien 1998, 1-45.

OPPITZ, MARTIN (2000), "Alternative Handelssysteme im österreichischen Börsenrecht", 48 Österreichisches Bank-Archiv, 2000, 1084-1094.

PFÜLLER, MARKUS/WESTERWELLE, KAI (2001), "Wertpapierhandel im Internet", in: Hoeren/Sieber (eds.), Handbuch Multimedia-Recht. Rechtsfragen des elektronischen Geschäftsverkehrs, München 2001, Part 13.7.

POSITIONSPAPIER (no date), "Alternative Handelssysteme und andere elektronische Kommunikationssysteme im Wertpapiergeschäft", Positionspapier der Internet-Projektgruppe der Bundes-Wertpapieraufsicht, at <www.bwa.at>.

PRIGGE, STEFAN (2000), "Recent Developments in the Market for Markets for Financial Instruments", Paper, Hamburg, October 2000.

RIEHMER, KLAUS/HEUSER, FREDERIKE (2001), "Börsen- und Internet", 4 Neue Zeitschrift für Gesellschaftsrecht, 2001, 385-391.

RUDOLPH, BERND/RÖHRL, HEINER (1997), "Grundfragen der Börsenorganisation aus ökonomischer Sicht", in: Hopt/Rudolph/Baum (eds.), Börsenreform. Eine ökonomische rechtsvergleichende und rechtspolitische Untersuchung, Stuttgart 1997, 143-285.

SCHERFF, DYRK (2001), "Alternative Handelssysteme und die traditionellen Börsen werden künftig kooperieren müssen", Frankfurter Allgemeine Zeitung, Nr. 89, 17. April 2001, 40.

SCHMIDT, HARTMUT/SCHLEEF, MICHAEL/KÜSTER SIMIC, ANDRÉ (2001), "Warentests für Handelsplattformen - Zur Anlegerfreiheit am Aktienmarkt", 13 Zeitschrift für Bankrecht und Bankwirtschaft, 2001, 69-83.

SCHWARK, EBERHARD (1997), "Börsen- und Wertpapierhandelsmärkte in der EG", 51 Wertpapier-Mitteilungen, 1997, 293-307.

SEC (1994), Securities and Exchange Commission, "Market 2000 - An Examination of Common Equity Market Developments", Washington, D.C. 1994.

SEC (1998), Securities and Exchange Commission, "Regulation of Alternative Trading Systems", Release No. 34-40760, at <www.sec.gov/rules/final/34-40760.txt>.

SEC (1999), Securities and Exchange Commission, "On-Line Brokerage: Keeping Apace of Cyberspace", November 1999, at <www.sec.gov>.

SEC (2000), Securities and Exchange Commission, "Special Study: Electronic Communication Network and After-hours Trading", June 2000, at <www.sec.gov/news/studies/ecnafter.htm>.

SPINDLER, GERALD (2001), "Internet, Kapitalmarkt und Kollisionsrecht unter besonderer Berücksichtigung der E-Commerce-Richtlinie", 165 Zeitschrift für das gesamte Handelsrecht und Wirtschaftsrecht, 2001, 324-361.

TETTERBORN, ALEXANDER (2000), "E-Commerce-Richtlinie – Erste Überlegungen zur Umsetzung in Deutschland", Kommunikation & Recht, 2000, 386-389.

VAUPEL, CHRISTOPH F. (2000), "IPOs Over the Internet", Butterworths Journal of International Banking and Financial Law, 2000, 46-52.

WASTL, ULRICH/SCHLITT, CHRISTIAN (2000), "Internetbörse - Revolution am Kapitalmarkt oder einfach nur juristisches Neuland?", Multimedia und Recht, 2000, 387-396.

WEBER, MARTIN (2000), "Die Entwicklung des Kapitalmarktrechts 1998-2000: Organisation, Emission und Vertrieb", 53 Neue Juristische Wochenzeitschrift, 2000, 2061-2075.

Judicial Jurisdiction In The Era Of E-Commerce

Masato Dogauchi[*]

Contents

[*]   Professor of Law, University of Tokyo, Graduate School of Law and Politics. Although the author has been a member of the Delegation of Japan to the Hague Conference on Private International Law with regard to the subject of jurisdiction and foreign judgments, the views expressed in this paper do not represent those of the Japanese government. This is the amended version of the paper that was submitted to the International Symposium on Electronic Commerce and Legal Issues held in Miyazaki on July 27-29, 2001. The author would like to express sincere thanks to the participants there for their comments.

TOSHIYUI KONO/ CHRISTOPH G. PAULUS/ HARRY RAJAK (eds.); THE LEGAL ISSUES OF E-COMMERCE
© 2002 Kluwer Law International. Printed in the Netherlands, pp. 127-144.

T. Kono et al. (eds.), Selected Legal Issues of E-Commerce, 127–144.
© 2002 *Kluwer Law International. Printed in the Netherlands.*

A.   INTRODUCTION

It seems to be an exaggeration to argue that the business activities through the Internet would require totally new set of rules in every field of law. It is, however, inevitable to reconsider appropriateness of the existing rules of law in some respects in consideration of unique features of the Internet. In the case of the rules of judicial jurisdiction in international dimensions, the following features of the Internet should be adequately evaluated:

-   Parties in the internet transactions cannot identify where the other parties are physically located;
-   Anyone can easily have information known by people all over the world;
-   Communication through the Internet can be recorded and evidenced by the technology of cryptography and certification with at least the same accuracy as in traditional transactions with tools of paper and signature or stamp on it.

The Hague Conference on Private International Law[1] has been pursuing the project of making a convention on jurisdiction and recognition/enforcement of foreign judgments in civil and commercial matters, because there is no worldwide mechanism to adequately allocate judicial jurisdiction among countries and to have judgments smoothly recognized or enforced in other countries.[2]

In the negotiation on this project one of the important issues is whether or not e-commerce needs special consideration in providing for rules of jurisdiction, and if affirmative, how such rules should be.

In Part II, the history of the Hague project and the basic structure of the Hague draft convention will be introduced. In Part III, it will be considered how the jurisdictional rules should be in consideration of the effect of the Internet with reference to the draft

---

[1]   This intergovernmental organization was established in 1955 in order to work for the progressive unification of the rules of private international law (Article 1 of the Statute of the Hague Conference on Private International Law). The origin of this conference, however, is found in the first private international law conference held in the Hague in 1893. This organization has since adopted forty conventions, including Convention on the Service Abroad of Judicial and Extrajudicial Documents in Civil or Commercial Matters (1965), Convention on the Civil Aspects of International Child Abduction (1980), etc. Japan has ratified six of them. The number of the member states was fifty-nine at the time of February 14, 2002. See, http://www.hcch.net/ .

[2]   With regard to arbitration, the so-called New York Convention, the Convention on the Recognition and Enforcement of Foreign Arbitral Awards of 1958, has succeeded in being accepted as a legal infrastructure shared by 126 countries. See, http://www.uncitral.org/en-index.htm. In contrast, with regard to court litigations, there are only some regional treaties: the Brussels Convention and the Lugano Convention in Europe, and the La Paz Convention of 1984 (24 ILM 468(1985)) in Latin America. As to the former, see, *infra* note 6.

articles of the Hague Draft Convention made in June 2001. Rules on jurisdiction in BtoB and BtoC contracts, jurisdiction in torts and choice of forum are to be considered. Part IV will be the conclusion of this paper.

B.   THE HAGUE DRAFT CONVENTION IN GENERAL

I.   History

The United States proposed making a convention on jurisdiction and recognition and enforcement of foreign judgments in civil and commercial matters in May 1992 at the meeting of the Hague Conference on Private International Law.[3] In response to this proposal, the Hague Conference organized a special commission to study this subject and prepare preliminary draft articles to be submitted to the Diplomatic Conference.[4] On October 30, 1999 the Special Commission adopted the Preliminary Draft Convention on Jurisdiction and Foreign Judgments in Civil and Commercial Matters (hereinafter cited as the "1999 draft convention").[5]

Since the 1999 draft convention was adopted by majority vote and many proposals of the United States were defeated by civil law countries' majority vote, the United States strongly opposed submission of such a "European" draft to the Diplomatic Conference as a starting point, and proposed having the Diplomatic Conference postponed. The European countries could not easily accept such proposal because they found that the 1999 draft convention seemed to be a good document for discussion at the Diplomatic

---

[3]   The concerns of the United States were, in addition to ensure having its judgments smoothly recognized and enforced in foreign countries, to limit the application of rules of exorbitant jurisdiction of other countries. Especially, it was of great interest for the United States to protect American parties from the enforcement of judgments that were founded on such an exorbitant basis of jurisdiction as the location of the defendant's assets found in German law or the nationality of the plaintiffs found in French law. This is because, at present, such judgment are recognized and enforced as they are in other European countries in accordance with the Brussels and Lugano Conventions, under which the jurisdictional bases of judgments of other contracting states cannot be verified at all.

[4]   In 1994 and 1996 a feasibility study was conducted by the Special Commission. And in October 1996, the 18th Session (the Diplomatic Conference) of the Hague Conference decided to make this theme as the subject of the 19th Session to be held in 2000 and newly established the Special Commission to make a preliminary draft convention on jurisdiction and foreign judgments in civil and commercial matters (Final Act of the Eighteenth Session, October 19, 1996, 35 I.L.M.1391, 1405 (1996). The Special Commission met five times: in June 1997; in March 1998; in November 1998; in June 1999; and in October 1999.

[5]   See, http://www.hcch.net/e/conventions/draft36e.html (on October 21, 2001). Japanese translation is found in "Jurist", No, 1172, pp.90-96 (2000) and "NBL", No.699, pp.26-43(2000) with English version. For the explanatory report of the 1999 draft convention, see, Preliminary Document No 11 - Report of the Special Commission, drawn up by Peter Nygh and Fausto Pocar (2000) (fttp://www.hcch.net/doc/jdgmpd11.doc.

Conference. On the other hand, some countries, including Japan, which do not have a multilateral framework in this field, such as Brussels and Lugano Conventions[6] among European countries, thought that the ratification by the United States in the final stage would be important for this convention to play its role effectively in the international field as a legal infrastructure for civil and commercial litigations. Accordingly, those countries supported the idea not to adhere to the original schedule of final adoption of the convention.[7] In May 2000, it was decided as a compromise that the Diplomatic Conference should be divided into two parts: the first part was scheduled to be held in June 2001, when all decisions would be made by consensus or on a near-consensus basis; and the second part was scheduled to be held at the end of 2001 of at the beginning of 2002, when a standard decision-making , which was majority vote, was expected to be adopted. Several informal meetings were held to review the 1999 draft convention not only from the viewpoint of e-commerce and intellectual properties[8], which review had been conducted in accordance with a decision made by the Special Commission at the time of the adoption of the 1999 draft convention, but also from the view point of finding a narrow way to make articles adoptable by every countries.

In June 2001, the first part of the Diplomatic Conference, the 19th Session, was held. As anticipated, many proposals were offered from the delegations to add the proposed ideas to the text of the draft convention, since, in accordance with the consensus method, no proposal would be dismissed so long as one country insisted on maintaining it in the text. As a result, in comparison with the 1999 draft articles which consisted of 12,000 words, the 2001 draft articles consists of 24,000 words, and the total number of words including notes explaining the meaning of alternatives and matters in parentheses id 48,000.[9]

At the end of the first part of the Session, it was decided again *by consensus* to postpone again the second part of the Session for adoption of the convention, since all the delegates acknowledged the need to consider how to proceed with this project. It was also decided

---

6   The Brussels Convention on Jurisdiction and Enforcement of Judgments in Civil and Commercial Matters 1968, which was entered into force by original six member states of the EEC, has been amended by subsequent Accession Conventions. By the end of February 2002, it was applied among fifteen member states of the EEC. Since march 1, 2002, Brussels Regulation, the contents of which are a revised version of Brussels Convention, has been implemented in principle among EU member states. On the other hand, Lugano Convention on the same matters is another convention concluded in order to apply almost the same rules as those of the Brussels Convention in larger area of Europe. The contracting states of the Lugano Convention is now 19 states including, among others, Switzerland in addition to 15 EEC member states.

7   In early 2000 Japan, Korea, Australia and the United States collectively wrote to the Bureau of the Hague Conference to that effect, and China separately wrote to the same effect.

8   With regard to the intellectual property matters, WIPO Forum on Private International Law and Intellectual Property was held on January 30 and 31, 2001, and an informal meeting with intellectual property experts on the next day in Geneva were held. In respect of the WIPO Forum, see, http://www.wipo.int/pil-forum/en/ .

9   See, Summary of the Outcome of the Discussion in Commission II of the First part of the Diplomatic Conference (http://www.hcch.net/e/workprog/jdgm.html).

that the Commission I of the Diplomatic Conference, whose task was to deal with general affairs,[10] was scheduled to be held within several months in order to decide the future of the project.

Participating governments are now considering what will be the most favorable way yo proceed with the project, as well as what will be the most favorable rules for themselves. In order to make their policy decision on the schedule of the second part of the Diplomatic Conference and on the decision-making method to be adopted there, they will have to make clear what should be their final objective for this project.

II. The Basic Structure: A "Mixed" Convention

The draft convention is a type of "mixed" convention.[11] It is different from a "single" convention in that, whereas a single convention provides only for the rules on recognition and enforcement of foreign judgments and controls jurisdiction of courts indirectly by checking the jurisdiction as one of requirements for recognition and enforcement, a mixed convention deals not only with the recognition and enforcement of foreign judgments but also with jurisdiction directly. However, a mixed convention does not provide for a full set of rules on jurisdiction, but rather provides for only a part of them. A convention that provides for a full set of rules on jurisdiction as well as rules on recognition and enforcement of foreign judgments is called a "double" convention. For example, the Brussels and Lugano Conventions are double conventions, under which no rules of jurisdiction other than those provided for in the conventions can be applied to the cases in which the defendant is domiciled in any one of the contracting states and judgments rendered by the courts of any one of the contracting states may be recognized and enforced without verifying the jurisdictional requirement. A mixed convention is different from a double convention in that a mixed convention allows contracting parties to apply their national rules of jurisdiction insofar as their application is not prohibited by the convention. Accordingly, in a mixed convention the jurisdictional rules are divided into three categories: jurisdictional rules in the white list, those in the grey area and those in the black list or black area. The jurisdictional rules in the white list shall be applied by contracting parties, and judgments based on such rules shall be recognized and enforced by other contracting states so long as other requirements are met. On the contrary, the

---

[10] It is the Commission II that is to make substantive rules of the convention.

[11] With regard to the idea of a mixed convention, see, von Mehren, Recognition of United States Judgments Abroad and Foreign Judgments in the United States: Would an International Convention Be Useful?, RabelsZ 57(1993), p.449; von Mehren, Recognition and Enforcement of Foreign Judgments: A New Approach for the Hague Conference?, 57 L.Comtemp.Probl.271 (1994); von Mehren, The Case for a Convention-mixte Approach to Jurisdiction to Adjudicate and Recognition and Enforcement of Foreign Judgments, RabelsZ 61(1997), p. 86; von Mehren, Enforcing Judgments Abroad: Reflections on the Design of Recognition Conventions, 24 Brook.J.Int'l L.17 (1998).

rules in the black list or area[12] shall not be applied by them, and in the case where a judgment is rendered based on the basis of such prohibited jurisdictional rules, other contracting parties shall neither recognized nor enforce such a judgment. Between the two sets of rules, there are some rules in the grey area. Each contracting party may apply such rules under its respective national laws, and the recognition and enforcement of judgments based on such rules are left to national laws of other contracting parties.

	Original Court ---	Receiving Court ---
Rules in the white list	shall apply them.	shall recognize/enforce judgments based on them.
Rules in the grey area	is free to apply them insofar as they are provided for under the national law.	is free to recognized/enforce or not to recognize/enforce judgments based on them under the applicable national law.
Rules in the black list or area	is prohibited to apply them.	is prohibited to recognize/enforce judgments based on them.

Initially, the United States proposed a mixed convention for the global convention, because the United States realized the difficulty of making a double convention among countries whose system of jurisdictional rules are so different from each other. Especially since the jurisdictional rules of the United States based upon the "due process" clause in

---

[12]   In a case where Article 18(1), which is a general clause to prohibit the application of jurisdictional rules under the national law if there is no substantial connection between the forum state and [either] the dispute [or the defendant], be maintained, there is the black area. In such a case, Article 18(2), which lists some notorious bases of jurisdiction, becomes just a nonexclusive example one. Instead, if Article 18(1) be deleted, Article 18(2) becomes an exclusive black list.

the U.S. Constitution[13] are unique in comparison with jurisdictional rules in civil law countries based upon the Roman law tradition, it was thought impossible to unify all jurisdictional rules in a world-wide convention.

The European countries, however, had been adhering to a type of double convention and argue every issue in reference to the Brussels and Lugano Conventions at the meetings of the Special Commission by June 1999, when an article permitting grey area was adopted.[14] Such article is now Article 17, which provides that, subject to certain provisions, "the Convention does not prevent the application by Contracting States of rules of jurisdiction under the national law, provided that this is not prohibited under Article 18", which is about the prohibited jurisdictional rules.

Japan had originally supported the idea of a mixed convention being the only method to make a truly worldwide convention. Within this framework Japan has been trying to realize its objectives as far as possible.

III.   Main Difficult Problems

The main problems at present over which delegations found difficulties in finding solutions to be accepted by all are as follows:[15]

-   (1) Should the rule on special "activity-based jurisdiction" be put in the white list?[16]
-   (2) Should the rule on general "doing business jurisdiction" be put in the black list?[17]

---

[13]   The XVIth Amendment reads in part "(N)or shall nay State deprive any person of life, liberty, or property, without due process of law...." See, Brand, Due Process, Jurisdiction and a Hague Judgments Convention, 60 U.Pitt.L.Rev. 661 (1999).

[14]   The adoption of the style of mixed convention was made 23 votes against no opposition.

[15]   An overall observation on these issues from a Japanese viewpoint, see, Dogauchi, The Hague Draft Convention on Jurisdiction and Foreign Judgments in Civil and Commercial matters from a Perspective of Japan, Japanese Journal of private International Law, No.3 (2001) (forthcoming).

[16]   The United States has been asserting to have "frequent or significant" activity of the defendant as the basis for jurisdiction in contract and tort cases directly relating to such activities. While such a jurisdictional notion is acknowledged in the United States, such a rule based on the nexus between the defendant and the court does not find easy acceptance by civil law countries, since the nexus between the claim and the court is the key concept in special jurisdictional rules for contract and tort cases.

- (3) Should choice-of-court agreements overcome the application of protective rules on jurisdiction, which allow such weaker parties as consumers and employees to file lawsuits against the business parties or the employers in the court of state where consumers or employees have their habitual residences?[18]
- (4) How should the activity through the Internet be evaluated in making the rules on jurisdiction?[19]
- (5) How should the intellectual property litigations be dealt with?[20]
- (6) How should be the relationship between the application of the future convention and the other conventions?[21]

---

[17] "Doing business" is one of the "activities" of the defendant. However, the "general" doing business jurisdiction is different from the "special" activity-based jurisdiction in that the former allows the courts to decide on any claims against the defendant, while the latter allows the courts to decide on the claim directly related to the activity there. This is also an American rule which has been accepted as constitutionally legitimate under the United States Constitution. The 2001 draft convention, however, lists this general doing business jurisdiction as one of the exorbitant jurisdictional rules under national laws, in addition to the rules based on the nationality of the plaintiff, service of a writ upon the defendant in the territory of the State and so on. Thus, Article 18(2) reads, "[In particular,] [where the defendant is habitually resident in a Contracting State,] jurisdiction shall not be exercised by the courts of a Contracting State on the basis [solely of one or more] of the following --- "(e) the carrying on of commercial or other activities by the defendant in that State, [whether or not through a branch, agency or any other establishment of the defendant,] except where the dispute is directly related to those activities." Such general doing business jurisdiction is notorious in business societies outside the United States and is deemed exorbitant in every country except in the United States, where it is constitutionally legitimate one. According to the United States delegation, as there are many strong opinions among American lawyers against inclusion of (e) in Article 18(2), it would cause difficulty for the United States ratification to prohibit the application of this jurisdictional rule under the future convention. In contrast, it would be the essential provision for other states to become parties to the future convention. Without Article 18(2)(e), the incentive for other countries to negotiate this convention would be fundamentally diminished.

[18] In accordance with the Brussels and Lugano Conventions, choice-of-court agreements in such cases are invalid. Therefore, the contracting states to these conventions are of opinion to the same effect. On the contrary, some other countries cannot easily accept such a solution.

[19] The e-commerce through the Internet is relatively new way of business. We have not yet understood its legal implications precisely. Tortuous activities can also be done through the Internet. In the context of jurisdictional rules, there are many unanswered questions. For instance, is information provision through the Internet included in "supply of goods" or "provision of services" under the jurisdictional rule based upon the place of performance in contract cases? Is the location of the server in which an interactive website operates a "branch" under the jurisdictional rule based upon the location of the defendant's branch? How should the place of damage be determined in such cases as defamation, unfair competition, or copyright infringement through the Internet? The businesses worry about such unclear issues which might cause unreasonable burden on their activities.

[20] The most debated problem here is whether the state of registration of patent or other industrial rights should have exclusive jurisdiction over infringement litigations. In such infringement litigation the issue of validity of the patent or other rights in question is often raised by the defendant. With regard to this problem, see, Dogauchi, "Jurisdiction over Firen Patent Infringement from a Japanese Perspective in Consieration of the Hague Draft Convention on Jurisdiction and Foreign Judgments in Civil and Commercial Matters as of June 2001", 44 Japanese Annual of International Law (2001) (forthcoming).

The problem (4) is the issue to be considered in this paper. The e-commerce through the Internet is relatively new way of business. We have not yet understood its legal implications precisely. Tortuous activities can also be done through the Internet. In the context of jurisdictional rules, there are many unanswered questions. For instance, is information provision through the Internet included in "supply of goods" or "provision of services" under a jurisdictional rule based of performance of obligation? How should the place of damage be determined in such cases as defamation, unfair competition, or copyright infringement through the Internet? With regard to choice-of-court agreement, is it a valid choice-of -court agreement made through the Internet by click a mouse, rather than made in writing on paper? It is possible for the businesses to validly agree with consumers on choice of court? The businesses worry about such unclear issues which might cause unreasonable burden on their activities.

As already mentioned, the conclusion of the convention in the Hague Conference on private International Law cannot be anticipated at this moment. However, from an academic viewpoint, the discussion done in the negotiation has shown many interesting problems to consider how the rules of jurisdiction should be. Among others, some provisions on jurisdiction represent the necessity to reflect the technological development in the electronic communication methods. The rules of jurisdiction in contracts, in torts and the rule on choice of forum will be explored in the next Part.

C.   THE EFFECT OF E-COMMERCE ON THE JURISDICTIONAL RULES

I.   Jurisdiction In BtoB And BtoC Contracts

In the draft convention made in June 2001 there are three provisions on rules of jurisdiction in contract cases: Article 6 on contracts in general, Article 7 on consumer contracts and Article 8 on individual contracts of employment. Articles 7 and 8 are special rules to protect weaker parties. Article 6 and 7 in particular concerns with the e-commerce.

> Article 6 provides for as follows:
> *Article 6Contracts*
> [Alternative A
> 1.   [Subject to the provisions of Articles 7 and 8,] a plaintiff may bring an action in contract in the courts of the State –

---

[21]   Especially, it has been discussed how the Brussels and Lugano Conventions should be applied in the matters which are also within the scope of the new Hague convention? This problem has been discussed without finding an appropriate solution yet. The parties to these conventions want to have their own regime untouchable, while other states want to have the application of the future convention not be diminished by such local regimes.

a)   in which the defendant has conducted frequent [and] [or] significant activity; [or

b)   into which the defendant has directed frequent [and] [or] significant activity;]

provided that the claim is based on a contract directly related to that activity [and the overall connection of the defendant to that State makes it reasonable that the defendant be subject to suit in that State].

[*Variant 1*

2.   For the purposes of the preceding paragraph, 'activity' means one or more of the following –

a)   [regular and substantial] promotion of the commercial or professional ventures of the defendant for the conclusion of contracts of this kind;

b)   the defendant's regular or extended presence for the purpose of negotiating contracts of this kind, provided that the contract in question was performed at least in part in that State. [Performance in this sub-paragraph refers [only] to non-monetary performance, except in case of loans or of contracts for the purchase and sale of currency];

c)   the performance of a contract by supplying goods or services, as a whole or to a significant part.]

[*Variant 2*

2.   For the purpose of the preceding paragraph, 'activity' includes, *inter alia*, the promotion, negotiation, and performance of a contract.

[3.   The preceding paragraphs do not apply to situations where the defendant has taken reasonable steps to avoid entering into or performing an obligation in that State.]]]

[Alternative B

A plaintiff may bring an action in contract in the courts of a State in which –

a)   in matters relating to the supply of goods, the goods were supplied in whole or in part;

b)   in matters relating to the provision of services, the services were provided in whole or in part;

c)   in matters relating both to the supply of goods and the provision of services, performance of the principal obligation took place in whole or in part.]

There are two alternatives for Article 6. The alternative A is based upon, in principle, the idea of the activity-based jurisdiction of the United States, where the defendant's frequent and/or significant activity in the forum state is the key to admit its jurisdiction. On the contrary, the alternative B focuses on the place of performance in the civil law tradition.[22] In the alternative A there are two variants with regard to paragraph 2: the variant 1, which

---

[22]   The alternative B consists of the text as it appeared in the 1999 Preliminary Draft Convention.

is trying to require "activity" to be substantial, is the civil law countries' resistance against the introduction of the American activity-based provision, whereas variants 2 represents the United States idea which does not define "activity" at all and leave it to case-by-case decision by the courts.

Paragraph 3 reflects the e-commerce consideration. This "safe harbor" rule, albeit using such vague condition as reasonableness, seeks to protect a party using electronic means who has taken measures to avoid entering into obligations in a particular country and thereby avoid becoming subject to the jurisdiction of the courts of that country.

On the other hand, Article 7 on BtoC contracts provides for as follows:

> [*Article 7   Contracts concluded by consumers*
> 1.   This Article applies to contracts between a natural person acting primarily for personal, family or household purposes, the consumer, and another party acting for the purposes of its trade or profession, [unless the other party demonstrates that it neither knew nor had reason to know that the consumer was concluding the contract primarily for personal, family or household purposes, and would not have entered into the contract if it had known otherwise].
> 2.   Subject to paragraphs [5-7], a consumer may bring [proceedings][an action in contract] in the courts of the State in which the consumer is habitually resident if the claim relates to a contract which arises out of activities, including promotion or negotiation of contracts, which the other party conducted in that State, or directed to that State, [unless [that party establishes that] –
>> *a)*   the consumer took the steps necessary for the conclusion of the contract in another State;[and
>> *b)*   the goods or services were supplied to the consumer while the consumer was present in the other State.]]
> [3.   For the purposes of paragraph 2, activity shall not be regarded as being directed to a State if the other party demonstrates that it took reasonable steps to avoid concluding contracts with consumers habitually resident in the State.]
> 4.   Subject to paragraphs [5-7], the other party to the contract may bring proceedings against a consumer under this Convention only in the courts of the State in which the consumer is habitually resident.
> [Alternative A [23]

---

[23]   This alternative is accompanied by the insertion of Article 25*bis* as the exception to the obligation to recognize or enforce a judgment based on a white list basis as follows:
[Article 25 *bis*

5.   Article 4 applies to a jurisdiction agreement between a consumer and the other party if the agreement is entered into after the dispute has arisen.

6.   Where a consumer and the other party have entered into an agreement which conforms with the requirements of Article 4(1) and (2) before the dispute has arisen, the consumer may bring proceedings against the other party in the courts of the State designated in that agreement.

7.   Where a consumer and the other party have entered into an agreement which conforms with the requirements of Article 4(1) and (2) before the dispute has arisen, Article 4 applies to the agreement to the extent that it is binding on both parties under the law of the State in which the consumer is habitually resident at the time the agreement is entered into.

[Alternative B
[*Variant 1*

5.   This provision may be departed from by a jurisdiction agreement provided that it conforms with the requirements of Article 4.

6.   A Contracting State may declare that –

    a)   it will only respect a jurisdiction agreement if it is entered into after the dispute has arisen or to the extent that it allows the consumer to bring proceedings in a court other than a court indicated in this Article or in Article 3; and

    b)   it will not recognise and enforce a judgment where jurisdiction has been taken in accordance with a jurisdiction agreement that does not fulfil the requirements in sub-paragraph *a)*.]

[*Variant 2*

5.   Article 4 applies to an agreement between a consumer and the other party if the agreement is entered into after the dispute has arisen; or to the extent that the agreement permits the consumer to bring proceedings in a court other than the consumer's habitual residence.

6.   A Contracting State may declare that in the circumstances specified in that declaration –

    a)   it will respect a jurisdiction agreement entered into before the dispute has arisen;

---

1.   A Contracting State may make a declaration that it will not recognise or enforce a judgment under this Chapter, or a declaration specifying the conditions under which it will recognise or enforce a judgment under this Chapter, where –

a) the judgment was rendered by the court or origin under Article 7(2) [or Article 8(2)]; and

b) the parties had entered into an agreement which confirms with the requirements of Article 4 designating a court other than the court of origin.

[2.   A declaration under this Article may not deny recognition and enforcement of a judgment given under Article 7(2) [or 8(2)] if the Contracting State making the declaration would exercise jurisdiction under the relevant Article in a corresponding case.]

3.   Recognition or enforcement of a judgment may be refused by a Contracting State that has made a declaration contemplated by paragraph 1 in accordance with the terms of that declaration.]]

      b)   it will recognise and enforce a judgment in proceedings brought by the other party given by a court under a jurisdiction agreement entered into before the dispute has arisen;

      c)   it will not recognise and enforce a judgment given by a court in which proceedings could not be brought consistently with a jurisdiction agreement entered into before the dispute has arisen.]]

[Alternative C

5.   Article 4 applies to a jurisdiction agreement between a consumer and the other party if the agreement is entered into after the dispute has arisen.

6.   Where a consumer and the other party have entered into an agreement which conforms with the requirements of Article 4(1) and (2) before the dispute has arisen –

      a)   the consumer may bring proceedings against the other party under the Convention in the courts of the State designated in that agreement;

      b)   the consumer may not bring proceedings against the consumer under this Convention in any other court, unless the agreement permits the proceedings to be brought in that court;

      c)   the other party may bring proceedings against the consumer under this Convention only if the agreement permits the proceedings to be brought in the courts of the State in which the consumer is habitually resident.]]

Article 7 consists of the first four common paragraphs with three different alternative solutions, including two variants of the alternative B. This is the result of divergent views on the validity of pre-dispute choice of court agreement in consumer contracts. This issue is especially critical in the e-commerce for the interests of both the business and the consumer side. Incidentally, there is another alternative solution, the forth one, that is to exclude BtoC contracts from the scope of the Convention.[24]

In the e-commerce, it is sometimes impossible to know who is on the other side of the line. The last clause in square brackets in Paragraph 1 reflects such concerns. The purpose of this part is to give some protection to the business party in the e-commerce, where the business party cannot easily ascertain with whom it is dealing. Although there was some oppositions in the discussion in the Hague to this point on the ground that it would be very difficult for a consumer to rebut an allegation that the business was unaware that the buyer was a consumer, it seems to be necessary to maintain these words

---

[24]   For that reason the whole of the Article is placed in square brackets.

in the paragraph 1 in order to keep balance between the interests of business and the consumer.

Paragraph 3 seeks to protect merchants using electronic means who take measures to avoid entering into obligations in a particular State and thereby avoid becoming subject to the jurisdiction of the courts of that State. This is based on the same idea as Article 6, Paragraph 3 as already mentioned.

II.   Jurisdiction In Torts

Article 10 on torts provides for as follows:

> *Article 10   Torts [or delicts]*
> 1.   A plaintiff may bring an action in tort [or delict] in the courts of the State –
>> *a)*   in which the act or omission that caused injury occurred, or
>> *b)*   in which the injury arose, unless the defendant establishes that the person claimed to be responsible could not reasonably foresee that the act or omission could result in an injury of the same nature in that State.
> [2.   A plaintiff may bring an action in tort in the courts of the State in which the defendant has engaged in frequent or significant activity, or has directed such activity into that State, provided that the claim arises out of that activity and the overall connection of the defendant to that State makes it reasonable that the defendant be subject to suit in that State.]
> [3.   The preceding paragraphs do not apply to situations where the defendant has taken reasonable steps to avoid acting in or directing activity into that State.]
> [4.   A plaintiff may also bring an action in accordance with paragraph 1 when the act or omission, or the injury may occur.]
> [5.   If an action is brought in the courts of a State only on the basis that the injury arose or may occur there, those courts shall have jurisdiction only in respect of the injury that occurred or may occur in that State, unless the injured person has his or her habitual residence in that State.]

Generally speaking, there is no significant difference on the basic rule of jurisdiction in tort case as far as the act or omission or injury shows both the court-defendant nexus and the court-claim nexus.[25]

Paragraph 3 is intended to protect merchants using electronic means who take measures to avoid acting in or directing activity into the state not to be subject to its jurisdiction. The idea in this paragraph is also found in Article 6, Paragraph3 and Article 7, Paragraph 3.

III.   Choice Of Court

As in the traditional transactions, choice of forum in the e-commerce gives the party predictability with respect to the forum of the disputes. Article 4 on choice of court provides for as follows:

> *Article 4   Choice of court*
> 1.   If the parties have agreed that [a court or] [the] courts of a Contracting State shall have jurisdiction to settle any dispute which has arisen or may arise in connection with a particular legal relationship, [that court or those] [the] courts [of that Contracting State] shall have jurisdiction[, provided the court has subject matter jurisdiction] and that jurisdiction shall be exclusive unless the parties have agreed otherwise. Where an agreement having exclusive effect designates [a court or][the] courts of a non-Contracting State, courts in Contracting States shall decline jurisdiction or suspend proceedings unless the [court or] courts chosen have themselves declined jurisdiction. [Whether such an agreement is invalid for lack of consent (for example, due to fraud or duress) or incapacity shall depend on national law including its rules of private international law.]
> 2.   An agreement within the meaning of paragraph 1 shall be valid as to form, if it was entered into –
>> *a)*   in writing or <u>by any other means of communication which renders information accessible so as to be usable for subsequent reference;</u>
>> *b)*   orally and confirmed in writing or <u>by any other means of communication which renders information accessible so as to be usable for subsequent reference;</u>
>> *c)*   in accordance with a usage which is regularly observed by the
> parties;

---

25   Therefore there is no consensus on the paragraph 2, which seeks to insert an American activity-based jurisdiction similar to that proposed in relation to Article 6 on contracts, the alternative A, paragraph 1.

> *d)* in accordance with a usage of which the parties were or ought to have been aware and which is regularly observed by parties to contracts of the same nature in the particular trade or commerce concerned.
>
> 3. Where a defendant expressly accepts jurisdiction before a court of a Contracting State, and that acceptance is in writing or evidenced in writing, that court shall have jurisdiction.
>
> [4. The substantive validity of an agreement conferring jurisdiction shall be determined in accordance with the applicable law as designated by the choice of law rules of the forum.]
>
> 5. [The parties cannot be deprived of the right to enter into agreements conferring jurisdiction.] [However,] [such agreements and similar clauses in trust instruments shall be without effect, if they conflict with the provisions of Article 7, 8 or 12.]

Traditionally, the form of choice has been limited to in writing. In considering the purpose of controlling the form of agreement[26], there is no need to stick to such conventional way. Paragraph 2 allows several ways, including "any other means of communication accessible so as to be useable for subsequence reference", which follows the definition in the UNCITRAL Model Law on Electronic Commerce of 1996.[27]

D.   CONCLUSION

The above observed special rules of jurisdiction in the Hague draft convention of June 2001 reflect the features of the Internet as mentioned in Chapter I as follows:

---

[26]   According to the Guide for Enactment for the UNCITRAL Model Law on Electronic Commerce, following non-exhaustive list indicates reasons why national laws require the use of "writings": "(1) to ensure that there would be tangible evidence of the existence and nature of the intent of the parties to bind themselves; (2) to help the parties be aware of the consequences of their entering into a contract; (3) to provide that a document would be legible by all; (4) to provide that a document would remain unaltered over time and provide a permanent record of a transaction; (5) to allow for the reproduction of a document so that each party would hold a copy of the same data; (6) to allow for the authentication of data by means of a signature; (7) to provide that a document would be in a form acceptable to public authorities and courts; (8) to finalize the intent of the author of the "writing" and provide a record of that intent; (9) to allow for the easy storage of data in a tangible form; (10) to facilitate control and subsequent audit for accounting, tax or regulatory purposes; and (11) to bring legal rights and obligations into existence in those cases where a "writing" was required for validity purposes."

[27]   Article 6 (Writing), paragraph 1 of the UNCITRAL Model Law provides for as follows: "Where the law requires information to be in writing, that requirement is met by a data message if the information contained therein is accessible so as to be usable for subsequent reference."

(1) Parties in the internet transactions cannot identify where the other parties are physically located.

Because parties in the Internet transactions cannot identify where the other parties are physically located, Article 6, Paragraph 2 provides that, where the defendant has taken reasonable steps to avoid entering into or performing an obligation in a certain country, he should not be subject to the jurisdiction of that country by the mere fact that he has in fact entered into or performing an obligation in that country. Also, Article 7, Paragraph 3 provides that activity shall not be regarded as being directed to a State if the other party demonstrates that it took reasonable steps to avoid concluding contracts with consumers habitually resident in the State.

The business parties in the Internet cannot also identify whether the customer is a consumer or not. Therefore, Article 7, Paragraph 1 provides that, when the business party demonstrates that it neither knew nor had reason to know that the consumer was concluding the contract primarily for personal, family or household purposes, and would not have entered into the contract if it had known otherwise, it should not be subject to the jurisdiction of the country where the consumer is habitually resident.

(2) Anyone can easily have information known by people all over the world.

In accordance with Article 10 on torts, a party shall be subject to the jurisdiction of the country in which the injury arose, unless he establishes that the person claimed to be responsible could not reasonably foresee that the act or omission could result in an injury of the same nature in that State. By posting information on the website, anyone can easily have information known by people all over the world and such feature of the Internet is well known and therefore such results as occurred in foreign countries are reasonably foreseeable. Without safe harbor rule, the business cannot enjoy such useful tool for fear of subjecting to jurisdiction of unintended countries. Article 10, paragraph 3, therefore, provides that, where the defendant has taken reasonable steps to avoid acting in or directing activity into a certain country, it should not be subject to the jurisdiction of that country.

In comparison with the similar rules in Articles 6 and 7 as above, the reasonableness of the rule in Article 10 may not be open to doubt. From the viewpoint of the victim of such tort, it is irrelevant whether the actor has taken steps to avoid causing injury in the country where the victim in fact suffered. However, a reasonable foreseeability test has already recognized generally and it is firmly built in Article 10, paragraph 1. Paragraph 3 can be seen as an e-commerce version of this reasonable foreseeablity test. Of course the level of reasonable step, which depends on the development of technology, should be high enough not to protect the business too much.

(3) Communication through the Internet can be recorded and evidenced by the technology of cryptography and certification with at least the same accuracy as in traditional transactions with tools of paper and signature or stamp on it.

Communication through the Internet can be recorded and evidenced by the technology of cryptography and certification with at least the same accuracy as in traditional transactions with tools of paper and signature or stamp on it. Therefore, it seems reasonable to admit "any other means of communication accessible so as to be useable for subsequence reference" in addition to writing as a form of choice of forum.

In conclusion, these modifications to the traditional rules of jurisdiction as discussed in the Hague Conference in the process of making a new convention seem to be valuable not only in making reasonable international jurisdictional rules in the age of the Internet but also in considering the domestic jurisdictional rules. In Japan, we do not have written rules on international jurisdiction. Such rules have been formulated by court decisions. Under Japanese case law, whether or not a Japanese court has jurisdiction shall be in general decided in accordance with the principle of justice that would require that fairness be maintained between parties, and a proper and prompt administration of justice be secured.[28] Therefore, the draft articles as discussed in the Hague Conference would have some impact in considering "the principle of justice" with respect to international jurisdiction of Japanese courts. In addition, the discussion made in the Hague in respect to the impact of the Internet on jurisdictional rules should be referred to in the future amendment of the Brussels Regulation and Lugano Convention.[29] In any event, the draft articles as introduced in this paper would be a starting point to formulate a set of sustainable jurisdictional rules in the era of e-commerce.[30]

---

[28]   See, Supreme Court judgment on 16 October 1981 (*Michiko Goto, et al. v. Malaysian Airline System Berhad*), *Minshu*, Vol. 35, No. 7, p. 1224; 26 Japanese Annual of International Law 122 (1983) and Supreme Court judgment on 11 November 1997 (*Family Co. Ltd. v. Shin Miyahara*), *Minshu*, Vol. 51, No. 10, p. 4055; 41 Japanese Annual of International Law 117 (1998). With regard to Japanese rules on international jurisdiction in general, see, Dogauchi, supra note 15.

[29]   See, supra note 6.

[30]   After the completion of this paper, an interesting document was published by the Hague Conference on Private International Law, that is "The Impact of the Internet on the Judgments Project: Thoughts for the Future" written by Avril D. Haines (Prel.Doc. No.17) (http://www.hcch.net/e/workprog/jdgm.html).

LEGAL PATHOLOGY AND THE CHALLENGES OF CYBERSPACE TRANSACTIONS

*Harry Rajak**

Contents

---

*   Professor of Legal Studies, University of Sussex, United Kingdom.

TOSHIYUI KONO/ CHRISTOPH G. PAULUS/ HARRY RAJAK (eds.); THE LEGAL ISSUES OF E-COMMERCE
© 2002 Kluwer Law International. Printed in the Netherlands, pp. 145-161.

T. Kono et al. (eds.), Selected Legal Issues of E-Commerce, 145–161.
© 2002 *Kluwer Law International. Printed in the Netherlands.*

A.   INTRODUCTION

I.   Outline Of A Legal System

It is, of course, part of the function of a legal system to describe authoritatively what human conduct is to be promoted and what is to be suppressed. At the public level, constitutions or other socially organising legislation and legal principles will seek to govern the relationship between individuals and the society as a whole, for example by advancing or reducing the freedom which any individual may have to express him or herself in various ways. At the private level, legal principles will seek to govern the relationships between one individual and another.

Although these public and private levels may be described in these separate terms and can be treated for many purposes as self-contained, it may be more accurate to see the private legal system as operating within the public legal system and as subordinate to it. Of both these systems, it may be said that they are in some measure the product of a particular history as well as individual and mass psychology. In these terms, the law carries with it the consolidated norms of the society as to how its members should behave in a wide variety of different circumstances. In addition, it describes the system by which these norms are to be put into effect. To adopt what may be a not inappropriate metaphor in the present surroundings, law both records the programme for how life is to be lived, as well as the operating system which enables the programme to function.

A further common and, some would say, essential feature of a legal system is its capacity to respond to new ideas and initiatives and to facilitate the attainment by the members of the society in which it operates of new practices and to enable them to exploit new ideas.

Norms within a legal system may thus seek to lead the community within which it operates as well as, sometime, to change existing patterns of behaviour. Both these, what we may call the historical and reformist aspects of a legal system will be relevant in our discussion of the appropriate legal norms for the governance of cyberspace dealings, interaction and transactions.

II.   The Indispensability Of Disease

It is, perhaps unfortunately, the human condition to wait for illness or disease or other unwanted event before seeking to alter the natural circumstances which produced or facilitated that which is considered to be unhealthy. Of course, there may be a certain efficiency in such an approach. Years and substantial resources, may otherwise be devoted to researching and discovering counteractive defences to conditions which may never arise. Equally, we have made some strides towards learning and internalising the necessity of care for the environment, preventive medicine and similar increasingly essential values. Given the potential for destruction which has been created in our generation, it is just as well that we have taken these, as yet, inadequate steps.

Similar observations may be made about aspects of a legal system. There is nothing quite like pathology to get it going! Where money is short and debtors cannot repay their debts, we have the fertile invention of a whole host of instruments which seek to elevate one set of creditors above other sets. Where, on the other hand, there is enough money to go round to ensure that all creditors are paid, no one bothers about invention in the world of credit and security.

The equivalent to preventive medicine in the legal system is the reduction or elimination of litigation, a development which, given its vast potential for complexity to a level hitherto unexperienced, is surely worthy of research in relation to the development of a legal system governing transactions and other interaction in cyberspace. In my view, three areas worthy of such research are first the nature of the business organisations which undertake internet business, secondly, the development of arbitration as opposed to litigation as the mechanism for resolving legal disputes and, thirdly, an insolvency system which can overcome the current myriad of problems of cross-border bankruptcy. Ideally these - and doubtless other relevant aspects of commercial transactions, should be considered as fit for an international treaty governing all countries in which residents conduct cyberspace commercial operations.

B.   THE LEGAL PROBLEMS OF CYBERSPACE

I.   Jurisdiction And Choice Of Law

Where legal problems extend beyond domestic borders, some form of international co-operation will often be necessary if the problem is to be solved satisfactorily. Such problems may be relatively uncomplicated. A may have a judgment for debt against B, but B may be resident in a different jurisdiction from A or may have assets in a jurisdiction different from that in which the judgment was granted. Further, the enforcement of foreign judgments has been facilitated by judicial comity, by bilateral treaties between countries and, most recently by multinational convention. The most notable convention is the Convention on Jurisdiction and the Enforcement of Judgments in Civil and Commercial Matters - "the Jurisdiction and Judgments Convention" - entered into by the member states of the European Union (and brought into force in the UK by the Civil Jurisdiction and Judgments Act 1982).

When asked to enforce a foreign judgment, a court may, for example, be concerned with whether the defendant was given adequate protection to know the case against him, to put his defence and so on. It may also be concerned by the principles of law under which the foreign judgment was rendered. But such reservations aside, no issues of policy arise in connection with the enforcement of a foreign judgment. In particular, enforcement will not generally be contrary to the law and policy of the enforcing state.

The enforcement in the United Kingdom of a French judgment based on a contract entered into in France should not, in consequence, compromise English contract law principles even if the contract would not have been enforceable under English law. Enforcement is, in general, a procedural matter with safeguards aimed principally at verifying the judgment obtained. The procedures are generally similar in most European countries and where the two countries are both members of the European Community, the judgment is enforceable in the same way as would be a domestic judgment. If this were not the case, a fresh action on the foreign judgment would be necessary as a prelude to enforcement.

A more complicated problem is the litigation of a dispute between parties from different legal systems and in circumstances where the issue or issues between the parties arose partly in the jurisdiction of one of the parties and partly in the jurisdiction of the other. Here it may be material to the dispute as to which legal principles are to be applied to resolve the dispute. Clearly this will be of the essence where the legal principles of each system would provide different answers to the dispute.

All developed legal systems will contain principles which purport to resolve this preliminary issue, but the procedure is costly, time-consuming and, occasionally, of supreme difficulty and complexity. Disputes arising out of transactions undertaken in cyberspace will raise further complications, for example that it may be impossible to establish the jurisdiction of one of the parties. A treaty governing transactions concluded in cyberspace may attempt two steps, first arbitration[1] rather than litigation of disputes and secondly, a clear and unambiguous method by which the legal system is selected for the resolution of the dispute. As to the latter, examples may be automatically the legal system of the place where the purchaser is resident or automatically that of the trader. The arbitrator or judge may also be given a discretion where it is impossible to establish which is the relevant legal system.

In relation to treaty attempts to reduce the problems of litigation in cross border disputes, the European Union has recently enacted the Distance Selling Directive[2] and a Council Regulation[3] which may have a significant effect on the resolution of disputes arising out

---

[1]   See below, para. B.III.
[2]   Directive 97/7/Eco f the European Parliament and of the Council passed on 20 May 1997 on the Protection of Consumers in respect of Distance Contracts.
[3]   Council Regulation (EC) No 44/2001 of 22 December 2000 on jurisdiction and enforcement of judgments in civil and commercial matters.

of cyberspace transactions between parties who are both resident within any of the fifteen member states of the EU.

The Directive places substantial obligations on the suppliers of goods and services and clearly favours consumers. While there is a substantial list of exceptions, the additional protection which the implementation of this Directive would give consumers includes the right to receive written confirmation of what they have bought and on what terms, as well as giving them the same rights they would enjoy in national law irrespective of where the sale is made within the internet market. The Council Regulation, which is a revision of the well established EU's Brussels Convention on Jurisdiction and the Enforcement of Judgments, gives consumers the right to sue a trader in the consumer's own country.

As long as litigation remains the staple form of dispute resolution, Conventions which reduce the scope for the application of private international law principles by imposing solutions as to issues of jurisdiction and choice of law are to be welcomed in the interests of speed and cost reduction. However, there is a balance to be struck. The substantial tilt of the recent EU legislation in favour of the consumer brought sharp criticism by the members of the trade. This in itself is not surprising but care does need to be taken in the negotiation of Conventions to ensure that traders are not subjected to such obligations as endanger the survival of all but a small oligopoly.

II.   Business Organisations

Initially we should consider the matter of the choice of organisation for a person or for people who conduct business on the internet. Before we do so, we need to discuss the issue of limited liability, something which often dictates the form of organisation chosen.

An enforceable contract creates an obligation on the part of a purchaser to pay for goods or services and on the part of a seller to supply goods or services or to pay commensurate damages. Each has a defined financially quantifiable liability. No apparent issue of unlimited liability arises as each is expected to pay a certain amount in discharge of a contractual obligation. However, a near opposite principle characterises the vast number of commercial jurisdictions around the world which provide for the establishment of incorporated organisations (usually called companies or corporations) and it is more than likely that the vast majority of those who conduct business on the internet will be incorporated entities with limited liability protecting the private estates of individuals within such organisations.

What are some of the arguments for and against limited liability for traders who conduct their business through the medium of a limited liability company? The experience of the United Kingdom may be helpful. Much of the infrastructure of the United Kingdom- the railways, canals, roads, electricity and gas industries developed in the wake of the industrial revolution – was built with private money invested in companies created by

Parliament ("statutory companies") and in which investors were protected against unlimited loss.

Statutory companies were seen as concerned with the development of the society. Registered companies on the other hand,[4] were much easier to set up and were available for small as well as large-scale business. The debate as to whether limited liability should be extended to investors - and by definition, directors - rumbled on throughout the rest of the nineteenth century and could only be said to have been settled in 1897 in the seminal case of *Salomon* v. *Salomon & Co.*[5] This decision made it clear that the use of the incorporated entity form by individuals not seeking investment from outsiders was perfectly legitimate and that these individuals were protected by limited liability.

An argument in favour of the extension of limited liability has always been thought to be that it is desirable in the interests of the society as a whole that individual people be encouraged to engage in business, to take risks and so on. It might also be argued that the distinction between companies that are and companies that are not dependent on outside investment can become unsustainable. Also, it may not always be possible to distinguish properly between an inside and an outside investor. Yet, equally it has been argued that the use of the incorporated entity might encourage unnecessarily risky and even fraudulent activity on the part of the investor/directors of the company.

It is true that all such jurisdictions also provide for the elimination of the protection of limited liability in certain circumstances. But these are often vague and discretionary to be applied by the courts. This does not detract from the fact that there remains a substantial area of commercial activity in which creditors will not be paid owing to the insolvency of the entity (most often an incorporated company) which undertook the liability. Should a treaty governing cyberspace transactions seek to regulate the ability of traders to escape liability by trading through the medium of another entity? If so what should be the basis on which the privilege of limited liability is forfeited by the trader?

We may begin with two simple examples of legal pathology, first the case of a contracting party who fails to honour his or her obligations, the second, the case of a debtor who is in debt to a number of creditors and has insufficient funds to pay all debts in full.

III.   Arbitration

"Arbitration is an ancient institution which has been deployed as the principal means of resolving disputes since trade began. Over the centuries,

---

[4]   First provided for by the Joint Stock Companies Act of 1844.
[5]   [1897] A.C. 22.

arbitration has responded to changes in trade, custom and practice and the underlying legal environment. More recently, arbitration was given a significant fillip when the major European trading nations updated and revised their arbitration laws in response to the challenges of the developing marketplaces. Arbitration is consensual and a tried and tested formula in commercial relations where the parties are from different states. This alone should support the contention that arbitration should be the preferred dispute resolution option for disputes arising in interactive sales channels."[6]

The advantages of arbitration over litigation in the settlement of disputes is now well established. Its speed and cheapness when compared to litigation must make it a serious contender for a substantial role in the resolution of disputes arising out of cyberspace transactions. Of course, one of the fundamental features of arbitration is the fact that it must be consensual and while this is one of its obvious strengths, it may deprive this method of dispute resolution of becoming a market leader.

Substantial international resources have already been deployed in seeking to increase the visibility and availability of arbitration to resolve distance selling disputes. Uncitral has adopted a Model Law on International Commercial Arbitration and a number of organisations has sprung up offering arbitration and mediation services for resolving disputes arising out of cyberspace transactions.[7]

Given the fundamental consensual nature of arbitration, there is a limit to the inroads which Conventions can make in this field. It is open to states, trade associations, consumer protection agencies and other related organisations to encourage arbitration for the settlement of cyberspace disputes. It may be a useful adjunct to the services or goods provided by an internet trader to include submission to an independent arbitration service in the event of a dispute. Such provision, like guarantees against credit card fraud, are likely to increase consumer confidence and attract business.

---

[6]   *De Zylva*, "Effective Means of Resolving Distance Selling Disputes" forthcoming, to be published in Arbitration International.

[7]   These are collected and briefly discussed in *De Zylva, op. cit.* Since this article has not yet been published, it may be helpful to list some relevant websites: www.clicknsettle.com   www.novaforum.com   www.ombuds.org   www.onlineresolution.com   www.squaretrade.com   www.webassured.com www.wordandbond.com.

IV. Bankruptcy And Business Rescue

1. Introduction

For hundreds of years, countries have sought to establish co-operation between themselves in matters of debt collection and bankruptcy. This reflected the relative ease with which a debtor might incur a debt in country A and then slip across the border to country B in an attempt to escape having to repay the debt. For at least three or four hundred years, there has been a stream of bilateral treaties between two neighbouring countries to establish the kind of co-operation necessary to eliminate this kind of opportunism. More difficult has been the search for co-operation in resolving the issues where the debtor is bankrupt and the bankrupt has assets and creditors in more than one jurisdiction. Here, too, we find quite early instances of inter-country co-operation, but now the holy grail is the establishment of international agreement among several countries so as to bring order to cross-border bankruptcies with assets and creditors in several of such countries.

International treaties of the kind envisaged can be dated back at least to the Montevideo and Bustamante treaties of 1889 and 1928 respectively among the countries of South America, the Nordic Bankruptcy Convention of 1933 among the Scandanavian countries.[8]

More recently, there has been substantial recent international legislative activity. Uncitral adopted a Model Law in 1997 and the European Union enacted a Regulation on Insolvency proceedings in 2000. These measures have, in turn, spurred on further efforts by the World Bank and the International Monetary Fund in the search for a harmonised bankruptcy system. While this search began in response to the crossborder complications which arise with the bankruptcy of large multinational corporations, the response is clearly not restricted to this large-scale level of bankruptcy. Bankruptcy of internet traders, large and small, is at least as prevalent as anywhere else and, given the international nature of so much of the internet trade, cyberspace stands to be a major beneficiary of a harmonised international bankruptcy system.

Despite these commendable efforts, we are still some way from a workable international bankruptcy system. What is desired is a system which can be credible in all or most countries which can provide a basis on which a quick but careful judgment can be made as to whether a particular trader can benefit from a rescue regime. If so, this regime should come immediately into operation to protect the debtor for a temporary period

---

[8]   See Prior, "Bankruptcy Treaties Past, Present and Future, Their Failures and Successes" in Rajak (ed.) Insolvency Law: Theory and Practice (Sweet & Maxwell, 1993) 225.

while the rescue is attempted; if not, the debtor's business must be liquidated as quickly as possible in accordance with an internationally recognised procedure.

2.   The Uncitral Model Law

The Uncitral Model Law approaches the problem of cross border insolvency through the slow co-operative route of voluntary harmonisation as opposed to the wild idealistic and now largely discredited route of enforced universalism. Under the auspices of Uncitral, a Model Law has been drafted which is a set of useful provisions providing mechanisms for dealing with the problems of seeking and offering judicial assistance for the resolution of cross border insolvency disputes. Some or all of these provisions can be slotted into the domestic laws of any country. Obviously the more common provisions that are inserted into national legislation, the more harmonisation there will be in the way in which different countries deal with cross border disputes. It must not be forgotten, however, that the courts of different countries are governed by different cultural traditions, something which may well result in different interpretations of the same provisions.

According to its preamble, the purpose of the Model Law

"is to provide effective mechanisms for dealing with cases of cross-border insolvency so as to promote the objectives of:

(a) cooperation between courts and other competent authorities of this State and foreign States involved in cases of cross-border insolvency;

(b) greater legal certainty for trade and investment;

(c) fair and efficient administration of cross border insolvencies that protects the interests of all creditors and other interested persons, including the debtor;

(d) protection and maximization of the value of the debtor's assets; and

(e) facilitation of the rescue of financially troubled businesses, thereby protecting investment and preserving employment."

The Model Law builds on the number of provisions already to be found in domestic legislation (for example section 426 of the UK's Insolvency Act of 1986 and section 304 of the USA's Federal Bankruptcy Code of 1978) under which countries seek to extend assistance to the representatives of other countries in matters of cross border insolvency. Any state may well need assistance for its own representatives abroad and to offer such assistance is an excellent way of trying to secure it.

The Model Law provides the mechanism by which a representative who is administering an insolvency may seek access to a foreign court (i.e, of a country which has enacted the appropriate Model Law provision) to request assistance in relation to assets or people under the control of that foreign court. The representative may need all kinds of assistance, from simply wanting a temporary freeze to protect an asset pending resolution of a dispute as to its ownership to authorisation to remove the asset or question the persons under the foreign court's control.

The Model Law would enable a country to determine which foreign insolvency proceedings it would recognise for the purpose of granting assistance to a foreign representative. Under article 2(a) of the Model Law, "foreign proceeding" is defined as meaning

> "a collective judicial or administrative proceeding in a foreign State, including an interim proceeding, pursuant to a law relating to insolvency in which proceeding the assets and affairs of the debtor are subject to control or supervision by a foreign court, for the purpose of reorganization or liquidation"

Other provisions of the Model Law seek to establish the transparency of insolvency regimes so as to ensure that assistance to foreign representative and creditors is not only conferred but is also readily capable of being understood and taken advantage of. Co-operation between courts is another matter addressed by the Model Law. Thus judges (and presumably other relevant officials) of different countries would be entitled to communicate directly or indirectly, as well as to request information or assistance from each other.

3.   The European Union Regulation On Insolvency Proceedings[9]

Before looking briefly at this most recent European Union initiative, the precise nature of the EU's legislative capacity should be considered. Traditionally the EU's law making powers were divided between the Regulation and the Directive, with the former representing legislation which emanated from Brussels complete in itself and binding throughout the territory of the EU. In particular, a Regulation was (and still is) entirely independent of any action by the individual member states for its effect. A Directive, on the other hand, is expressly said to be dependent upon implementing legislation by individual member states and until that stage was thought to represent legislation between the EU and the governments of the member states, alone, that is to say without effect as between individual citizens. However, a series of decisions by the ECJ has given effect to unimplemented Directives, as least in litigation between a state and a citizen of that state. ("vertical effect"). There is still something of a controversy as to whether an

---

[9]   Council Regulation (EC) No. 1346/2000.

unimplemented Directive can have "horizontal effect", that is to say between one citizen and another.

Finally, it should be pointed out that the EU as a body has the power to enter into Conventions, certainly with other internationally recognised entities, including independent countries, but also inter se, that is to govern relations between the member states of the EU themselves. In some ways, a Convention of the latter kind would overlap with the legislative instruments of the Regulation and the Directive, but may suggest a slightly looser binding effect than that of either of the latter two instruments.

The search among the member states of the EU for agreement on matters of bankruptcy began in the very early 1960's – in fact by means of a Convention among member states - and was originally part of the negotiations which led to the successful Convention on Jurisdiction and Judgments concluded in 1968. In fact the reference to insolvency matters originally included in these negotiations, had to be excluded for feat that lack of agreement in this regard would jeopardise the entire initiative. After 1968, the search for a Bankruptcy Convention among the EU member states continued and looked like it had been successfully concluded in 1995 with an agreed draft which had been signed by all but one of the members of the EU well in advance of the 6 month period set aside for this final legislative stage. The United Kingdom, however, refused to sign this draft Convention which, therefore, lapsed in May 1996.

Surprisingly, however, these negotiations were revived shortly after and the form of the intended agreement was converted from a Convention to a Regulation, which was agreed among the members of the EU in May 2000, to come into effect on 31 May 2002.

A preliminary point should be made about the nature of this Regulation, the Council Regulation on insolvency proceedings as it is styled. It has an exceedingly long preamble, some 33 paragraphs, many of them more appropriate to an explanatory memorandum, others repetitive of what is in the body of the Regulation, yet others as provisions which are essential to a system catering for cross border bankruptcy and, therefore, more appropriate to being within the body of the Regulation rather than its preamble.

It is difficult to avoid the conclusion that the preamble in its present form may cause more problems than it may resolve. If it were possible to draft a preamble for the simple purpose of setting out the broad context for the Regulation as well as setting out the broad objectives which it is to be hoped that the Regulation might assist in achieving, and at the same time inserting into the body of the Regulation those provisions of substance in the management of cross border bankruptcy, a great step towards simplification and clarification would have been taken. The unfortunate suspicion which arises is that the present unstructured and convoluted form of the preamble masks serious divisions of policy between member states as to the form and function of the Regulation. This is a pessimistic assessment which might well be confounded by a bold European Court of Justice ("ECJ") acting as swiftly as it can to simplify this Regulation and enable it to reveal the many positive features which are undoubtedly intended.

The Regulation is expressed to "apply to *collective* insolvency proceedings which entail the partial or total divestment of a debtor and the appointment of a liquidator"[10] but insolvency proceedings concerning insurance undertakings, credit institutions, investment undertakings and collective investment undertakings are excluded.

The major insolvency-related terms are defined and an annex (Annex A) which is expressed to form an integral part of this Regulation, sets out for each member state the proceedings which fall within the definition of "collective insolvency proceedings. The requirement of partial or total divestment of the debtor raises an interesting theoretical question. With the growing popularity – at least in principle – of regimes based on Chapter 11 of the United States Bankruptcy Code, where the debtor remains in possession and control of the insolvent estate, the question may be asked whether the debtor is, even partially, "divested" of the insolvent estate.

It is, of course, of central significance to the functioning of this Regulation, that there should be agreement as to which legal principles will apply to the conduct of the bankruptcy of any debtor with establishments in at least two of the member states of the European Community. The ideal, but clearly unattainable solution is one set of comprehensive insolvency legal principles for all member states. The next best stage is agreement as to whose legal principles will apply in given circumstances and the Regulation achieves this (in principle) by the agreement among the Member States that the legal principles of the Member State where the debtor's main interests are situated will apply.[11]

This is a major step forward, despite the formidable list of exceptions. It is brought to life by the enunciation of a list of circumstances which, it is anticipated, will be governed by the legal principles of the chosen state. It must also be assumed that where circumstances arise which are not provided for in this list - and while it is a bold and interesting list it cannot and does not claim to be comprehensive - the Regulation authorises the use of local legal principles.

The Regulation also lays down the requirement that all Member States should recognise any judgment made by any court of the country which has jurisdiction to deal with a particular insolvency.[12] This is an obvious corollary to the requirement of agreement as to which country's legal principles govern the insolvency, but as the Regulation itself makes clear, it does not prevent the opening of secondary bankruptcy proceedings where appropriate.

---

[10]   Article 1.1.
[11]   Article 4.1.
[12]   Article 16.1.

The European Union is not yet at a stage where procedural and institutional unity can be achieved as say in the United States, but this Regulation makes great strides in the direction of mutual recognition of each country's insolvency institutions and officers.

4.   Business Rescue

Nowhere to be found in any bankruptcy harmonisation measure is an attempt to grapple with the notion of a harmonised business rescue procedure. Yet given the very widespread nature of such regimes throughout the world and the substantial number of common features of such regimes, it might have been thought that such a goal is both highly desirable and attainable.

Despite the absence of any such formal agreement, there has been a not inconsiderable incidence of rescue proceedings started in one country and which have sought to impose their authority on assets and debtors in other jurisdictions. An example of this can be found in *Felixstowe Dock and Railway Co. v. United States Lines*,[13] where the giant American carrier, U.S. Lines was placed in the U.S. business rescue regime, known as Chapter 11 (because its provisions are contained in Chapter 11 of the U.S. Bankruptcy Code). Those responsible for the affairs of U.S. Lines attempted to bring the assets of U.S. Lines outside the jurisdiction of the U.S. Bankruptcy Court within that Court's control, in that instance with mixed success.

There have been many examples some with greater success than in the Felixstowe case, some with less. One thing has become clear and that is the importance of judicial activism in seeking co-operation between courts of different jurisdictions to attempt to bring unified order to what would otherwise be the chaos of a cross border bankruptcy where the potential of rescuing the bankrupt is a distinct possibility.

Business rescue needs to be taken seriously in the world of cyberspace commercial transactions. The high incidence of bankruptcy in this world may become extremely wasteful in terms of the resulting unemployment, the failure of investment and, especially, in the losses and inconvenience to creditors. Some of these bankrupt businesses will, of course, be beyond salvation, in need of a decent burial and here, it would certainly increase the waste by seeking to save what have become mere corpses. Others, however, and their creditors might benefit from temporary protection against what would otherwise be lethal pursuit of claims by creditors. Having a brief respite, may enable a restructuring, perhaps a slimming down of operations ultimately to the benefit of all interests concerned, including those creditors who wanted to take the destructive action.

---

[13]   [1989] Q.B. 360, [1989] 2 W.L.R. 109.

Nowadays almost all industrial countries have business rescue regimes, all of which share many characteristics, so the job of establishing international agreement should be within our grasp. Bankruptcy, generally, however, and business rescue in particular, however, is seemingly prone to cultural influences and fascinating, sometimes frustrating, differences can be found among the various regimes. That notwithstanding, however, the search for harmonised or co-ordinated international business rescue is a worthy and attainable goal.

5.   The Common Components Of A Modern Business Rescue Regime

Essentially all business rescue regimes share a number of features. In the first place the business placed in the rescue regime is temporarily protected against any court processes (usually for an average of about three months). During this protective period, negotiations are conducted with the various interests in the business to try to reach agreement as to how the business may recover and emerge from protection into the market place. In a successful case, terms will be agreed which may involve the reduction in the business's staff or activities; they may involve a reduction in the indebtedness of the business to its creditors. On such agreement, the business is restored to the market place. If there is no agreement, the most likely outcome is the liquidation of the business.

While the structure of a modern business rescue regime is very similar from jurisdiction to jurisdiction, legal culture and different historical evolution has produced a number of fascinating but quite deep-seated variations. Among such - which are problems which need to be addressed in the search for a harmonised business rescue regime - are the following questions:

a)   By What Process Should An Eligible Entity Move From Unprotected To Protected Status?

A society which introduces temporary protection for insolvent business debtors is, by definition one where free enterprise plays a large role in the organisation and development of the economy. It is highly likely to be a society which enjoys a developed set of principles of contract which enable contracting parties to seek fulfilment of promises made or, at least, compensation for promises broken. The failure of a borrower to repay a loan will invariably give rise to a power in the hands of the lender to seek the assistance of the courts in enforcing the claim for repayment. Thus to protect a debtor by making it impossible for a lender whose debt is due to seek enforcement of that debt is an interference with the principle which is likely to underpin almost all sets of contractual principles, namely that contracts should be maintained ("pacta sunt servanda").

It is thus a sensitive matter to frame legislation which provides for this interference, but which does not undermine confidence in the normally anticipated consequences in commercial dealings. One approach, therefore, is to require a debtor who wants the protection to petition a court to show that it satisfies certain stated requirements (for example that it is insolvent and that it is likely that given the protection, it will successfully return to the market place. This approach obviously confers a substantial discretion on the judge

A different mechanisms for this process can be seen in the United States. Here, the only involvement of the Bankruptcy Court at this stage, in the mechanism by which the protection comes into operation, is to receive the filing of the notice by the debtor. It is simply that filing which triggers the protection which, unless lifted will last until the time the case is closed, or the case is dismissed or a discharge is granted or denied. Here there is neither the exercise of discretion, nor, in the initial stage anyway, any investigation as to eligibility requirements. There are, indeed, no eligibility requirements as such. A debtor seeking and obtaining protection from suits by creditors may do so when solvent. On the other hand there is a general requirement of good faith and much of the litigation which follows consists in creditors asking for the stay to be lifted on the grounds that there is no genuine possibility of a realistic plan acceptable to the creditors under which the debtor can be restructured. The difference between the respective approaches may be described in/terms of onus of proof. In the UK system, the onus is on the debtor to establish its entitlement to protection. In the US the onus is on the creditors to establish a lack of good faith on the part of the debtor.

b)   The Meaning Of Rescue

The term "rescue" obviously includes cases where the debtor's recovery is complete, that is to say where the debtor emerges from the protective period, solvent, with the business intact and capable of being continued successfully from the point where the protection began. All creditors will have been or will be paid in full. "Rescue" must, however, also be understood to encompass cases where the debtor's recovery is partial but where the overall result is one of greater benefit to the various interests concerned (including the public interest) than would have arisen on liquidation. Thus, for present purposes, "rescue" includes the case where the debtor emerges from the protective period solvent and capable of carrying on without protection, but where this will have been due to some surgery conducted during the protective period. The result of this surgery might be all or any of the following:

(i)   a slimmer business,
(ii)   with fewer employees,
(iii)   with certain activities reduced or eliminated,
(iv)   with the agreement of the creditors as a body to accept a particular percentage of their claims - with or without agreement that the balance be paid over an agreed period.

It is, in theory, axiomatic that debtors who seek and obtain the protection of a limited moratorium, are potentially able to survive a temporary liquidity crisis. It is inevitable, however, that the survival prospects of debtors in temporary protection will span a wide range. The following represent some fixed points along this range.

(i)   Debtors with genuine recovery prospects who do, in fact recover
(ii)   Debtors with genuine recovery prospects who do not recover
(iii)   Debtors with little chance of recovery, who do recover
(iv)   Debtors with little chance of recovery who do not recover
(v)   Hopeless debtors who, at the outset, have no chance of recovery

It would seem obvious that any successful business rescue regime would first want to ensure that (i) and (ii) - debtors with genuine recovery prospects - receive the protection of the moratorium and that (v) - hopeless debtors - do not. Further fine tuning might enable the regime to distinguish between case (iii) and case (iv), but it must be remembered that no rescue regime however well devised will always be able to avoid the pitfalls of providing a haven for those that eventually fail and denying protection for those that would have succeeded.

c)   *Who Should Take Charge Of The Debtor?*

The two poles may be said to be represented by the U.S. and U.K. positions. In the U.S., the system known as the "debtor in possession" applies, implying no change in the administration of the debtor. If the debtor is a corporation, the existing board of directors remains as much in control as it was before the onset of the moratorium. This is probably the aspect of U.S. bankruptcy law which has provoked the sharpest criticism in the U.K.; where the system is one of having a licensed insolvency practitioner appointed as administrator in an administration or an administrative receiver in an administrative receivership. The insolvency practitioner takes complete control of the debtor to the exclusion of the directors where the debtor is a company or of the partners in a partnership.

A third model for the management of the debtor while under protection is that in operation in Holland and France, and possibly elsewhere. Here the debtor may remain in possession of the assets and retain management powers but only in conjunction with a neutral third party who is appointed by the Court and who has parallel authority with the debtor. In general, such appointees tend to be professionally qualified, usually as lawyers. There are obvious dangers with such a diarchy. Disagreement may paralyse the debtor's attempts to resume financial health and render the debtor incapable of acting with the speed which is sometimes essential in these circumstances. On the other hand co-operation may also bring a benefit which can be lacking where there is one authority. In the main, it may be thought that the spirit which characterises the institution is as important as the structure of the institution itself.

If, then a diarchy, who are to be the monitors? Professionals, it may be argued, are unsuited to this role. Possibly qualified accountants may be considered but their training and orientation may deny them the entrepreneurial skills needed to manage a business from insolvency to solvency. Another possibility is to employ successful retired or semi-retired businesspeople in this role.

d)   *What Powers Should Be Exercisable By The Insolvent Debtor During The Rescue Period?*

The first part of this question is relatively easy. If the debtor is undertaking a genuine rescue attempt, it must be permitted all the powers it had when solvent but subject to acceptable outside monitoring. The second part is infinitely more difficult, namely how should these powers be split between debtor and monitor? The latter question must be debated in good faith by the various apparently conflicting interests each being aware that to press for too great an advantage will jeopardise a scheme which is designed to break a logjam which is detrimental to all.

C.   CONCLUSION

The development of appropriate legal principles depends so often on disease and failure to direct the area of necessary reform. The rapid development of e.commerce has thrust upon the commercial worlds of individual countries and, spectacularly, the international commercial world, a need to face major new challenges. The development of appropriate legal principles is essential if this wonderful but as yet frail creature is to survive and prosper.

INSOLVENCY LAW IN CYBERSPACE

Christoph G. Paulus[*]

Contents

A.   INTRODUCTION

To set insolvency law in a new context – namely cyberspace with its new media – touches on a number of issues. How, for example, contemporary insolvency administrators, trustees, and other bankruptcy officers could make use of those modern media? This in turn leads on to questions such as the organisation of a creditors' assembly (or committee) via Internet or the lodging of claims by a click of a mouse-click. We may, indeed, learn much simply by investigating the specific bankruptcy problems of

---

[*]   Professor of Law, Humboldt-University at Berlin, Germany.

TOSHIYUI KONO/ CHRISTOPH G. PAULUS/ HARRY RAJAK (eds.); THE LEGAL ISSUES OF E-COMMERCE
© 2002 Kluwer Law International. Printed in the Netherlands, pp. 163-171.

T. Kono et al. (eds.), Selected Legal Issues of E-Commerce, 163–171.
© 2002 *Kluwer Law International. Printed in the Netherlands.*

today's dot.com companies under current bankruptcy laws and practices and how bankruptcy officers cope with this most modern of bankruptcy phenomena.

In this paper, I will be discussing what changes to the present law will be necessary in order to enable bankruptcy regimes adjust this law to the specific needs of cyberspace commerce? Of course, this will only be an issue if e-commerce really becomes the huge world encompassing market which some predict.[1] Based on this (somewhat shaky) assumption it is admitted right away, that the conclusions of this paper necessarily carry much speculation

B.   LOOKING INTO THE FUTURE

In order to engage in this speculation, we need to clarify precisely the nature of this assumption. For this, it is helpful to adopt the position of a future legal historian looking at our present situation. He or she may characterize our present times as those when the legal world was captured by a mania for insolvency law. The year 1978 was the year when the US Bankruptcy Reform Act came into force, which, in turn, was the starting point of an ongoing reform of insolvency law all over the world. This mania intensified in the late1990s when –following the East Asian financial crisis – global institutions such as the International Monetary Fund[2] and the World Bank[3] entered upon this stage and drafted general principles of insolvency law to form the basis for further insolvency legislation, both in transition economies as well as advanced, industrial countries. In addition, UNCITRAL developed model laws for both international insolvency law and domestic insolvency law[4] to try to deal with the failure of enterprises in circumstances where the economies of different countries around the world were fast becoming more and more inter-dependent. These developments are likely to carry much weight with out future legal historian, given the strong authority of these organisations and the scholastic weight of those who helped shape the relevant proposals.

This future legal historian will recognize that, roughly at the same time, something like cyberlaw emerged and that e-commerce became a new branch of the general commercial law. And by correlating these parallel developments, he or she will discover that all the new insolvency laws – praised as modern and farseeing as they might have been at the time of their enactment – had at least one flaw - they had no adequate tool for dealing with the break-down of those firms or legal entities which acted in e-commerce. To be sure – in our present day, there is an even increasing number of insolvencies of dotcoms

---

[1]   Cf. Thomas Hoeren's article in this volume.
[2]   Orderly and Effective Insolvency Procedures, International Monetary Fund, Legal Department, 1999.
[3]   Principles and Guidelines for Effective Insolvency and Creditor Rights Systems, 2001.
[4]   To be sure, whether this model law will be approved by the UN Plenary Assembly (and whether the draft will be propelled until that stage) or not is at the present time unpredictable.

and other actors in the telecommunication area. And of course, all these insolvencies are dealt with under existing insolvency laws. Yet it is already clear to us that these insolvency laws do not offer the tools, which would be appropriate to resolve the many new issues which the bankruptcy of these more or less virtual enterprises gives rise to. Our future legal historian, in other words, will probably note that all our very modern laws were already old fashioned at the time of enactment, although those who made the proposals and those who implemented them were unable to see this.

C.   A TELLING HISTORICAL DEVELOPMENT

To help us speculate as to what future legal historians will say of our period, let us look back, into our own history. By having an idea as to where we come from should put us into the position of having some idea as to where we are heading. Thus, it becomes necessary to look at how insolvency law has developed so far – obviously, not in detail, but in rough outline.[5]

I.   Liquidation

The beginning of any insolvency law is liquidation – first of the debtor's physical person, thereafter – and this is important for our context – of the debtor's assets. The ancient Romans had already subdivided these assets into movables, immovables and claims (mobilia, immobilia, nomina); and they had also prepared the legal instruments for transferring and alienating these goods. For almost two millennia such assets formed the main part of any estate. Thus, in order to satisfy, at least in part, the creditors of a bankrupt person, it sufficed to sell the debtor's assets in the traditional manner and to hand over to the creditors the proceeds of such sale. This, in briefest outline, might be said to be the predominant scenery in a production-based economy.

II.   Reorganisation

At the end of the second millennium a new "invention" entered upon the insolvency stage – namely reorganisation of the debtor. It became famous because of the US legislation (the renowned chapter 11 proceedings) even though the concept of reorganisation as a mechanism for dealing with a bankruptcy other than by means of a complete financial destruction of the debtor and the alienation of all his or her or its assets can be traced back at least to the Roman emperor Augustus who introduced the "cessio bonorum".

---

[5]   Cf. Paulus, Entwicklungslinien des Insolvenzrechts, Zeitschrift für Insolvenzrecht (KTS) 2000, 239 seq.

There are, of course, major differences between ancient and modern debtor reorganisation. The latter contemplates something quite specific - the fresh start of the debtor - and its debt to the history of the US and especially its pioneers who were willing to start a new business even though they had failed with their old one is almost palpable.

Even this modern idea of reorganization has already undergone some change as it becomes a worldwide phenomenon. As modern economies change from production into service societies (Dienstleistungsgesellschaften) the old division of assets into immovable, movables and claims comes under pressure. When one considers, for example, a software developer, a music producer, or a premier league soccer team, one will not find too many of the old-fashioned assets. They will have been replaced by goods which might be as valuable as the assets of former times but which are not, for example, as trafficable. Consider, in this context, for example, goodwill, know-how, customers lists, to name but a few. Since these goods are generally closely linked with the debtor, the creditors are – at least in many cases – better helped, not by the attempted sale of such intangible assets, but by leaving them with the debtor and helping the debtor to get back into successful business. This is exactly what insolvency law calls reorganisation.

D.   LESSONS FROM HISTORY

The point of this short and one-sided description of the history of insolvency law is the close connection between the general economic development of a society and its law. On this basis we could now seek to develop some basic speculations as to the future of the insolvency law governing cyberspace transactions. Of course, this must be done with care. As a first step, we must seek to clarify what the peculiarities of cyberspace might be, followed by considering what sort of problems are now apparent visible in today's insolvency cases in the dotcom-area and finally seek to understand what can be done for the creditors in order to meet their demands as far as this is possible. We may than have some, perhaps somewhat difficult to discern clearly, vision of how such insolvency law might look like in the cyberspace era to come.

I.   What Are The Peculiarities Of Cyberspace?

Cyberspace is invisible.[6] Even though we see something, for example, on our computer screens we know that this is just a glimpse into a world behind – a world, which is virtual and therefore ubiquitous. In this world the traditional borderlines on which so much

---

[6]   Cf. Paulus, Multimedia als Herausforderung an das internationale Wirtschaftsrecht, Multimedia und Recht (MMR) 1999, 443 seq.

domestic legal thought is predicated are non-existent, although has not stopped domestic legislatures from seeking to regulate this world with traditional forms of legislation.

It is important to make the point that if the predominant peculiarities of cyberlaw are, indeed, its virtualness and its ubiquity, we can readily observe that here there is nothing really new. Suffice it is to mention a simple claim of a creditor against his debtor. This claim is transferable and is in general treated by lawyers as if it were a corporeal thing. But as a matter of fact, it is as virtual and therefore as ubiquitous as cyberspace. We have never seen a claim, never touched one, yet, we have incorporated the notion of a claim into our daily legal toolbox to such a degree that it needs some effort to recall the artificiality of this legal instrument.

Why is this so? How can we have so incorporated the notion of a claim as to forget its virtualness? Clearly, we have found a way to deal with it so its real nature has become uninteresting or, at least, has lost its importance. Thus it has become legally manageable. The answer is that we have found a connecting point between the virtual phenomenon and the world of tangible things – something that might be called "reification". Thus, if a creditor, assigns his or her claim to a third party, he or she does so by means of a contract, something which we recognise as a real legal act. For lawyers, this reification is the decisive thing – not the material substance of the claim. If this is a correct observation, the lawyers' task in organizing cyberspace will be to develop cyberlaw by finding acceptable points of reification and thereby to organize cyberspace.

II. What Are The Problems Of Today's Dotcom Insolvencies?

To be sure, virtualness and ubiquity are not the only peculiarities of cyberspace, yet they are probably its most distinctive. The failure of today's dotcom companies also reveals that speed is a prominent factor to be taken into account. Since these companies act and – up to a certain point – even exist only in the virtual world of the net they share the latter's fate, especially its speed. Worldwide communication without delay and prompt delivery of goods and services are just a few of the catchwords with which the net and, more specifically, e-commerce has represented the uniqueness of its operations. These are the big promise of the internet and all who use it to do business. Current studies now reveal that if the average user has to wait more than 20 seconds before the screen shows a selected homepage in full, he or she will have become uninterested and will search or surf elsewhere.

Therefore, efficient and successful commercial performance on and via the internet requires presence at any time without any interruption. And if a participant suffers a financial crisis, these very wonders of the internet - its speed, its immediacy, its constant presence, will, in turn, become the source of its enemy. The causes of financial crisis are obvious: The connecting line (whether to the provider, to the common telecommunication net, elsewhere) might be interrupted on account of a payment delay; or the transporter of goods sold over the internet may be refusing to deliver goods ordered on account of an unsettled account for a previous delivery. In the traditional world, there may be a little time to sort out these financial embarrassments but now speed and its companion, all-time omnipresence, will have raised the customers' expectations who, with the benefits (if such they are) due to the increasing and worldwide competition, are likely to seek attention from one of the many alternative providers at hand. Even a short absence from constant availability may lead to an increasing number of disastrous losses of customers which in turn will accelerate the financial decline moving swiftly to insolvency proceedings.

III.   How Might Creditors Get Their Money?

Quite often such an insolvency proceeding will result in the distribution of little or nothing, given the relative valuelessness of the rather few assets. Dotcom-companies generally do not have many goods in the traditional sense to be transformed into money in, order to satisfy their creditors. Their assets are more likely to be an idea and, maybe, connections or addresses, assets which I have already described as being of value primarily only when linked to the person of the debtor. Therefore, seen from the creditors' point of view, it would appear to be preferable to try to get the debtor's business back on track rather than to liquidate the assets.

But unlike the case of a common service enterprise or company, the usual plan proceeding is probably not the appropriate tool. This is likely to be too time consuming in that it requires the debtor's insolvency, followed by a certain period of plan drafting, thereafter a plan discussion and, finally, its acceptance by means of a somewhat complicated voting procedure. If an e-commerce participant were to be put through these proceedings, it will be long forgotten long before the proceedings are completed.

E.   WHAT WILL THE INSOLVENCY LAW OF THE FUTURE LOOK LIKE?

I.   General Observations

What lessons can be learned from what has been described? Obviously, an appropriate insolvency regime for cyberlaw has to provide an extremely speedy proceeding, which, therefore, must be simplified in comparison to the present shape of reorganisation.[7] To be sure, there are already attempts to speed up reorganisation proceeding, especially by

---

[7]   In case of a liquidation, nothing needs to be changed because speed is there only of secondary interest.

means of the so called "option model".[8] However, this trading of share-options after a "debt for equity swap" is still quite time consuming, leaving aside the general questionability of the underlying idea.[9]

In terms of speed, the optimal solution would be that an option should be at hand as soon as the company's financial difficulties arise, thereby avoiding the hiatus which would inevitably arise at this point were traditional insolvency proceedings to ensue. Indeed, the insolvency option should be clear right from the start of an internet company's existence. Ideally, it should appear in the foundation charter of any such enterprise. This, of course, is quite a dramatic shift from today's realities. Here, usually, the foundation of a company gives reason to dream about a flourishing future with minor obstacles on the path to prosperity; the thought of the opposite - however realistic - is ignored and suppressed. The company's insolvency is rarely the subject of any consideration at this point of time. Sober balancing of possible options is replaced by wishful thinking.

II. Current Similarities

The proposed idea - anticipating insolvency at the start-up stage - is not completely new. In some countries - perhaps more in the US more than elsewhere - insolvency proceedings are used as a strategic tool. Developed insolvency systems have what is sometimes called a pre-packaged plan, bearing a close resemblance to what I have suggested is needed in e-commerce: Before the company reaches financial turmoil, a plan is prepared as to how it is to be restructured, transferred or whatever; and when the proceedings commence – generally on the grounds of an imminent illiquidity –, the plan is swiftly put in place according to the previously secured agreement of all interested parties.

A striking example of the likely applicability of some current insolvency practices to insolvency in cyberspace, can be seen in the US, in the insolvency of Toysmart.com, whose major investor was the Walt Disney Co.[10] This dotcom company announced its plans to sell its database of customer information in order to raise money. This, however, created such an enormous public outcry, that it will probably lead to an amendment of the Bankruptcy Code so as to provide some data protection for customers of a bankrupt entity. What is interesting is that as a consequence of the Toysmart proceedings, some

---

[8]   For a discussion of the concepts of, e.g., Bebchuk, Aghion, Hart, and Moore cf. Balz, Simplifying Bankruptcy (to appear early 2002 in Festschrift für das Max-Planck-Institut für ausländisches Recht und Rechtsvergleichung in Hamburg).

[9]   The basic idea of the debt-equity swap and the succeeding tradability of options shifts those tasks to the creditors, who then become part of the administrator's business. Whether this form of job swap is a prudent idea remains to be seen.

[10]   Cf. www.siliconvalley.com/docs/news/depth/priv031601.htm.

websites in the US have now changed their appearance so as to describe their privacy policy including information as to how they would handle customers' personal informations in the case of bankruptcy. This might be seen as an example of envisaging one's own insolvency and inviting the consumers to decide whether or not they are willing to accept this proposal. If they do not like it , they will look for another provider.

This is now a notion which is the subject of quite intense debate in the US.[11] Some argue that substantial areas of insolvency law – including its procedural rules – should be subject to pre-insolvency contractual agreements. Thus, it should be possible for example, effectively to exclude certain assets from the automatic stay. This view, however, ignores the essential feature of any insolvency law – namely to be *ius cogens*, to be a law which can be contractually changed only to a very limited degree and by specified means alone. The reason and justification for this enforcement character of insolvency law is, seen from a very general perspective, to ensure that from the commencement of an insolvency proceeding law the creditors collectively will replace the debtor as the dominant interest in the enterprise.[12] Because of this plurality of interests, the existing insolvency rules must necessarily be fixed or changed – if at all – only by an agreement of all parties involved.

III. Possible Solutions

At this point of the discussion we might be in the position to develop some considerations about the future shape of an insolvency law for the new market of e-commerce. The contractual approach as described suprabove will not do because of the lack of the indispensable consent of all those who happen to be creditors of the debtor in question at the commencement of the proceeding. This is true for both alternatives as described above, namely restricted to what will happen to creditor information or more widely than that. Even if stated in the general terms of agreement as to what will happen with the debtor's assets, this does not bind the insolvency administrator. Once a proceeding has been initiated, the power to dispose of such assets is solely with the person in charge according to the applicable insolvency law.

However, it is undeniable that such a pre-packaged solution as to what should be done in the case of the debtor's insolvency, increases the speed of the proceeding dramatically.

---

[11]   See Rasmussen, Debtor's Choice: a Menu Approach to Corporate Bankruptcy, 71 Texas L.R. 51 (1992); A. Schwartz, A Contract Theory Approach to Business Bankruptcy, 107 Yale L.J. 1807 (1998); idem, Bankruptcy Contracting Reviewed, 109 Yale L.J. 343 (1999); S. Schwarcz, Rethinking Freedom of Contract: A Bakruptcy Paradigm, 77 Texas L.R. 517 (1999); with further references; For a profound discussion of this concept see J. Westbrook, A Global Solution to Multinational Default, 98 Mich. L.R. 2276, 2303 (2000).

[12]   To be sure, this is only a very rough outline of the concept of the existing insolvency laws in this world. Nevertheless, as a fundamental consideration the outline holds true.

Therefore, a clause like the one described above need not necessarily be null and void; it has to be made subject to the approval of the administrator of the insolvency proceeding or the creditors. If this condition is fulfilled, nothing prevents insolvency law from accepting this general contractual term as a kind of pre-packaged plan with respect to certain assets. As a matter of fact, such "sales offers" might be feasible especially by group (Konzern) members, who might thereby, declare another member of the group (for example the mother company) to be the offeree.

Thus, if such a group member goes bankrupt, the sale will be perfected if the person in charge – the administrator and/or the creditors – gives his or their consent. However, this acceleration of the proceeding need not be restricted to group member insolvencies and to sales of assets. The insolvency law in general could provide for incentives to prepare such pre-packaged solutions, for example, by reducing the minimum period before which the first creditors' assembly has to meet, or by changing the necessary quorum for the creditors' consent, or by reducing the time span between the filing of the petition and the initiation of the proceeding.

The latter idea, however, demonstrates where the borders are of the idea in the present paper. The insolvency law cannot waive the fundamental requirement that the debtor has to be insolvent, however that might be defined, and to have it replaced by such a pre-package clause. While the latter approach would certainly lead to an immense acceleration of the process in dealing with an insolvent debtor, it would be open to widescale abuse by a debtor who might seek to make use of it at practically any time.[13] To allow this would be in clear contradiction of what has been said above as to the peculiarity of insolvency law – namely the replacement of the debtor by his creditors as the dominant interest in the business. This is only justified if the debtor is proved to have failed according to common commercial standards. These standards do not allow a "flight" into the protected area of insolvency law and to, thereby, escape competition, etc. If this were permissible it would be consistent to introduce the above-mentioned contractual insolvency system. Since then insolvency law were just one more tool in the surrounding of the ordinary course of business.

---

[13] This is, as a matter of fact, the big attraction of the US chapter 11 proceeding.

INDEX

Law and Electronic Commerce

1. V. Bekkers, B.-J. Koops and S. Nouwt (eds.): *Emerging Electronic Highways*. New Challenges for Politics and Law. 1996   ISBN 90-411-0183-7
2. G.P. Jenkins (ed.): *Information Technology and Innovation in Tax Administration*. 1996   ISBN 90-411-0966-8
3. A. Mitrakas: *Open EDI and Law in Europe*. A Regulatory Framework. 1997   ISBN 90-411-0489-5
4. G.N. Yannopoulos: *Modelling the Legal Decision Process for Information Technology Applications in Law*. 1998   ISBN 90-411-0540-9
5. K. Boele-Woelki and C. Kessedjian (eds.): *Internet*: Which Court Decides? Which Law Applies? Quel tribunal décide? Quel droit s'applique? 1998   ISBN 90-411-1036-4
6. B.-J. Koops: *The Crypto Controversy*. A Key Conflict in the Information Society. 1999   ISBN 90-411-1143-3
7. E. Schweighofer: *Legal Knowledge Representation*. Automatic Text Analysis in Public International and European Law. 1999   ISBN 90-411-1148-4
8. L. Matthijssen: *Interfacing between Lawyers and Computers*. An Architecture for Knowledge-based Interfaces to Legal Databases. 1999   ISBN 90-411-1181-6
9. K.W. Grewlich: *Governance in "Cyberspace"*. Access and Public Interest in Global Communications. 1999   ISBN 90-411-1225-1
10. B.-J. Koops, C. Prins en H. Hijmans (eds.): *ICT Law and Internationalisation*. A Survey of Government Views. 2000   ISBN Hb 90-411-1505-6; Pb 90-411-1506-4
11. C. Girot: *User Protection in IT Contracts*. A Comperative Study of the Protection of the User Against Defective Performance in Information Technology. 2001   ISBN 90-411-1548-X
12. J.E.J. Prins (ed.): *Designing E-Government*. On the Crossroads of Technological Innovation and Institutional Change. 2001   ISBN 90-411-1621-4
13. E. Lederman and R. Shapira (eds.): *Law, Information and Information Technology*. 2001   ISBN 90-411-1675-3
14. A.R. Lodder and H.W.K. Kaspersen (eds.): *eDirectives: Guide to European Union Law on E-Commerce*. Commentary on the Directives on Distance Selling, Electronic Signatures, Electonic Commerce, Copyright in the Information Society, and Data Protection. 2002   ISBN 90-411-1752-0
15. J.E.J. Prins, P.M.A. Ribbers, H.C.A. van Tilborg, A.F.L. Veth and J.G.L. van der Wees (eds.): *Trust in Electronic Commerce*. The Role of Trust from a Legal, an Organizational and a Technical Point of View. 2002   ISBN 90-411-1845-4
16. T. Kono, C.G. Paulus and H. Rajak (eds.): *Selected Legal Issues of E-Commerce*. 2002   ISBN 90-411-1898-5

KLUWER LAW INTERNATIONAL – THE HAGUE / LONDON / BOSTON